83 DAYS
IN MARIUPOL

A War Diary

by

DON BROWN

CLARION BOOKS
Imprints of HarperCollins*Publishers*

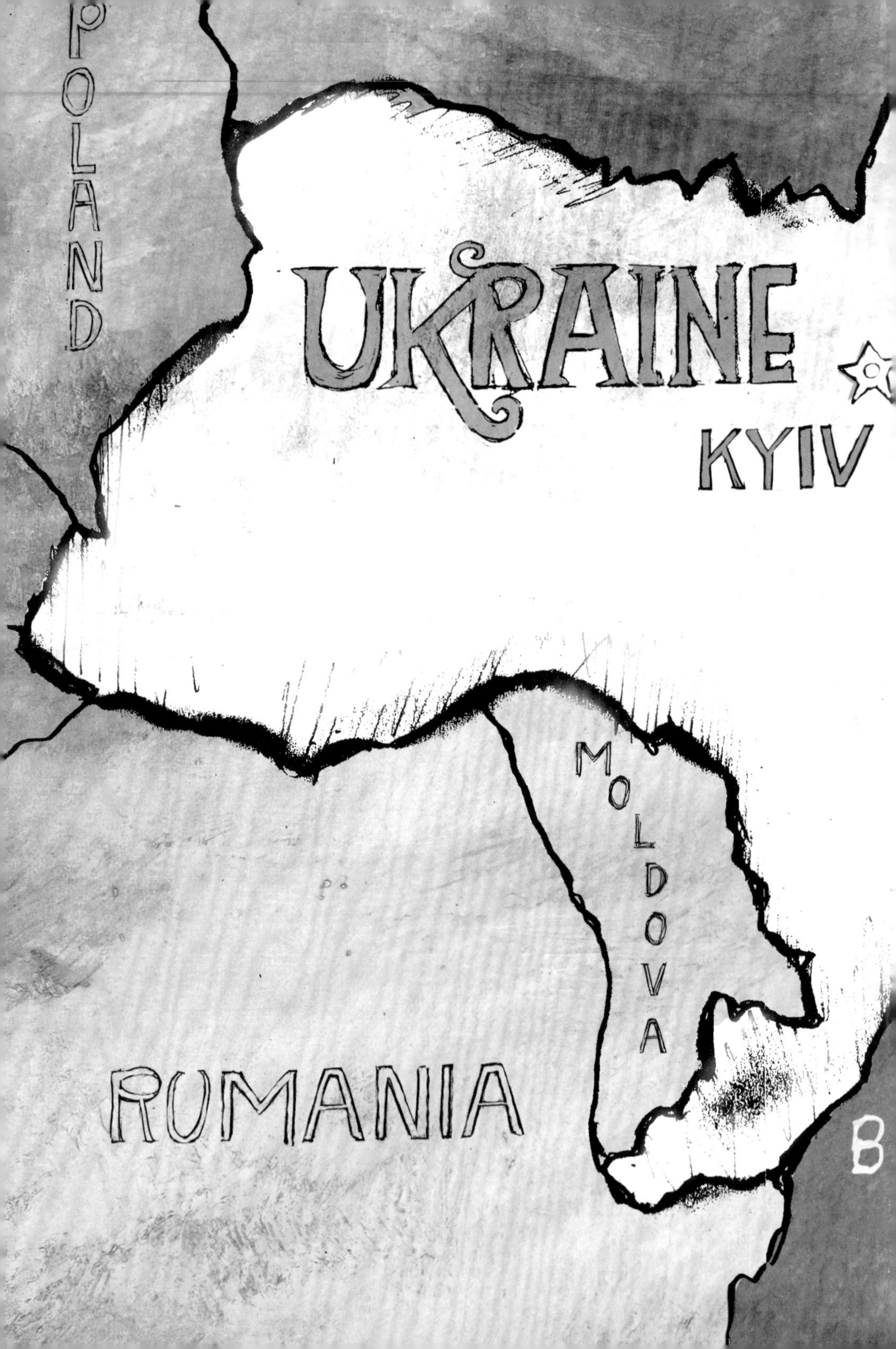
POLAND
UKRAINE
KYIV
MOLDOVA
RUMANIA
B

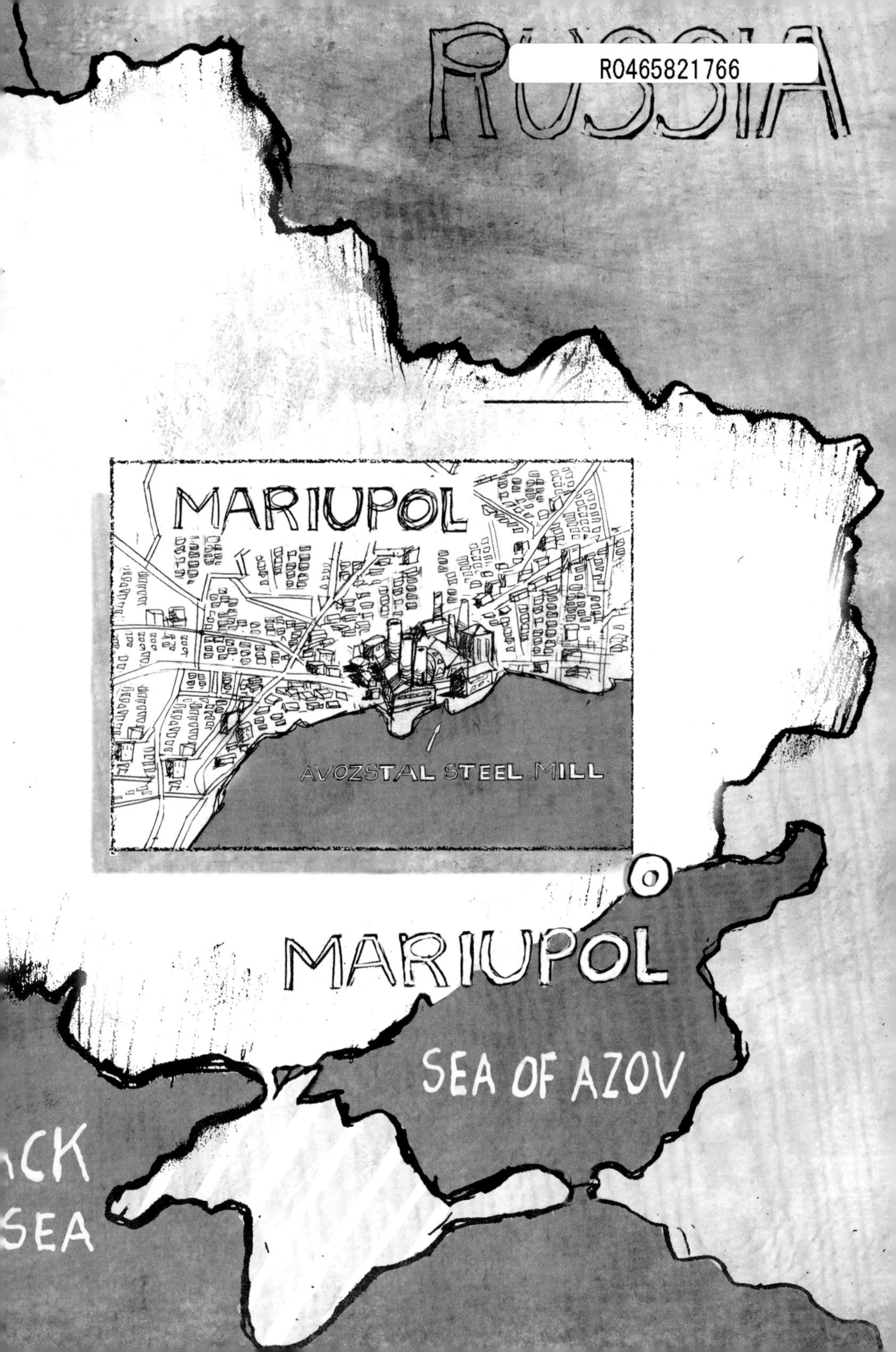
RUSSIA
MARIUPOL
AVOZSTAL STEEL MILL
MARIUPOL
SEA OF AZOV

PROLOGUE:

UKRAINE, RUSSIA, AND THE CLATTER OF HISTORY

More than a thousand years ago, the Slavic kingdom of Kyivan Rus was the cradle for both Ukraine and Russia. It is this history that leads President Vladimir Putin and some other Russians to insist that they and the Ukrainians are "one people, a single whole."

History suggests something else.

Over centuries, the fortunes of Russians and those who had come to see themselves as Ukrainians diverged. Parts of modern-day Ukraine were incorporated into different empires until 1793, when most of it was absorbed by Russia. Though dominated by Russians, deep-rooted Ukrainian culture held on. When in the turbulent wake of World War I the Russians traded monarchy for communism, Ukrainians fought an unsuccessful war for their independence. Despite their loss, the Ukrainians remained a thorn in the side of what was now the Soviet Union rule. To subdue them, Soviet leader Stalin contrived a famine against the Ukrainians, killing millions of them in the 1930s.

With the tragedy fresh in their memory, many Ukrainians celebrated the Nazis as liberators from Soviet tyranny when Germany invaded Russia at the start of World War II. Wide factions of Ukrainians allied themselves with Germany's Hitler and assisted in the murder of their Jewish neighbors; some of the most hideous episodes of the Holocaust occurred in Ukraine.

After Germany's defeat, Ukraine remained tethered to Russia for decades. Then, in 1991, the corrupt and oppressive Soviet Union collapsed, and Ukraine declared its independence. It also found itself the proprietor of nuclear weapons once under the control of the Soviets. Rather than keep them for their own protection, they returned them to Russia, but only after Russia, Great Britain, and the United States signed an agreement to honor Ukraine's borders and not ever use force against her.

Over the previous years of domination, Ukraine had seen an influx of Russians, many of whom retained their Russian language and identified more with Russia than Ukraine. When thousands of Ukrainians agitated for greater integration with Europe in 2004, many ethnic Russians, living mostly in the eastern portion of Ukraine bordering Russia, disagreed. It was a critical political fissure.

In 2014, Russian president Vladimir Putin seized Ukraine's Crimea, a large peninsula bordering Russia, justifying the grab on invented claims of Ukrainian victimization of Russian Crimeans. Shortly afterward, Russian sympathizers in the eastern Ukrainian province of Donbas declared independence from Ukraine. Most unbiased observers saw them as a mere puppet regime of Russia. Ukraine fought to recover the lost territory.

Then in 2022, Putin ignored internationally accepted norms and earlier agreements and invaded Ukraine. He claimed it was in the defense of ethnic Russians being terrorized by Ukrainians and for the denazification of Ukraine. Neither was true. (Ukraine's president Volodymyr Zelensky is, in fact, Jewish.)

The truth lay elsewhere: Putin wanted to resurrect the expansive empire of the old Soviet Union; to undercut a thriving democracy on his doorstep, one that Russians might imitate at the cost of his own autocracy; and to undermine Ukraine's bid to join NATO, the European defensive, military alliance created in opposition to Russia.

Russian soldiers poured into Ukraine with the widespread expectation that the Russian superpower would overwhelm and defeat Ukraine in days.

For the port city of Mariupol, geography was destiny. Sitting on the eastern edge of the country, it was close to both the Donbas province of Russian separatists and Russia. Bombs and bullets began to fall on it at the very start of the war. Soon, it was cut off and beyond rescue. But like Thermopylae, the Alamo, and Corregidor before it, Mariupol became a rallying cry of a people's resolve.

83 Days in Mariupol is its war diary.

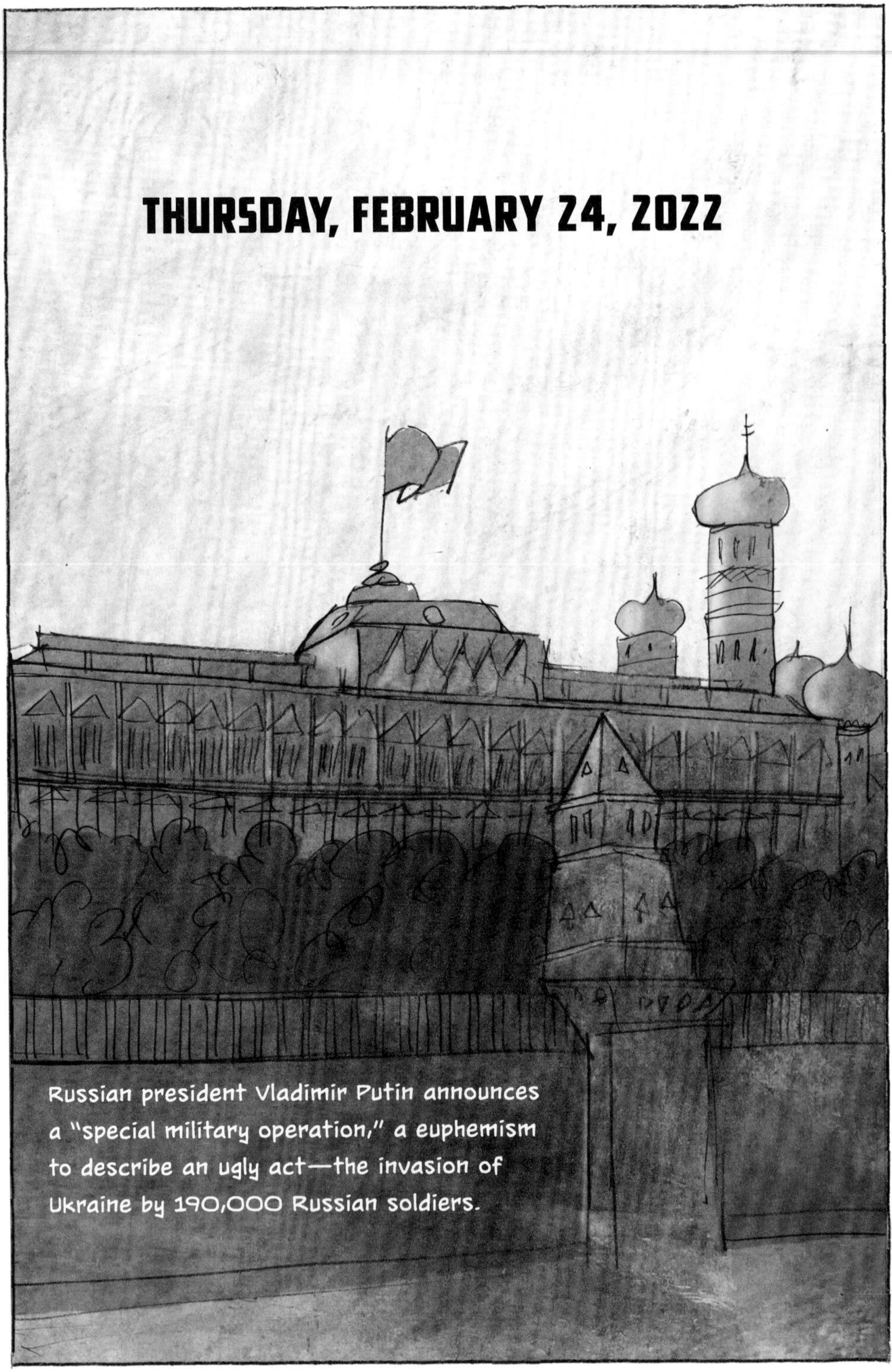
THURSDAY, FEBRUARY 24, 2022
Russian president Vladimir Putin announces a "special military operation," a euphemism to describe an ugly act—the invasion of Ukraine by 190,000 Russian soldiers.

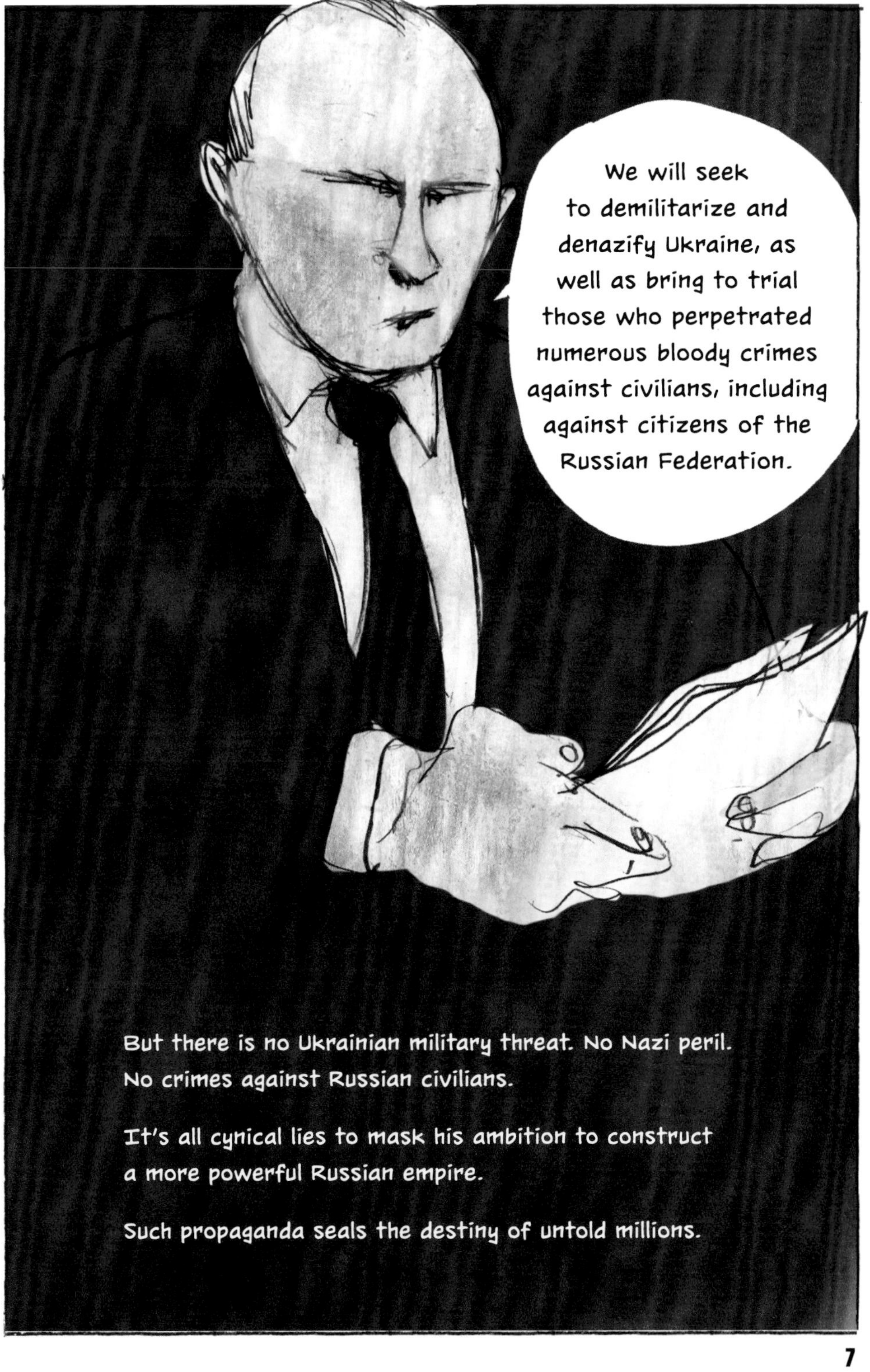
We will seek to demilitarize and denazify Ukraine, as well as bring to trial those who perpetrated numerous bloody crimes against civilians, including against citizens of the Russian Federation.
But there is no Ukrainian military threat. No Nazi peril. No crimes against Russian civilians.
It's all cynical lies to mask his ambition to construct a more powerful Russian empire.
Such propaganda seals the destiny of untold millions.

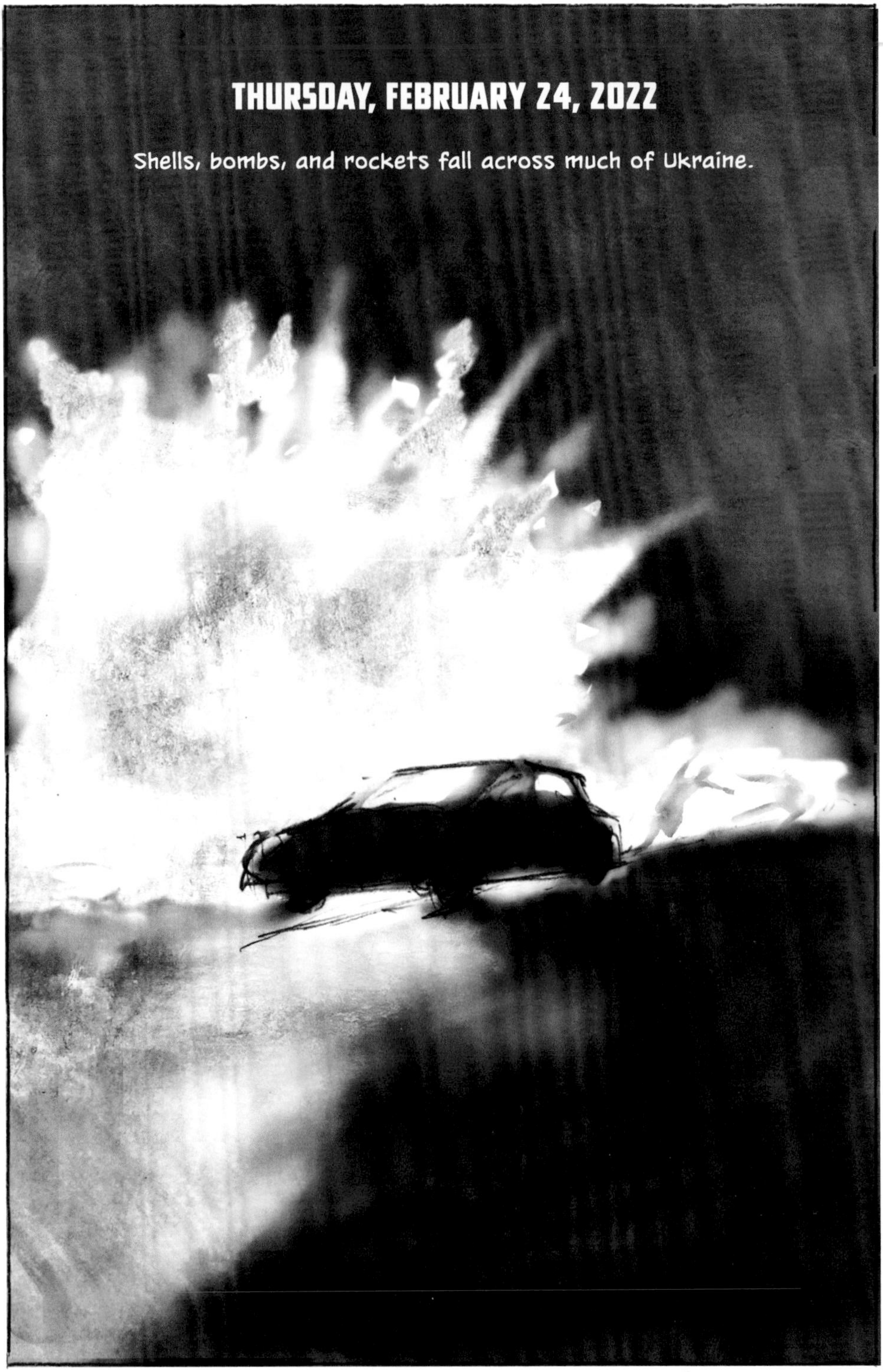
THURSDAY, FEBRUARY 24, 2022
Shells, bombs, and rockets fall across much of Ukraine.

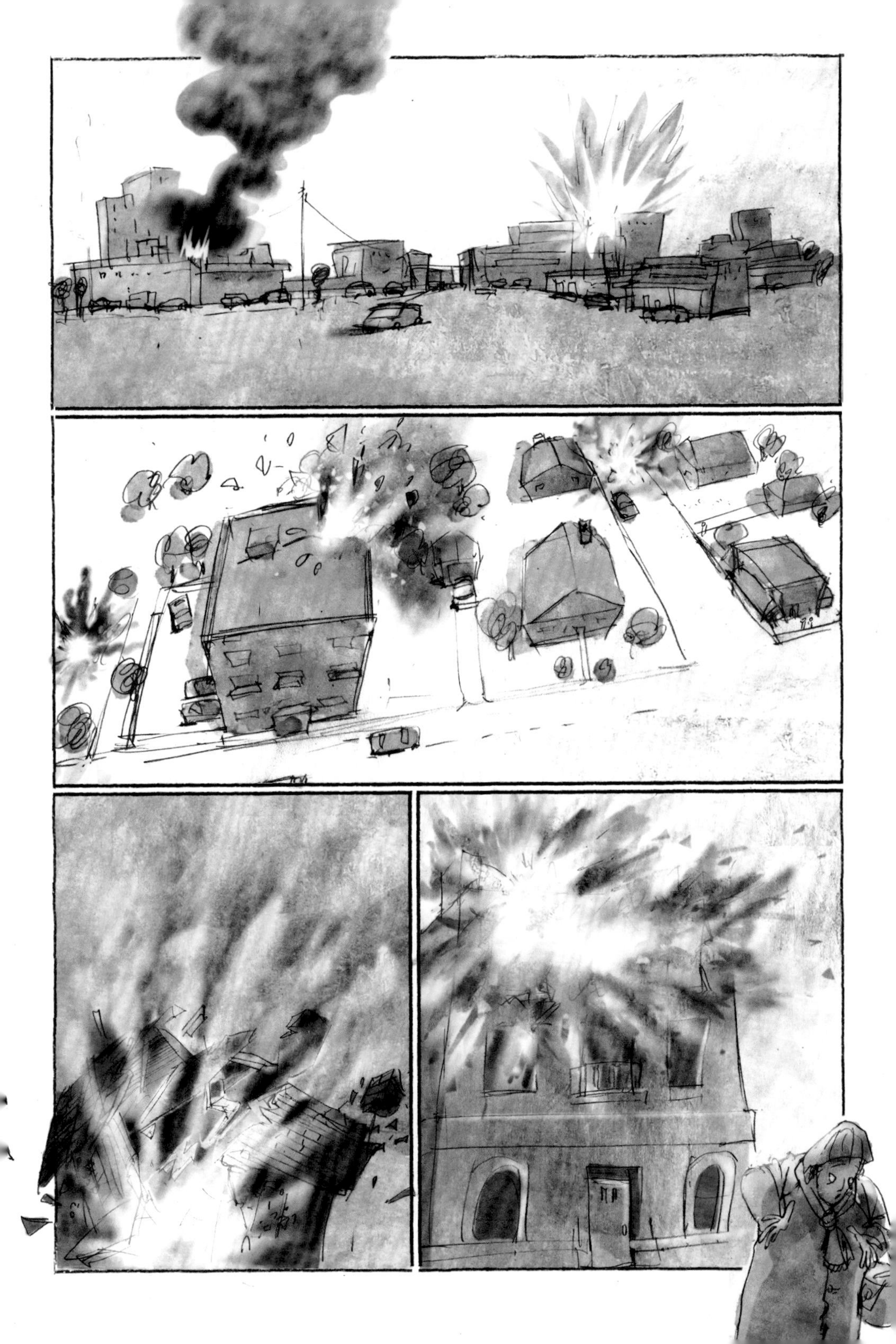

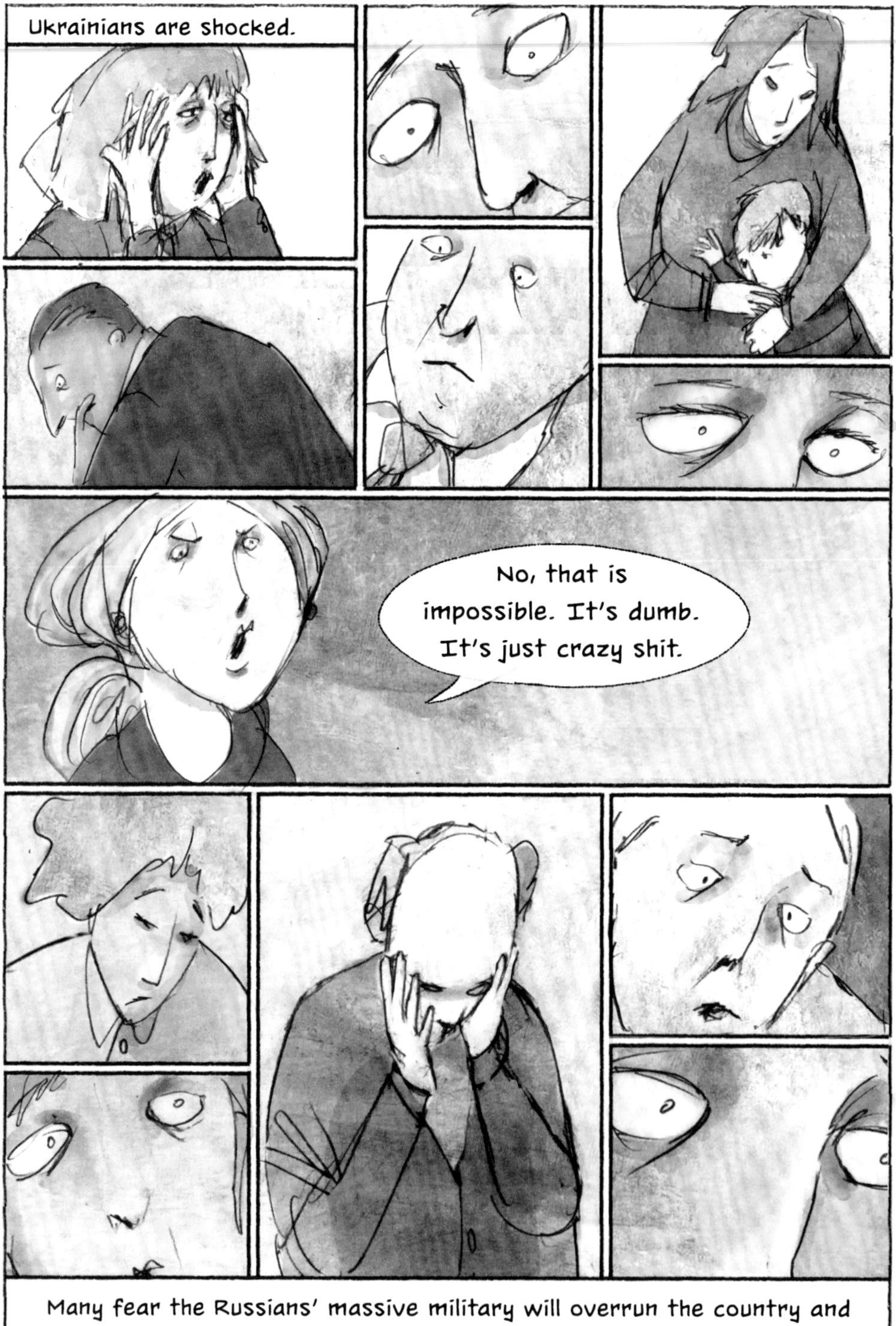
Ukrainians are shocked.
No, that is impossible. It's dumb. It's just crazy shit.
Many fear the Russians' massive military will overrun the country and be in the capital city, Kyiv, in days.

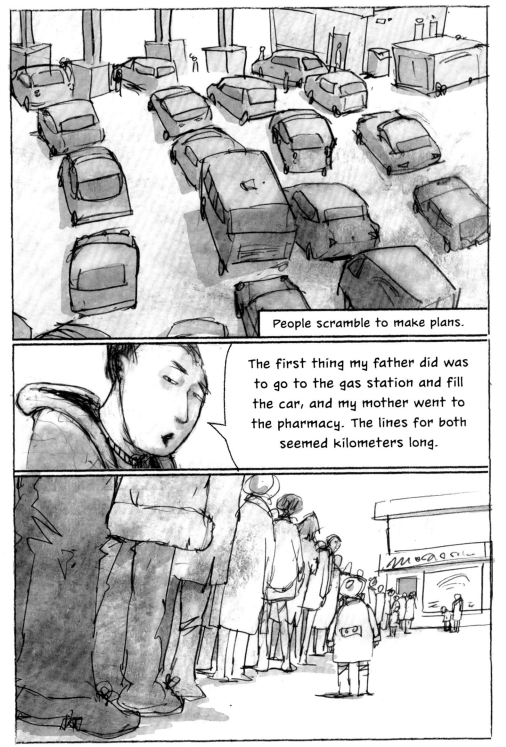

People scramble to make plans.

The first thing my father did was to go to the gas station and fill the car, and my mother went to the pharmacy. The lines for both seemed kilometers long.

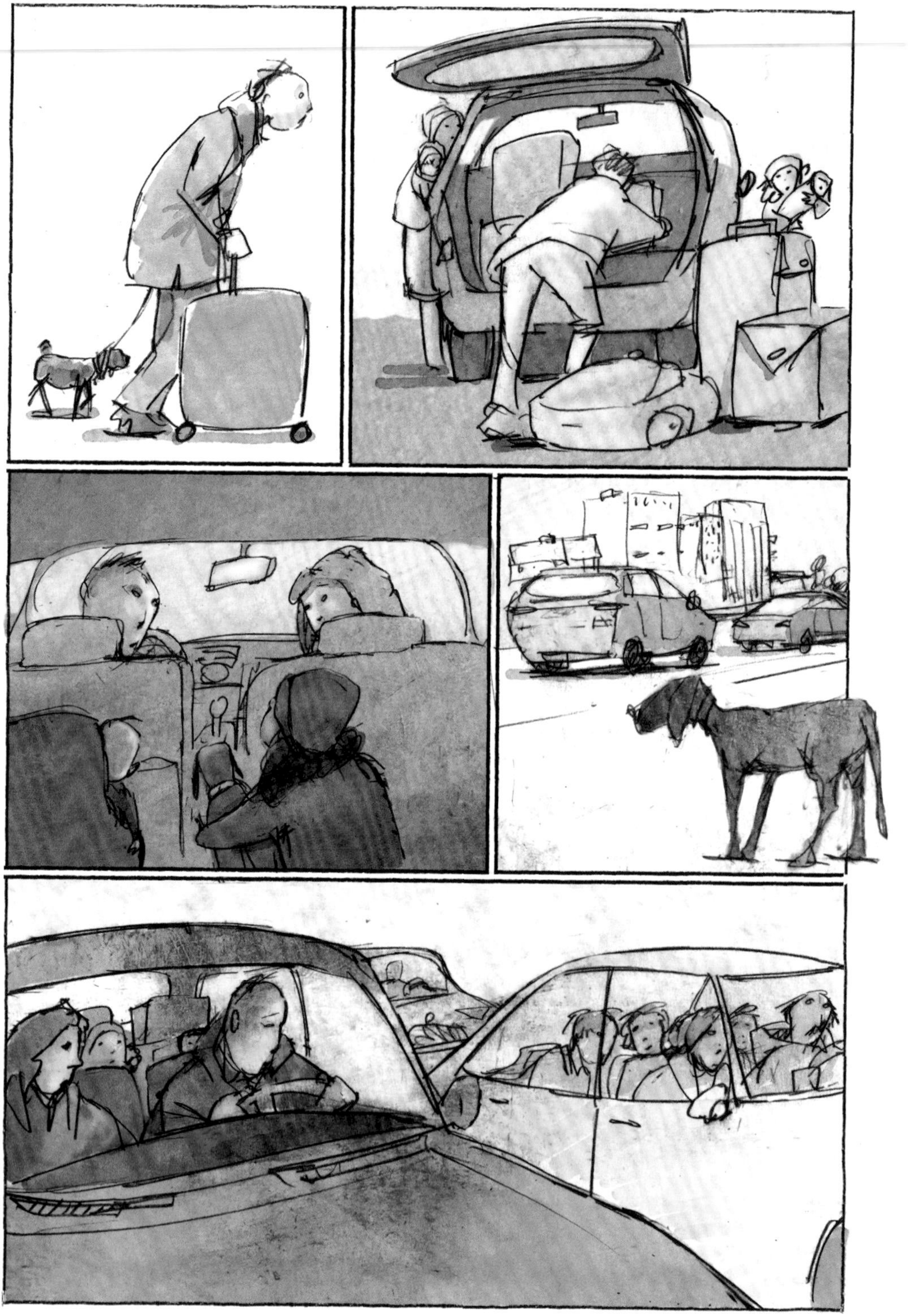

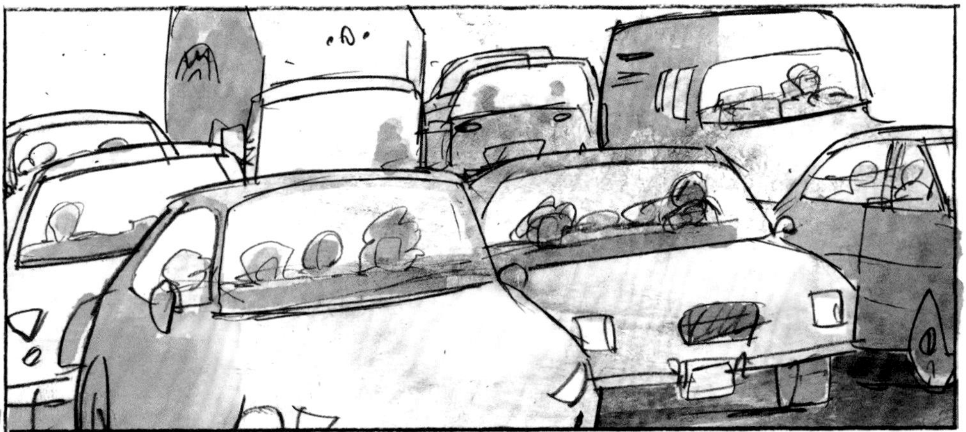

Roads are jammed with cars heading away from the Russians.

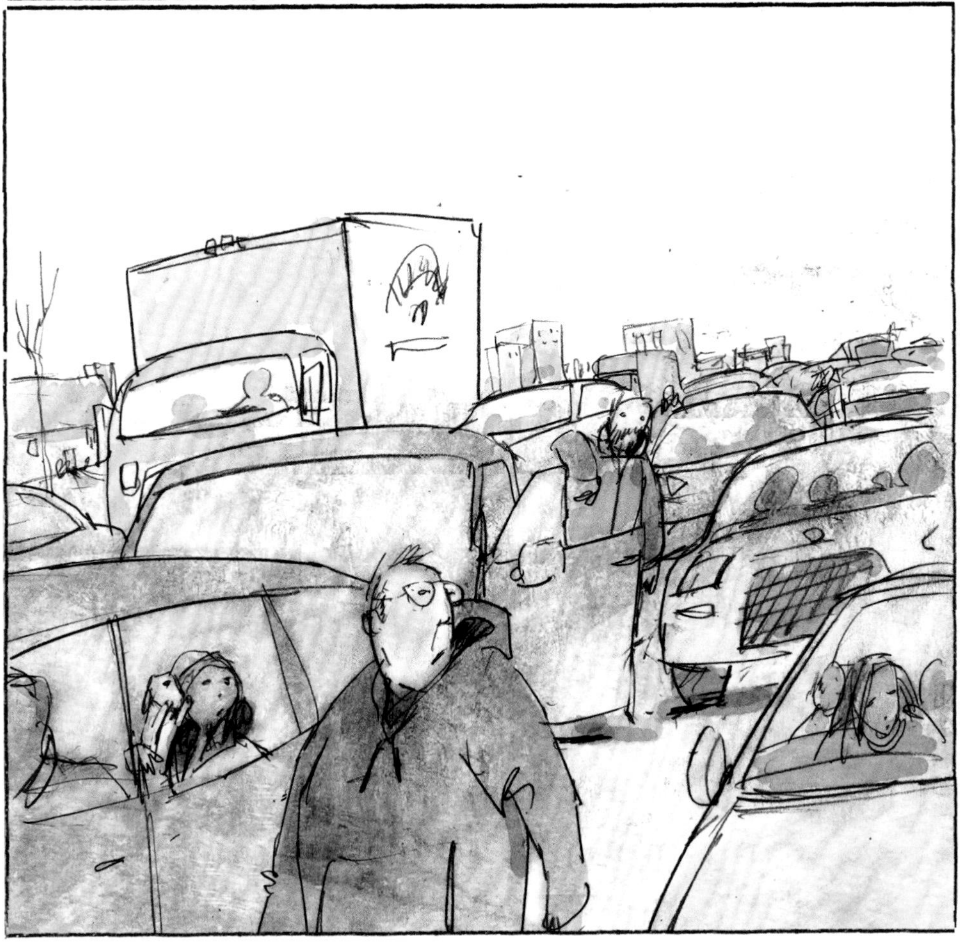

Violence quickly finds the coastal city of Mariupol, Ukraine's principal port on the Sea of Azov.

It sits only about 36 miles from the Russian border and close to the Donbas region, where Russian-backed residents had broken away from Ukraine in 2014, setting off something of a civil war between the separatists and Ukrainian forces.

The Russians mean to seize all of Ukrainian land bordering the Sea of Azov, crippling Ukraine's ability to ship its profitable farm products and making a "land bridge" to the Russian forces in the occupied territory of Crimea.

The first step is to seize the gateway to the sea, Mariupol.

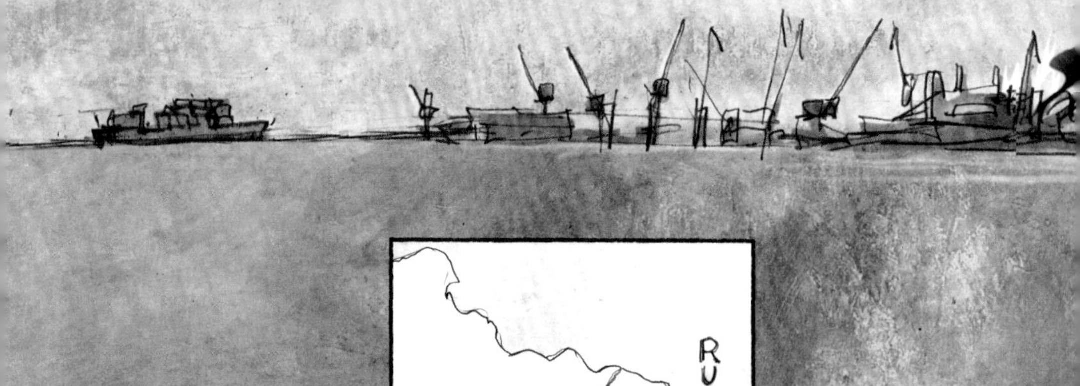

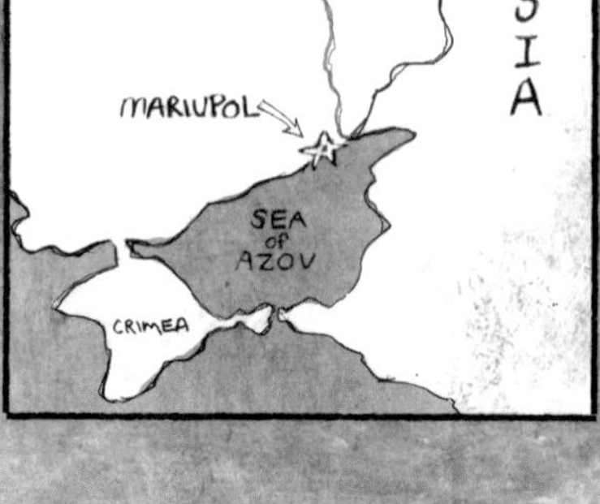
UKRAINE
RUSSIA
DONBAS
MARIUPOL
SEA of AZOV
CRIMEA

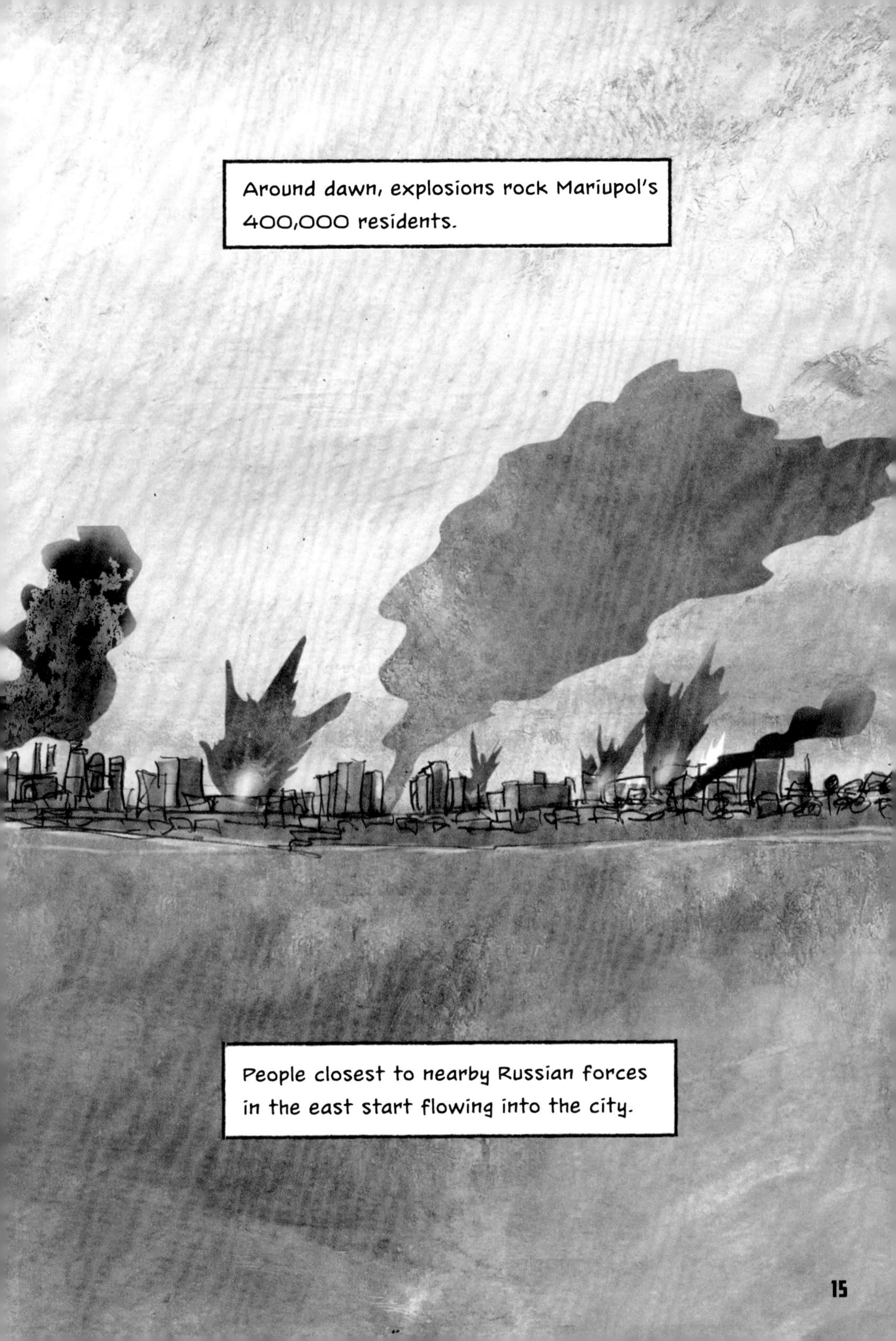
Around dawn, explosions rock Mariupol's 400,000 residents.
People closest to nearby Russian forces in the east start flowing into the city.

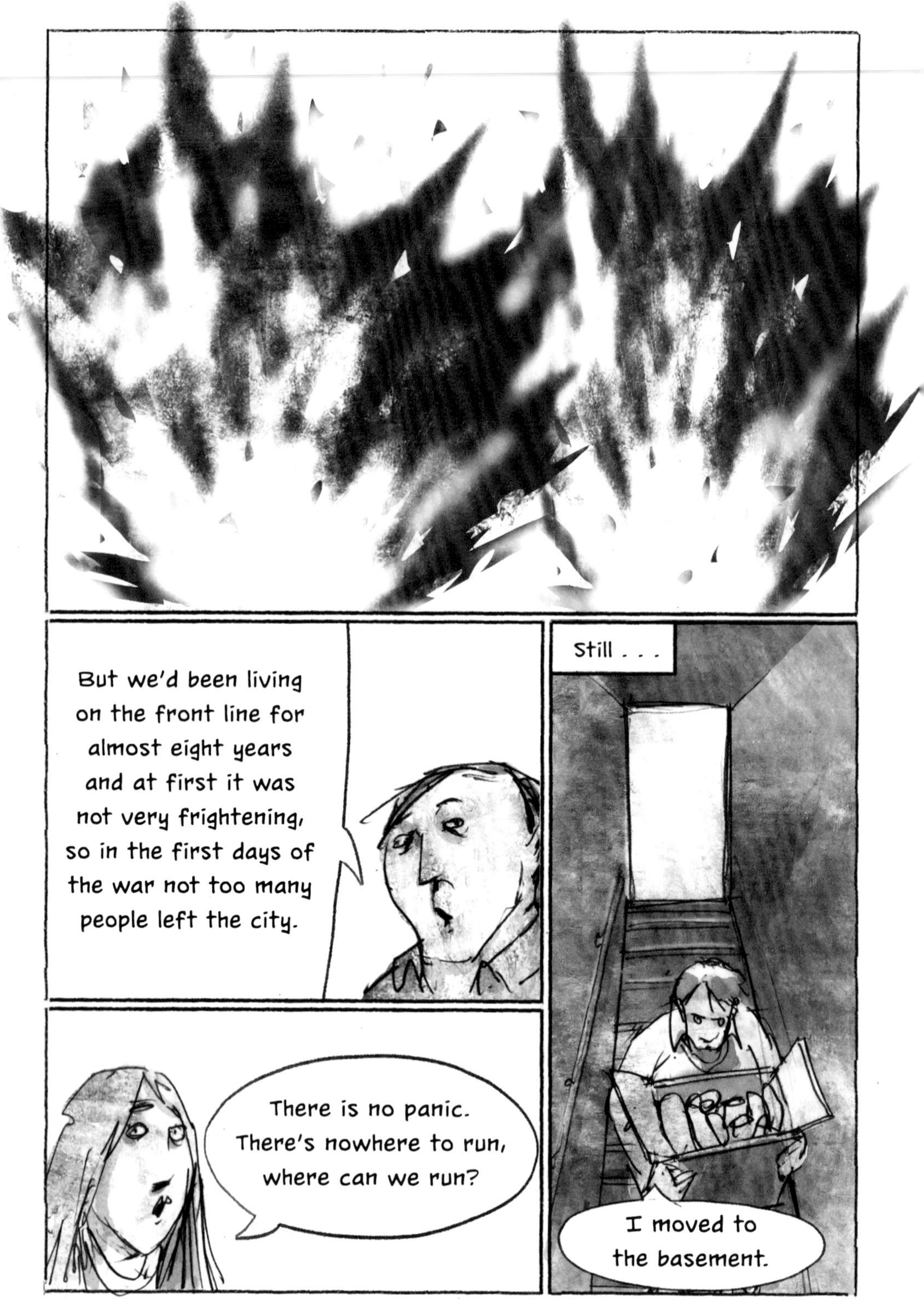
But we'd been living on the front line for almost eight years and at first it was not very frightening, so in the first days of the war not too many people left the city.
Still . . .
There is no panic. There's nowhere to run, where can we run?
I moved to the basement.

Some head to the Azovstal steel plant. The huge factory is known to house deep underground bomb shelters dating back to WWII that are stocked with food and water to nourish people for weeks.

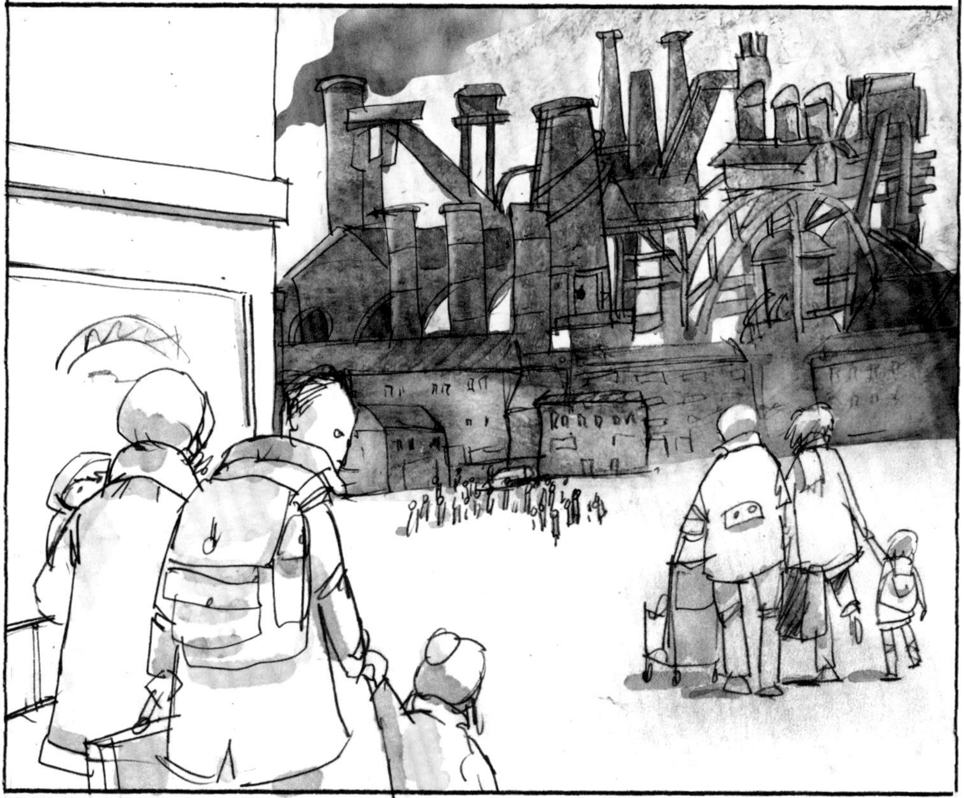

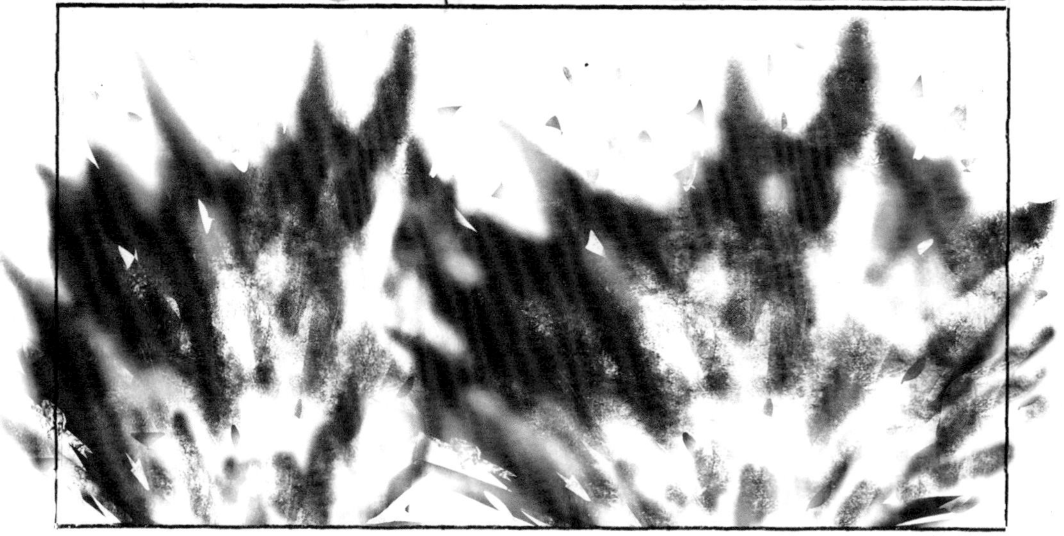

TUESDAY, MARCH 1, 2022

Ukrainian president Volodymyr Zelensky tells the world Ukraine is

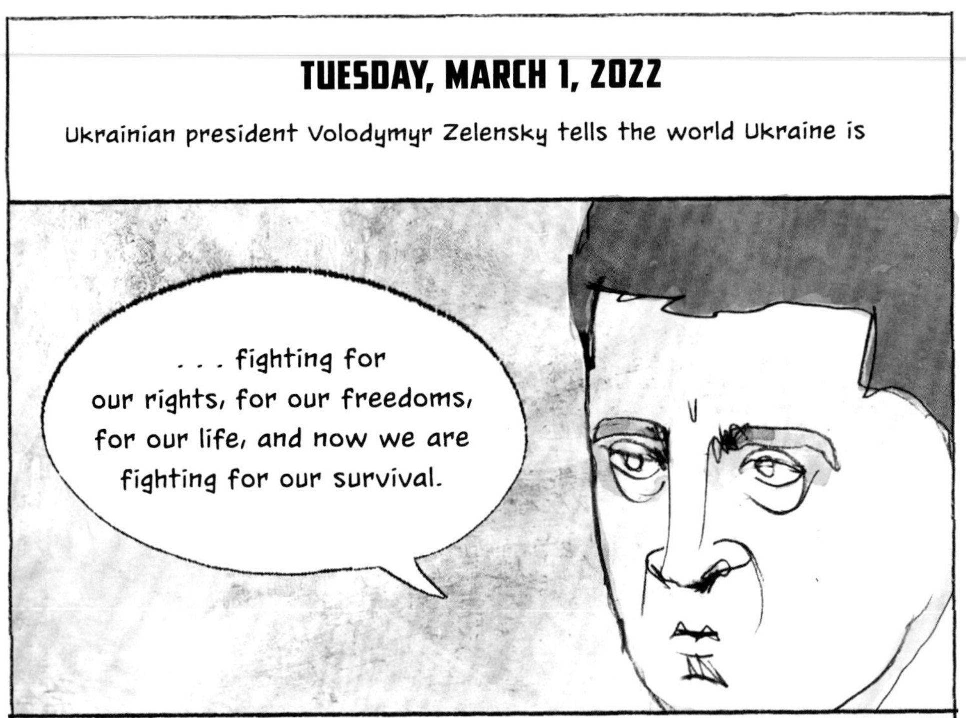
. . . fighting for our rights, for our freedoms, for our life, and now we are fighting for our survival.

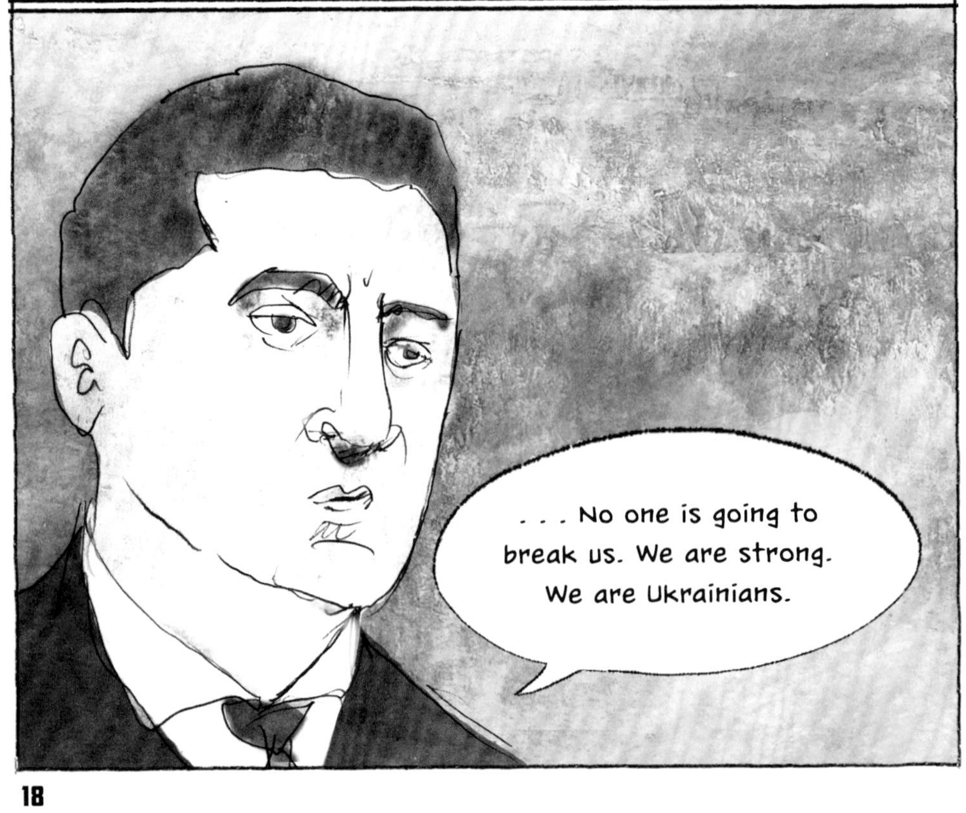
. . . No one is going to break us. We are strong. We are Ukrainians.

Finding shelter in basements or parking garages, some civilians concoct Molotov cocktails—gasoline-filled bottles—as simple fiery weapons to be heaved at Russian troops.

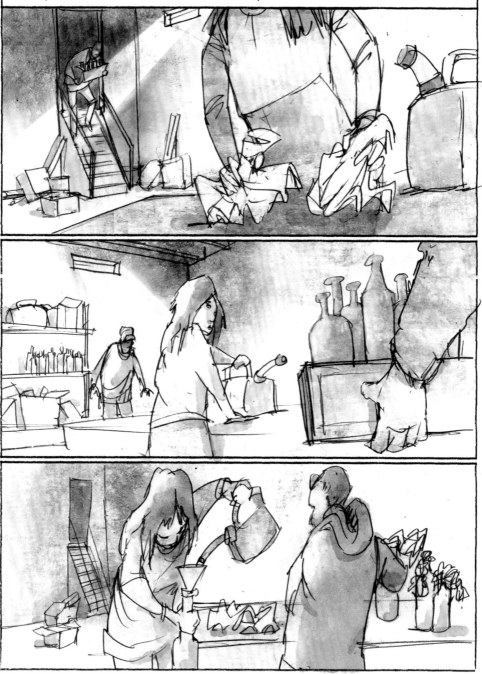

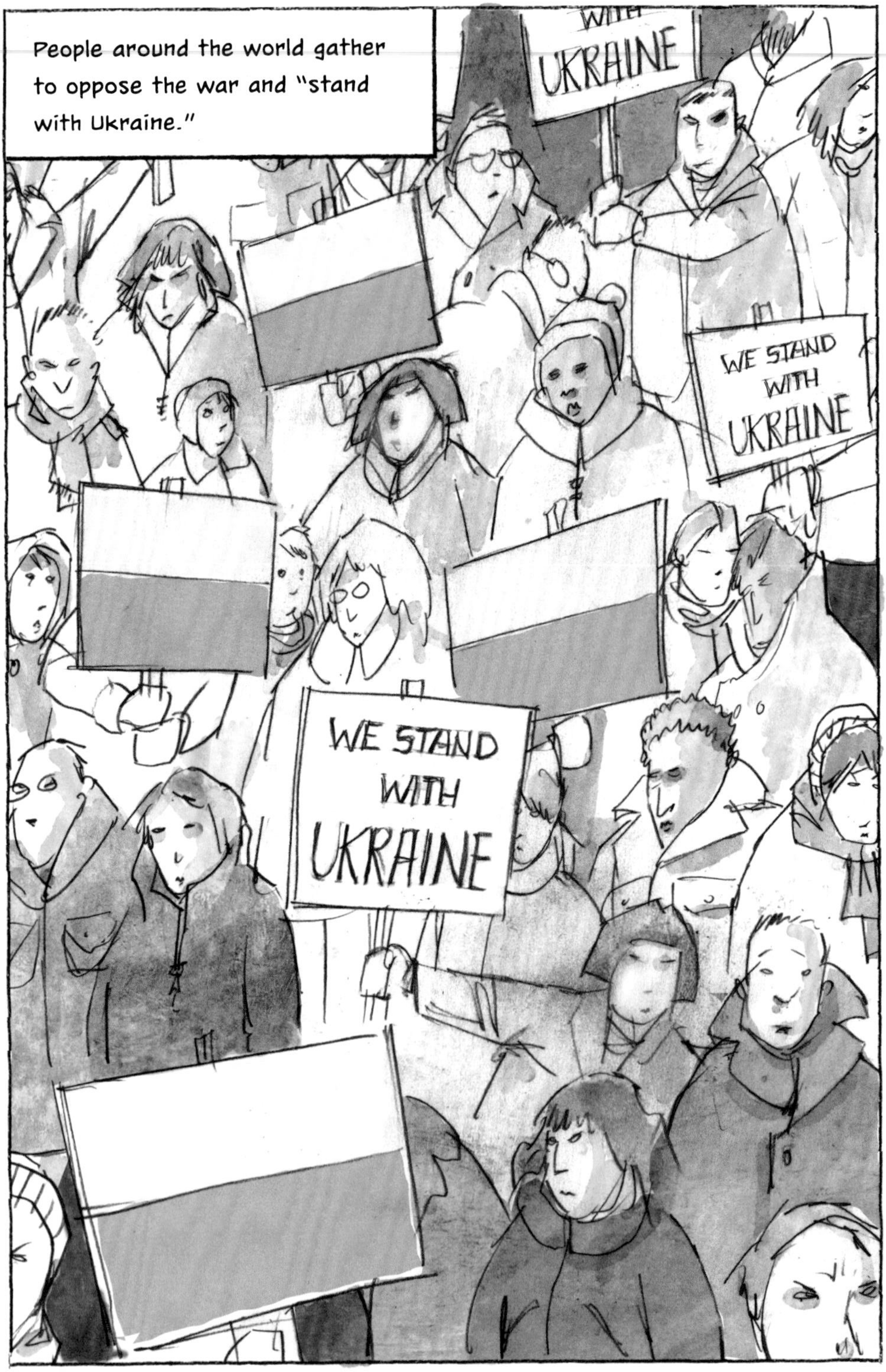
People around the world gather to oppose the war and "stand with Ukraine."
UKRAINE
WE STAND WITH UKRAINE
WE STAND WITH UKRAINE

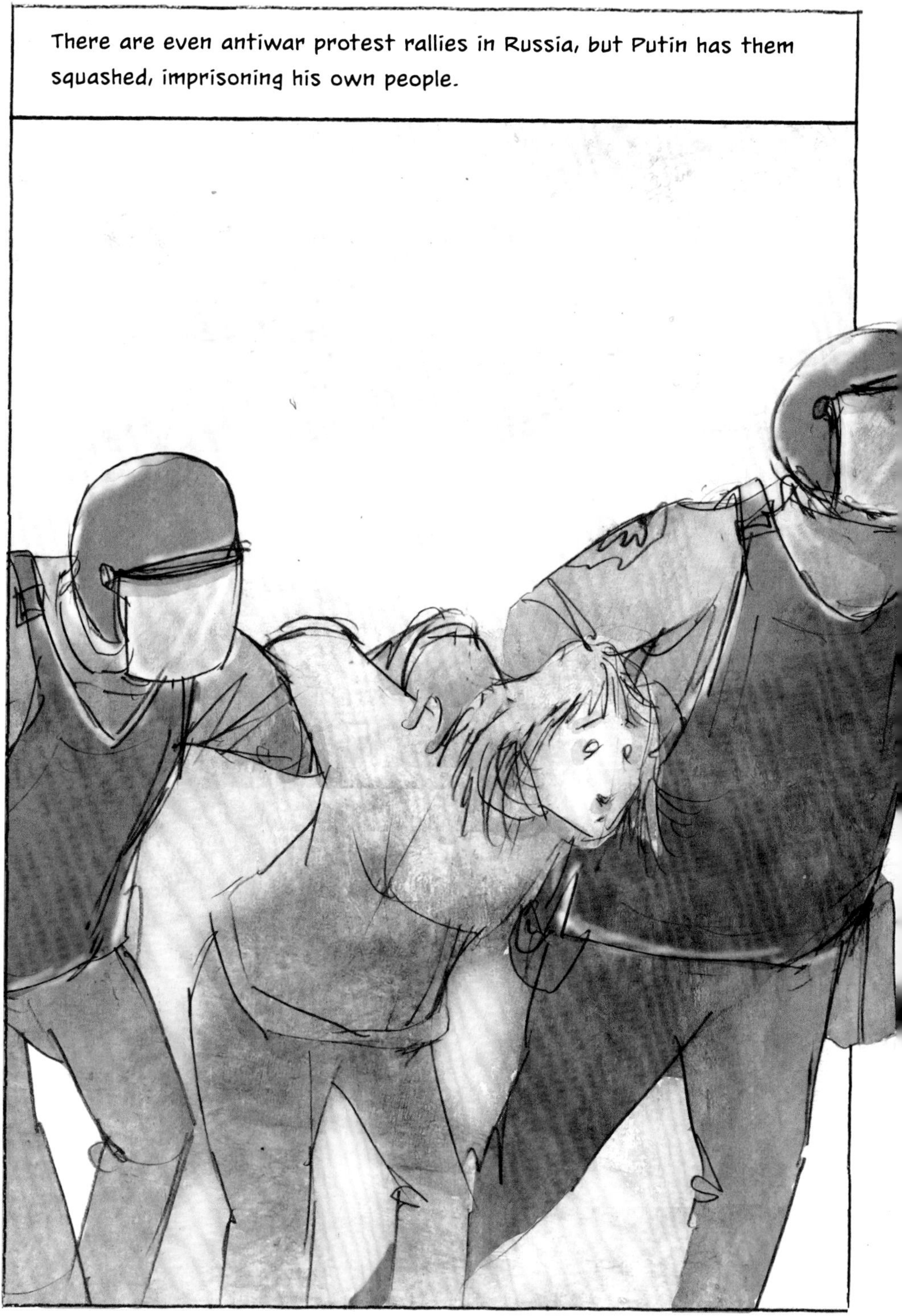
There are even antiwar protest rallies in Russia, but Putin has them squashed, imprisoning his own people.

WEDNESDAY, MARCH 2, 2022

Russian mortars, cannons, rockets, and jets pound the city for 14 straight hours.

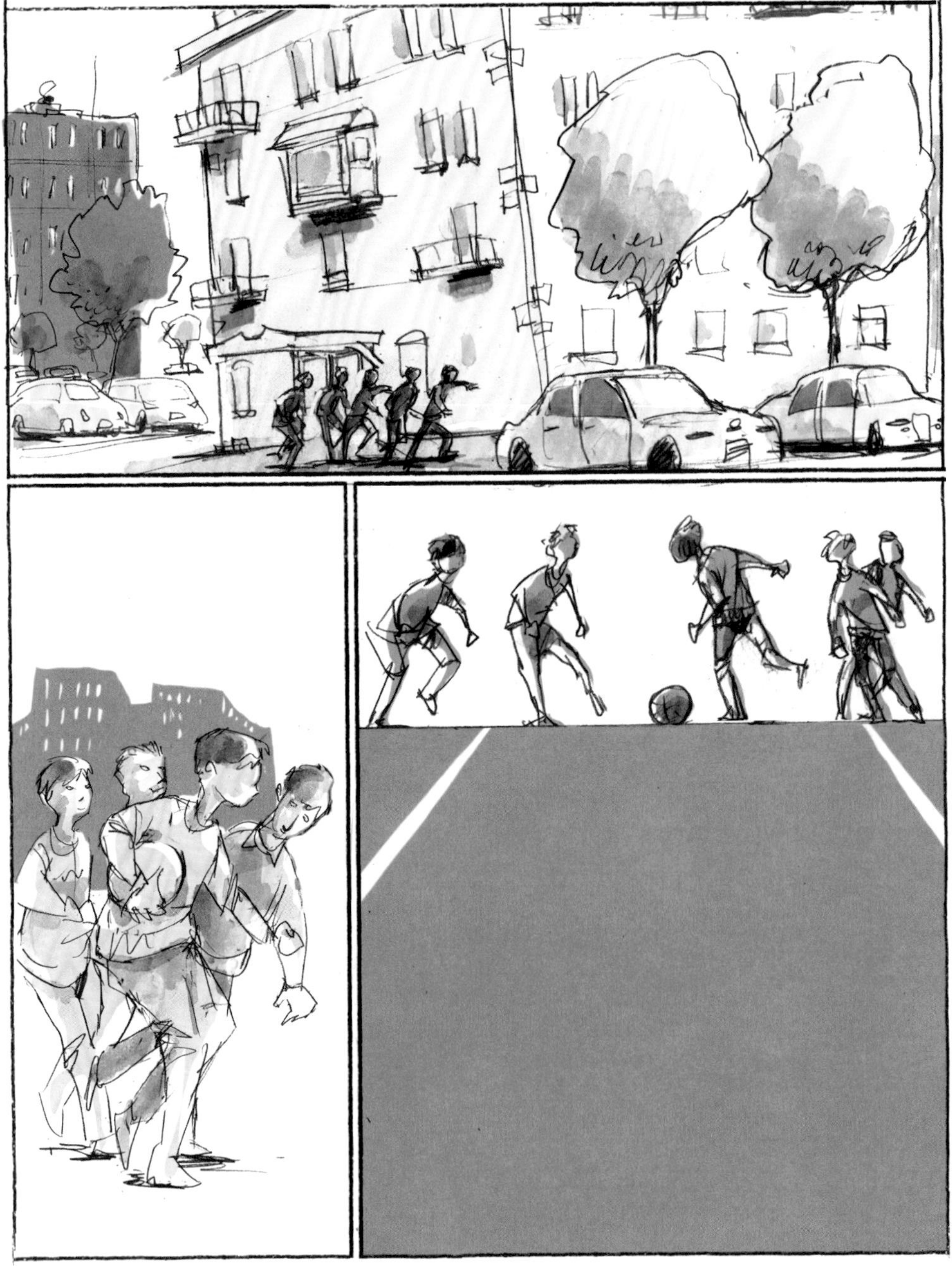

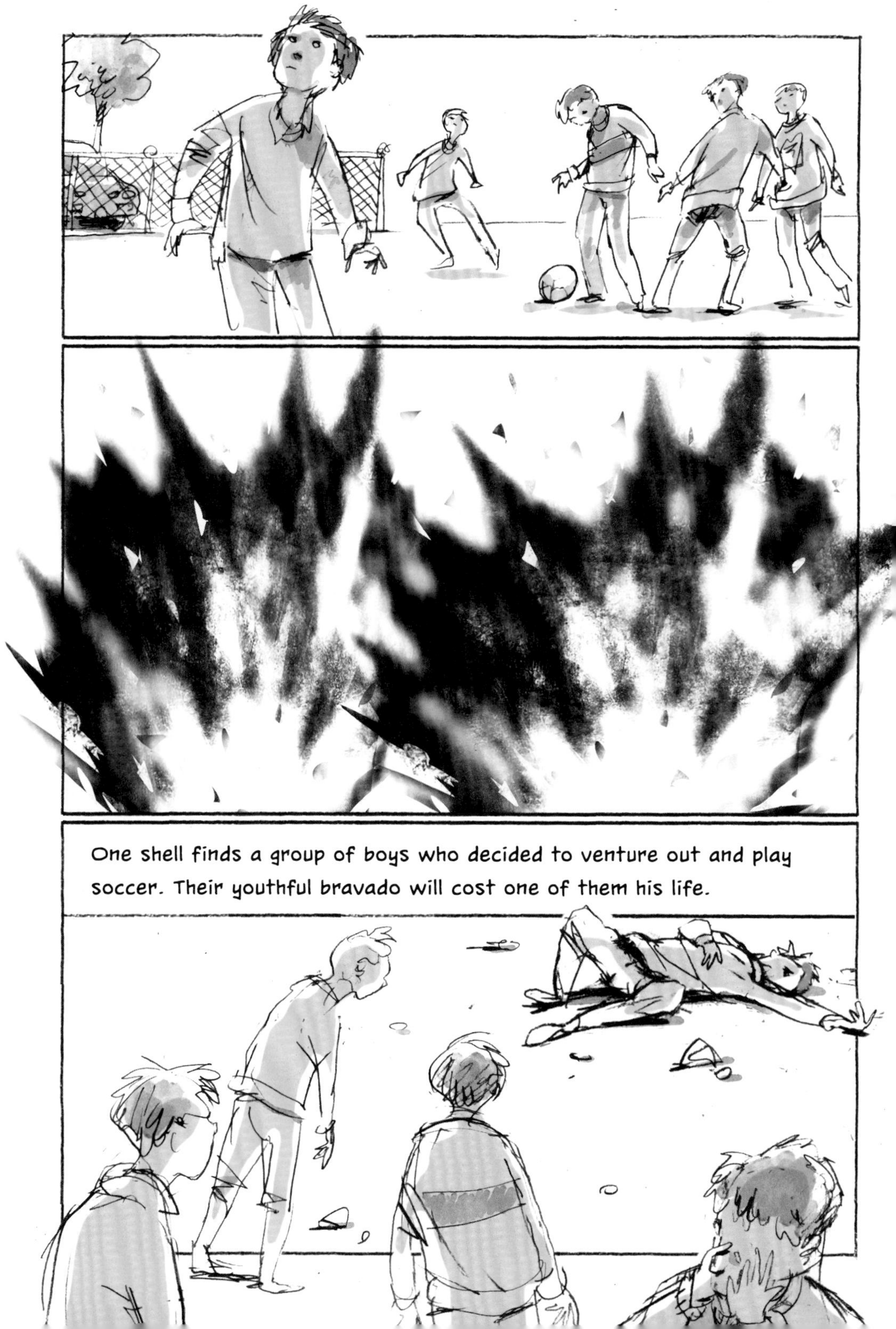
One shell finds a group of boys who decided to venture out and play soccer. Their youthful bravado will cost one of them his life.

THURSDAY, MARCH 3, 2022

The fighting disrupts electricity and heating across the city.

It is below freezing.

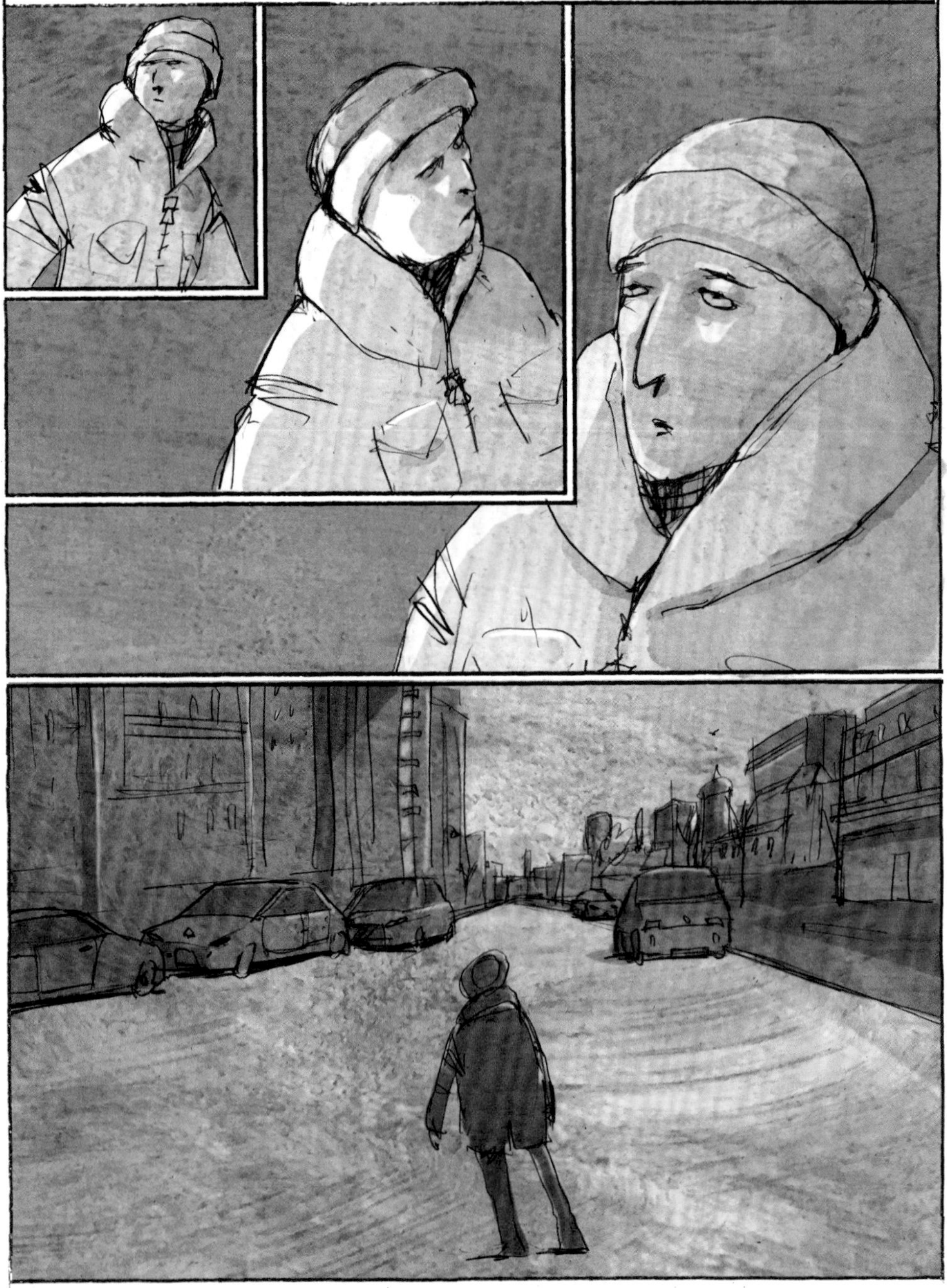

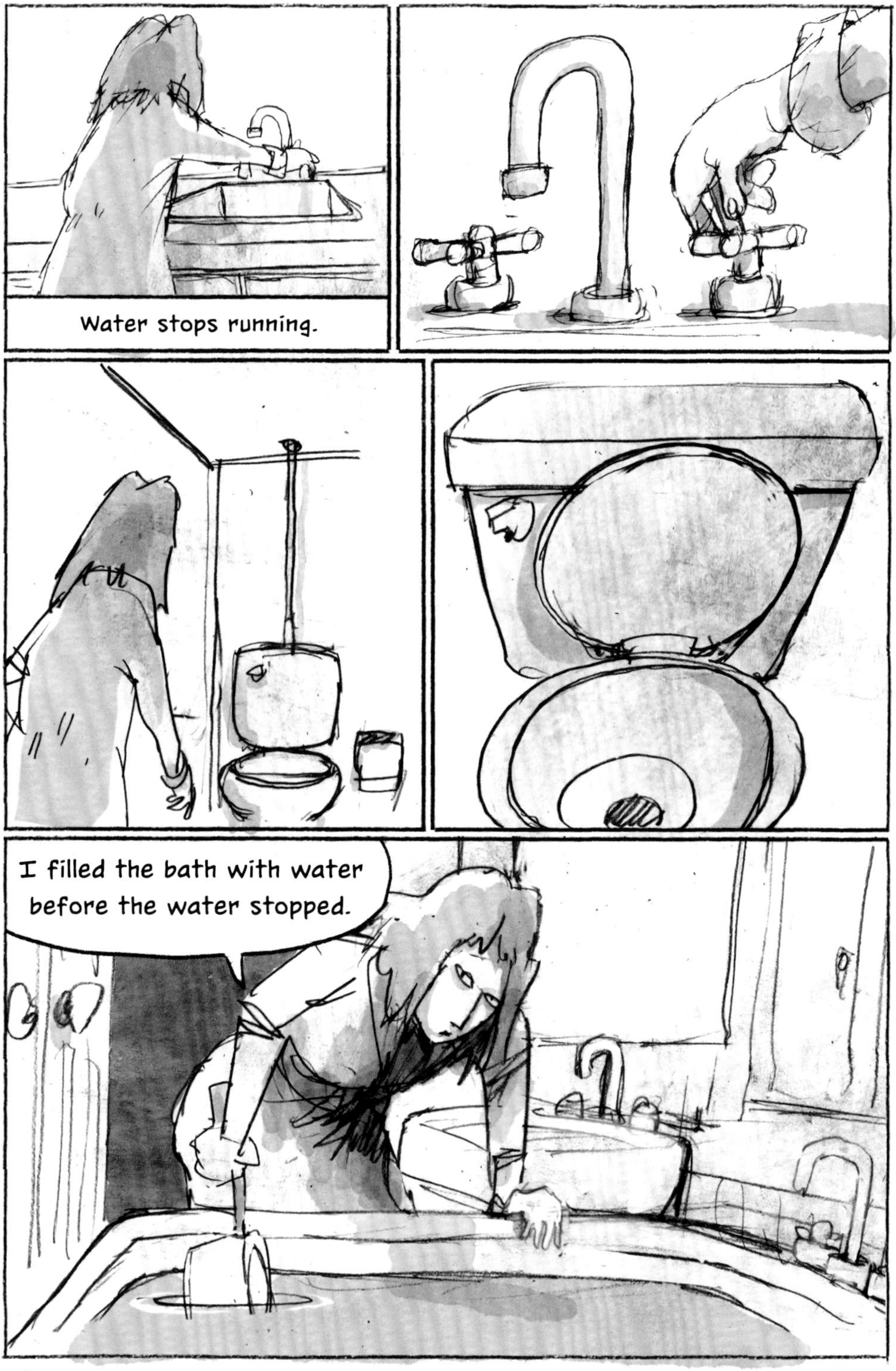
Water stops running.
I filled the bath with water before the water stopped.

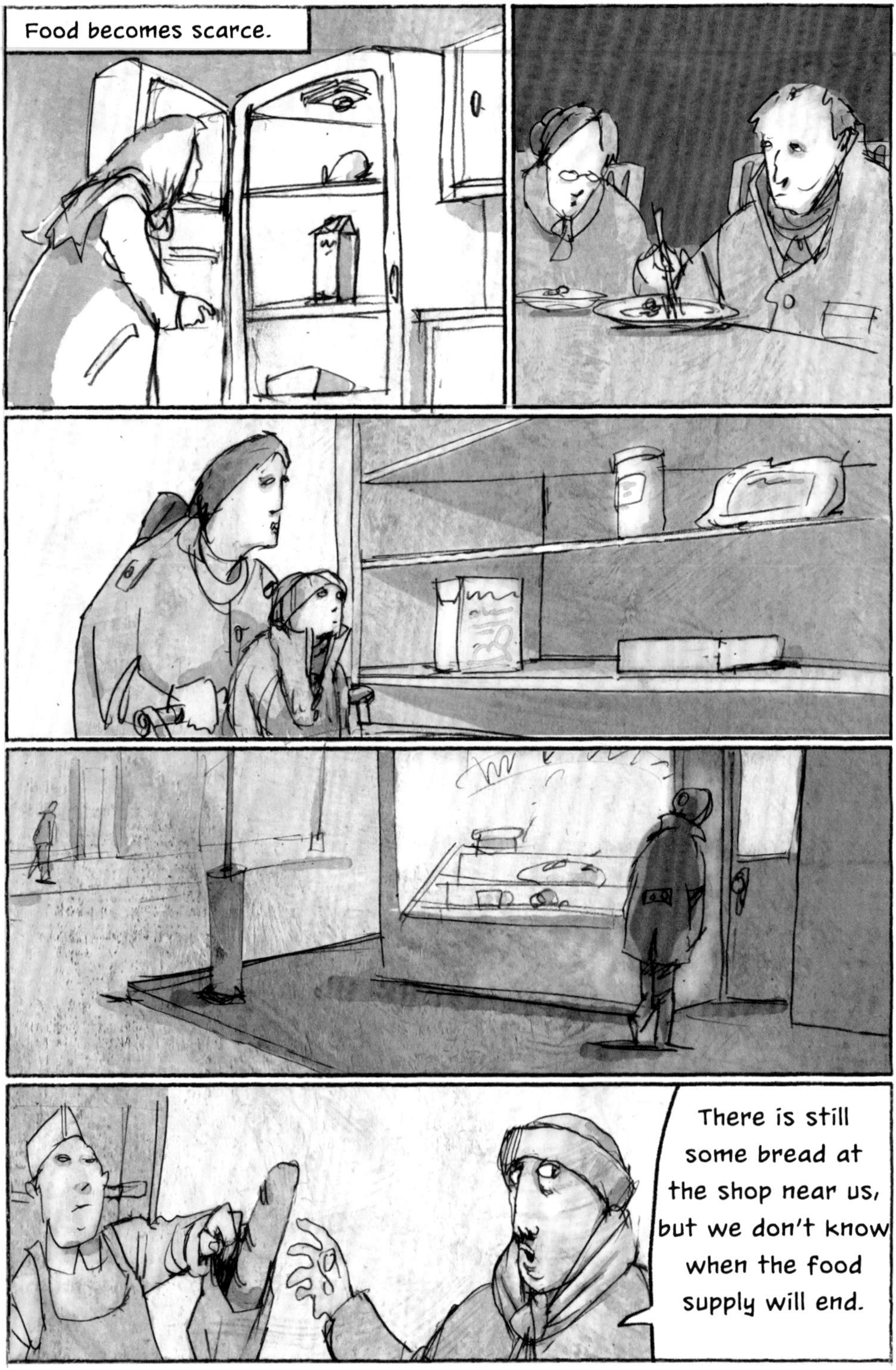
Food becomes scarce.
There is still some bread at the shop near us, but we don't know when the food supply will end.

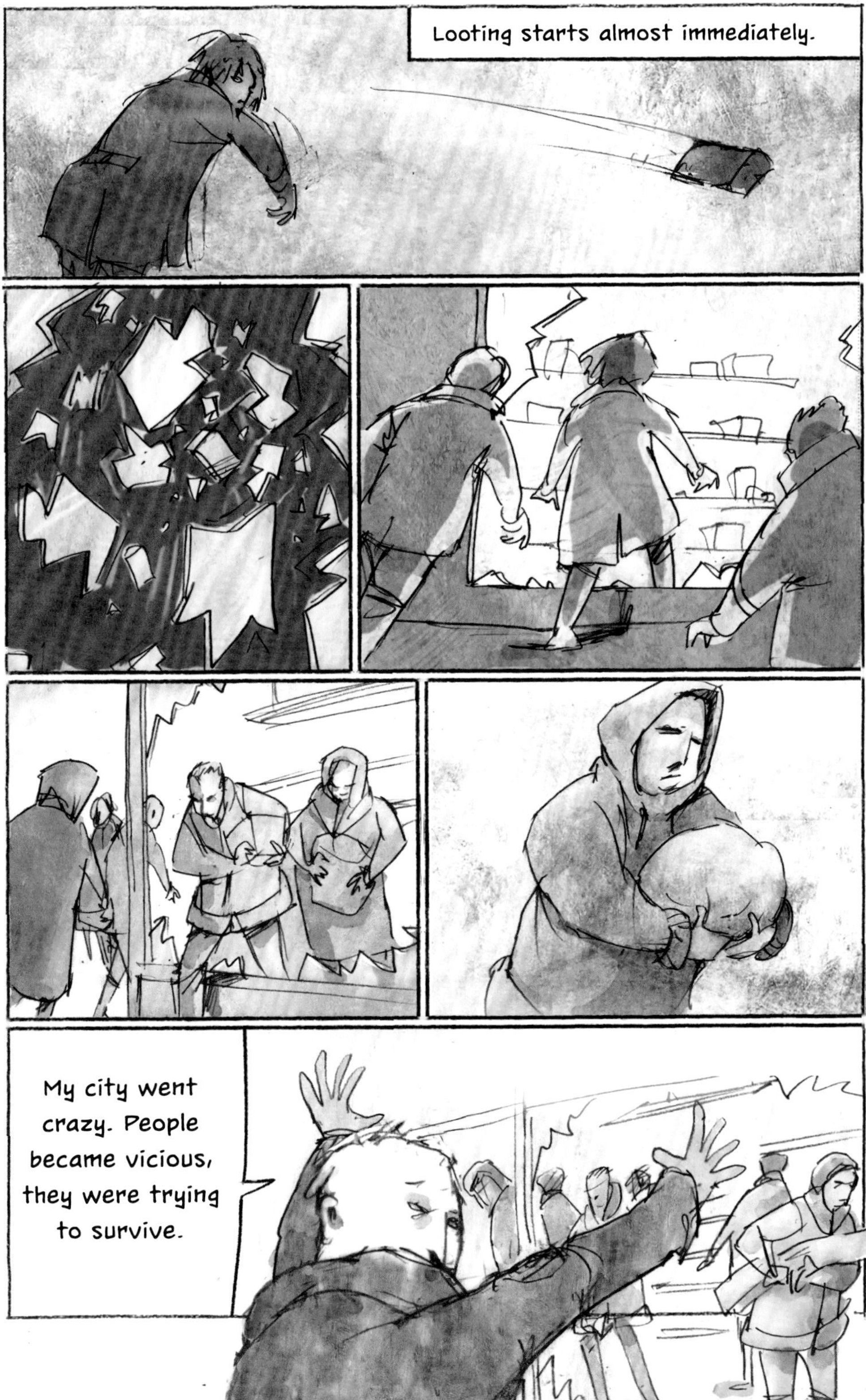
Looting starts almost immediately.
My city went crazy. People became vicious, they were trying to survive.

Whatever food they can scrounge is heated outside over open fires.

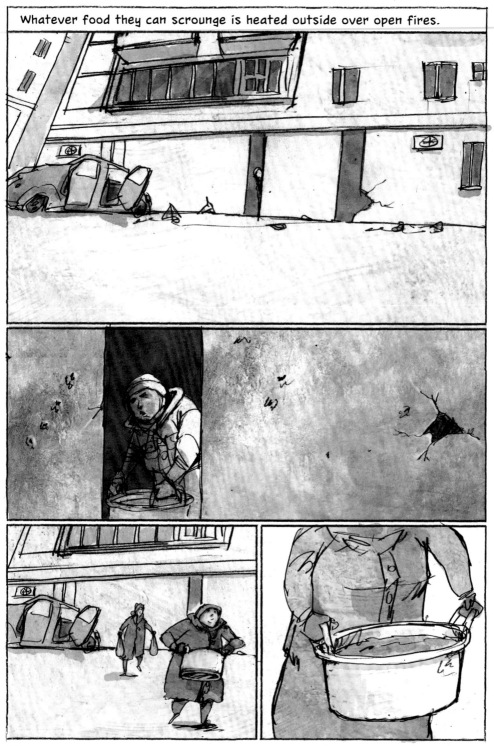

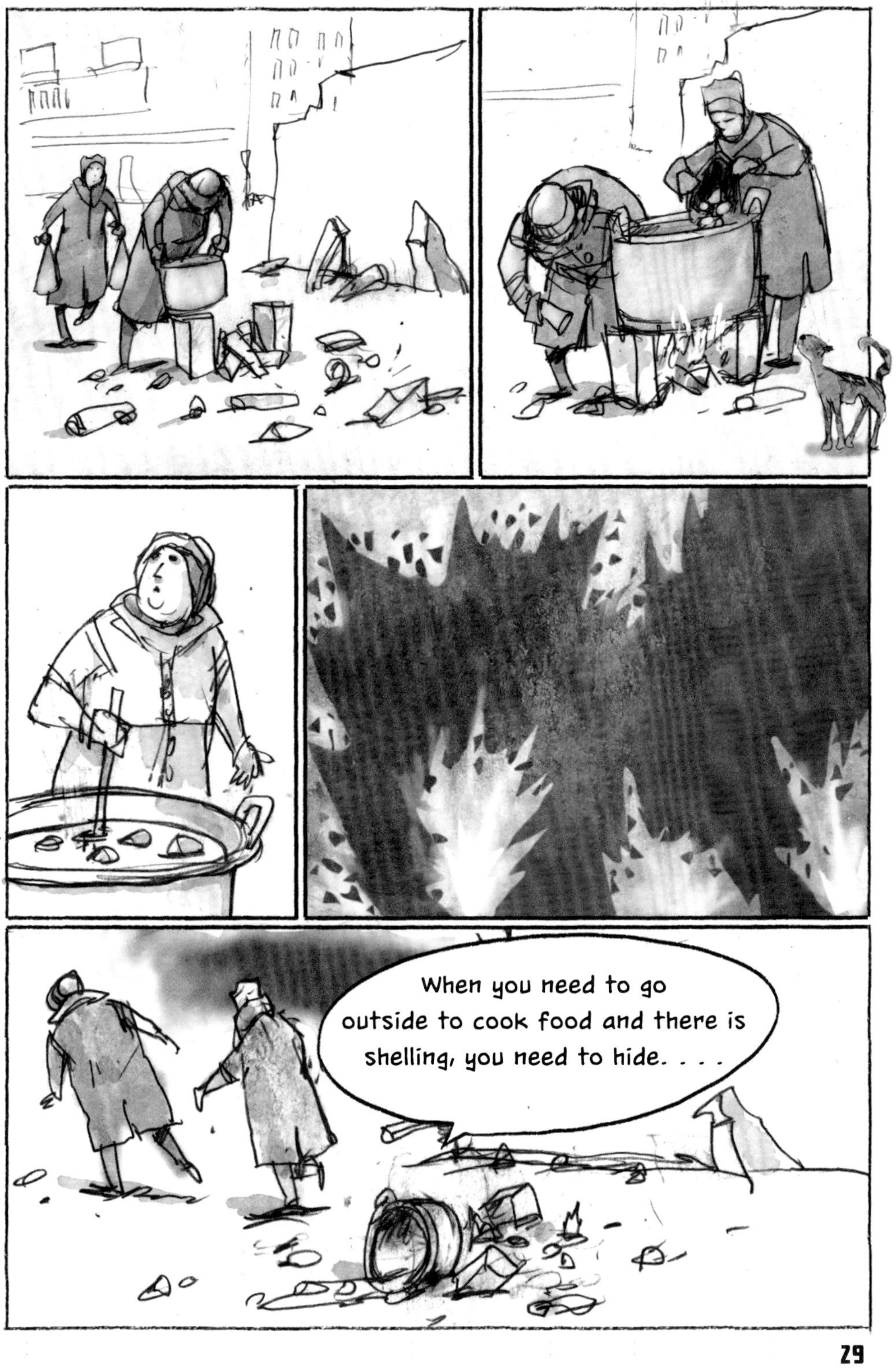
When you need to go outside to cook food and there is shelling, you need to hide. . . .

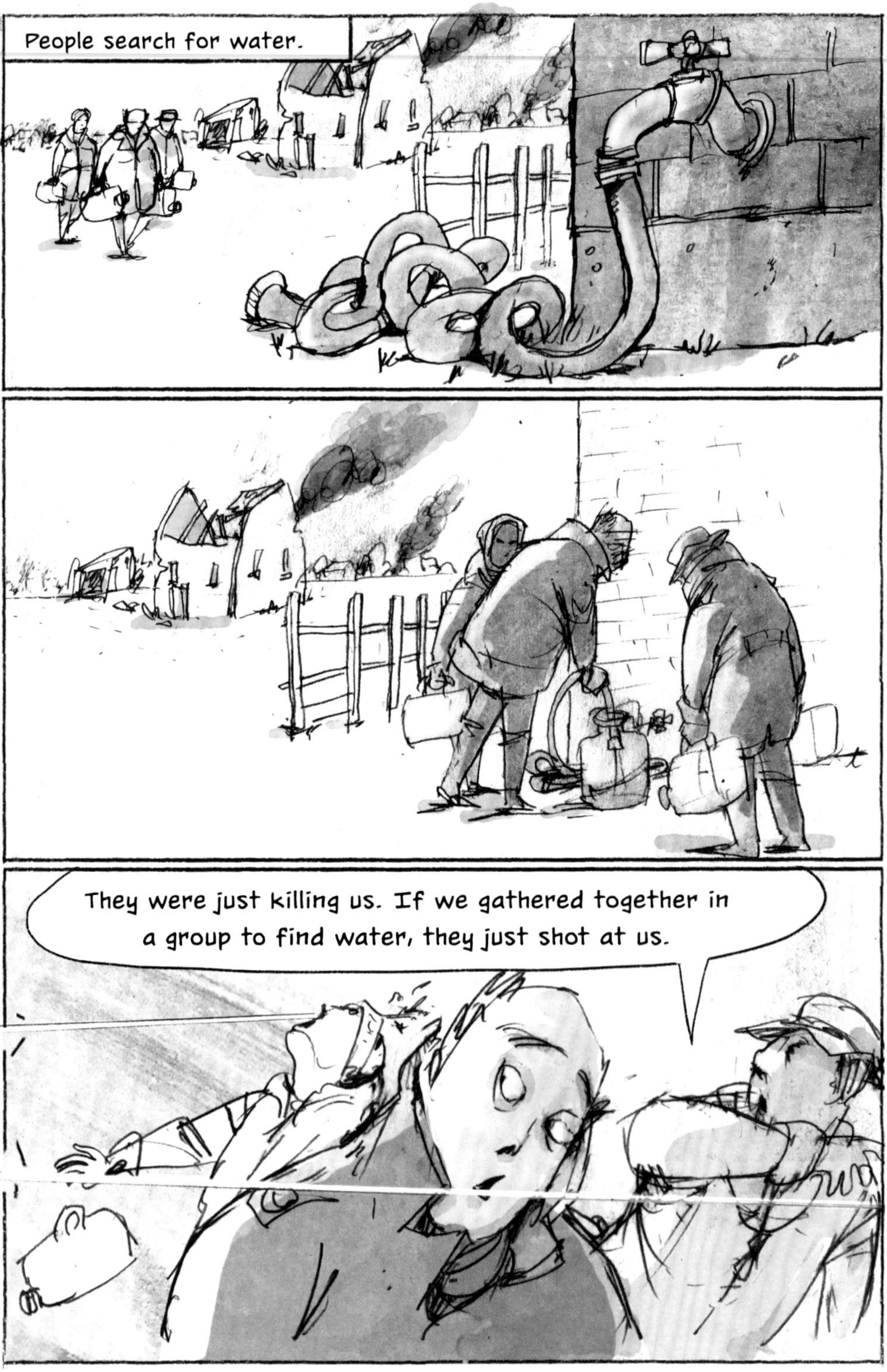

People search for water.
They were just killing us. If we gathered together in a group to find water, they just shot at us.

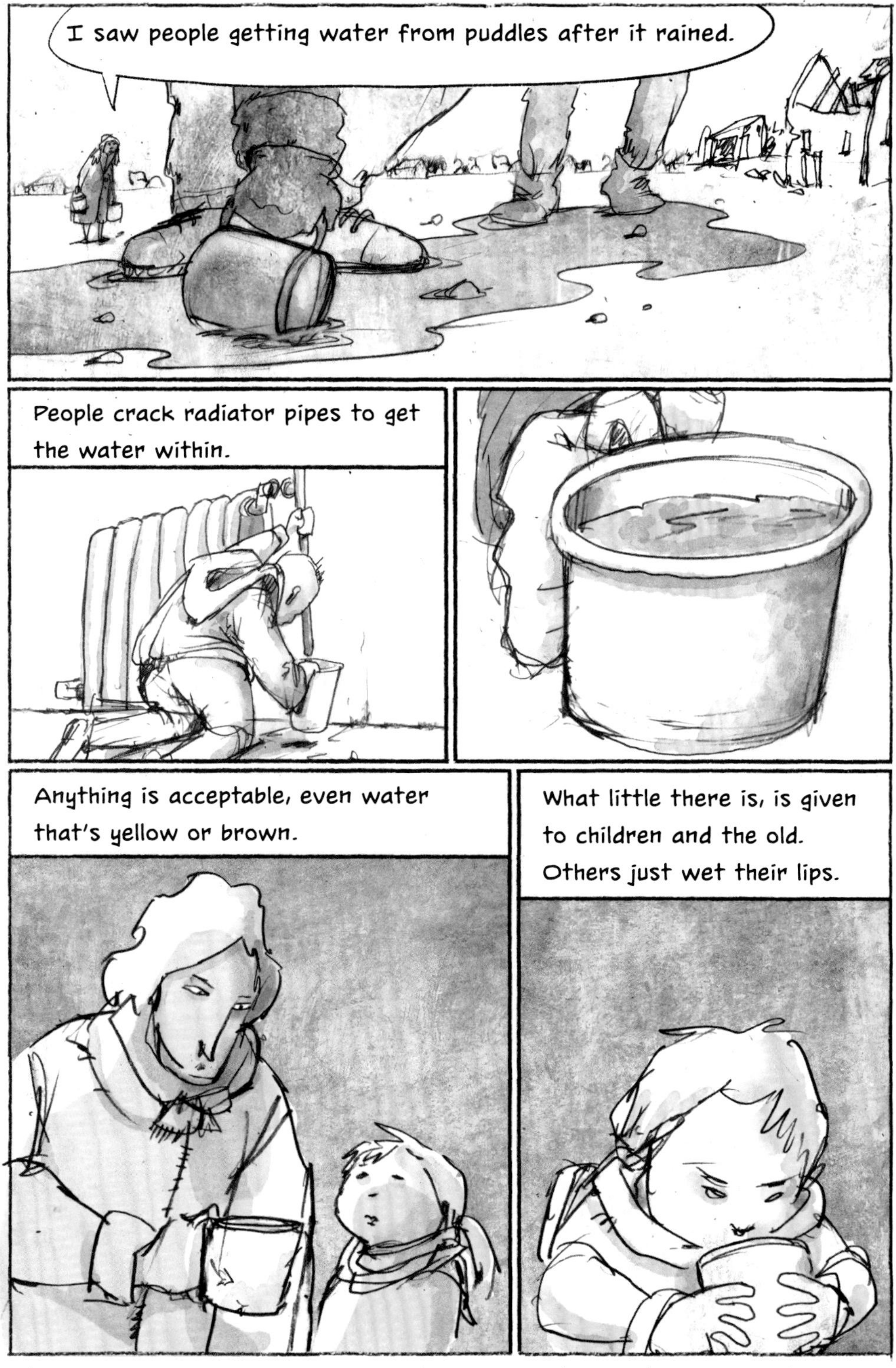
I saw people getting water from puddles after it rained.
People crack radiator pipes to get the water within.
Anything is acceptable, even water that's yellow or brown.
What little there is, is given to children and the old. Others just wet their lips.

A humanitarian organization, the International Committee of the Red Cross, reports, "Hundreds of thousands of people in Ukraine have no food, water, heat, electricity, or medical care."

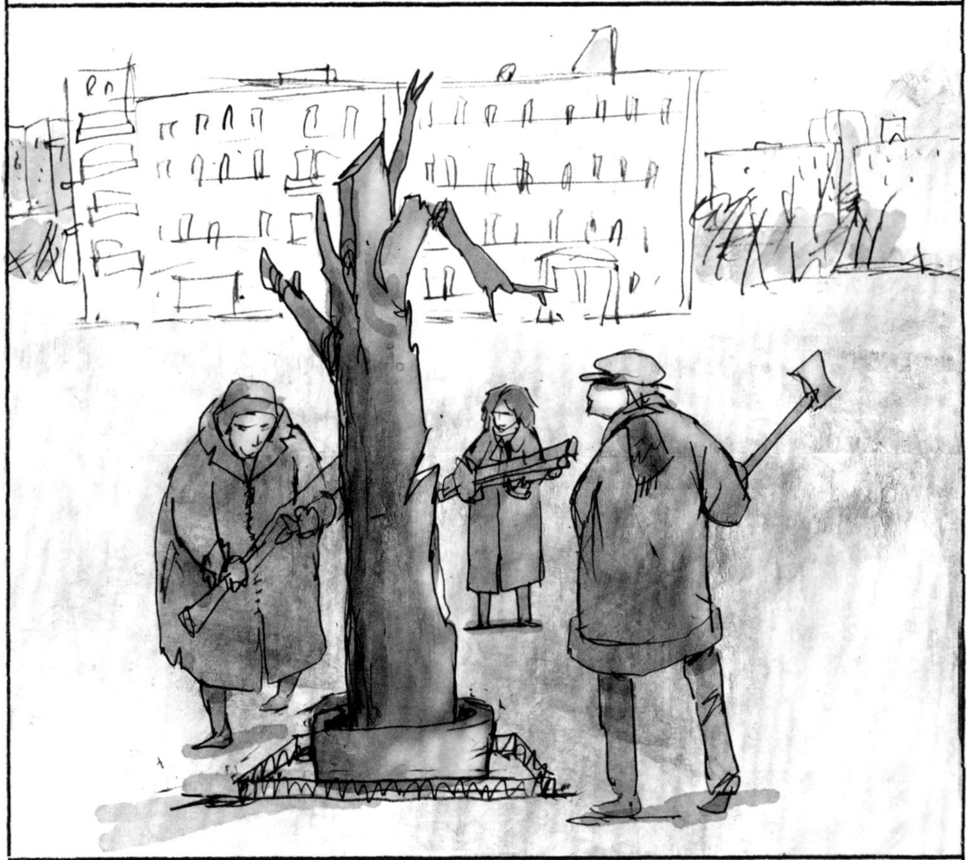

Freezing weather adds to the misery. Trees disappear as people cut them for firewood.

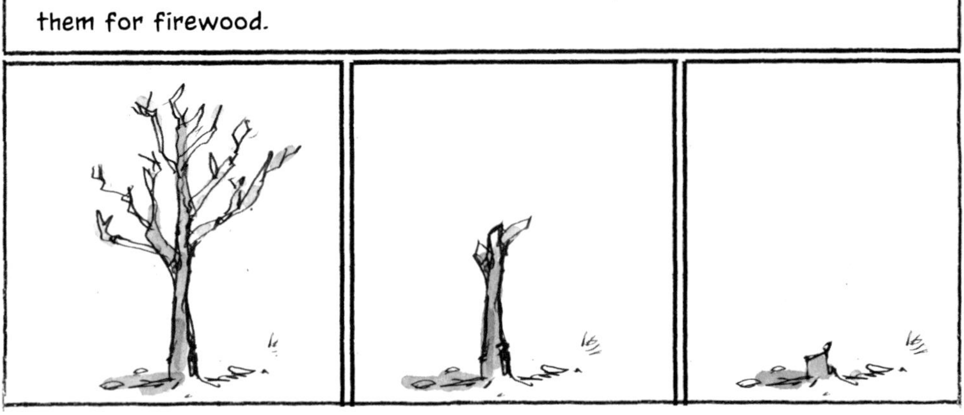

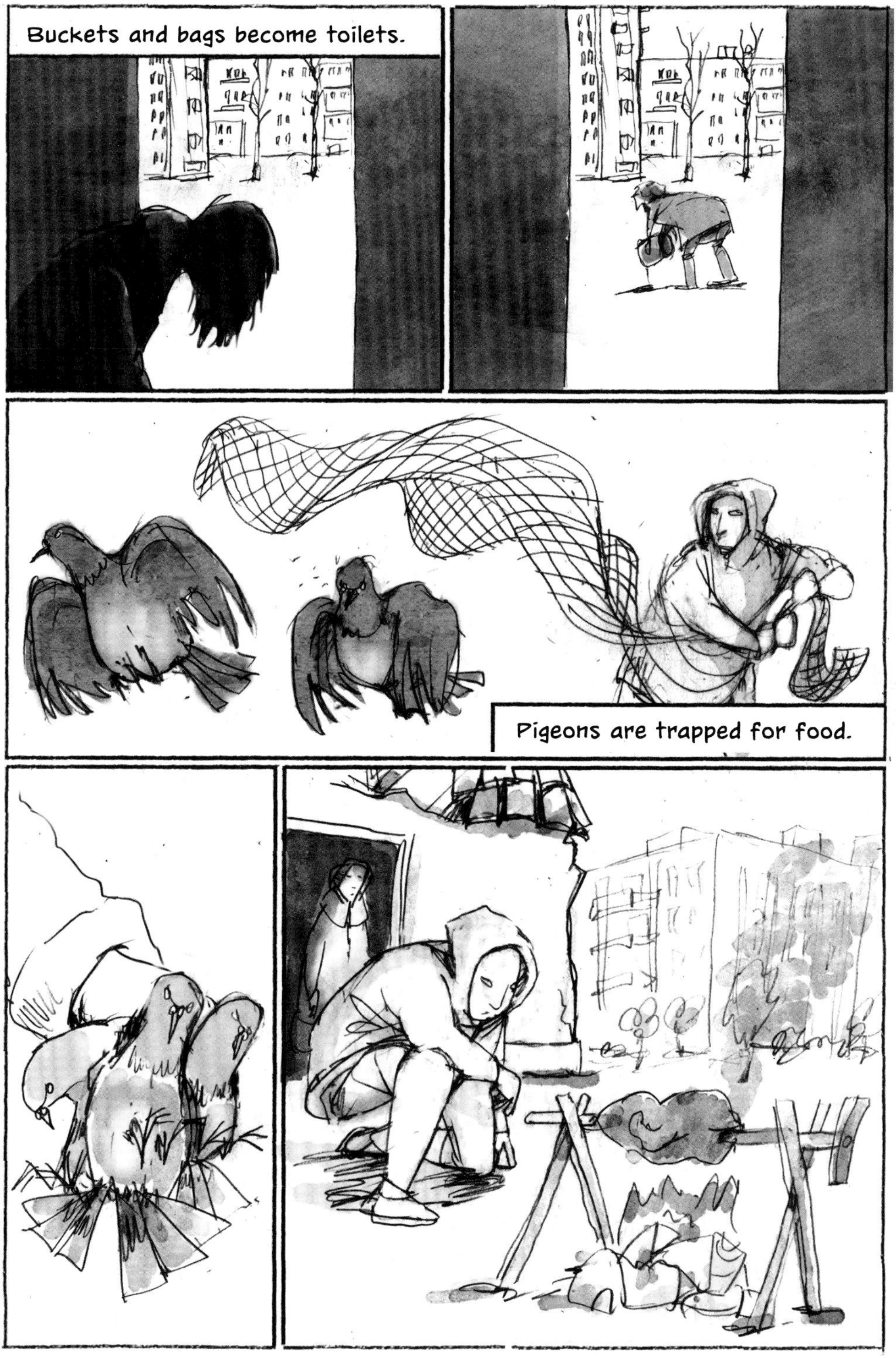
Buckets and bags become toilets.
Pigeons are trapped for food.

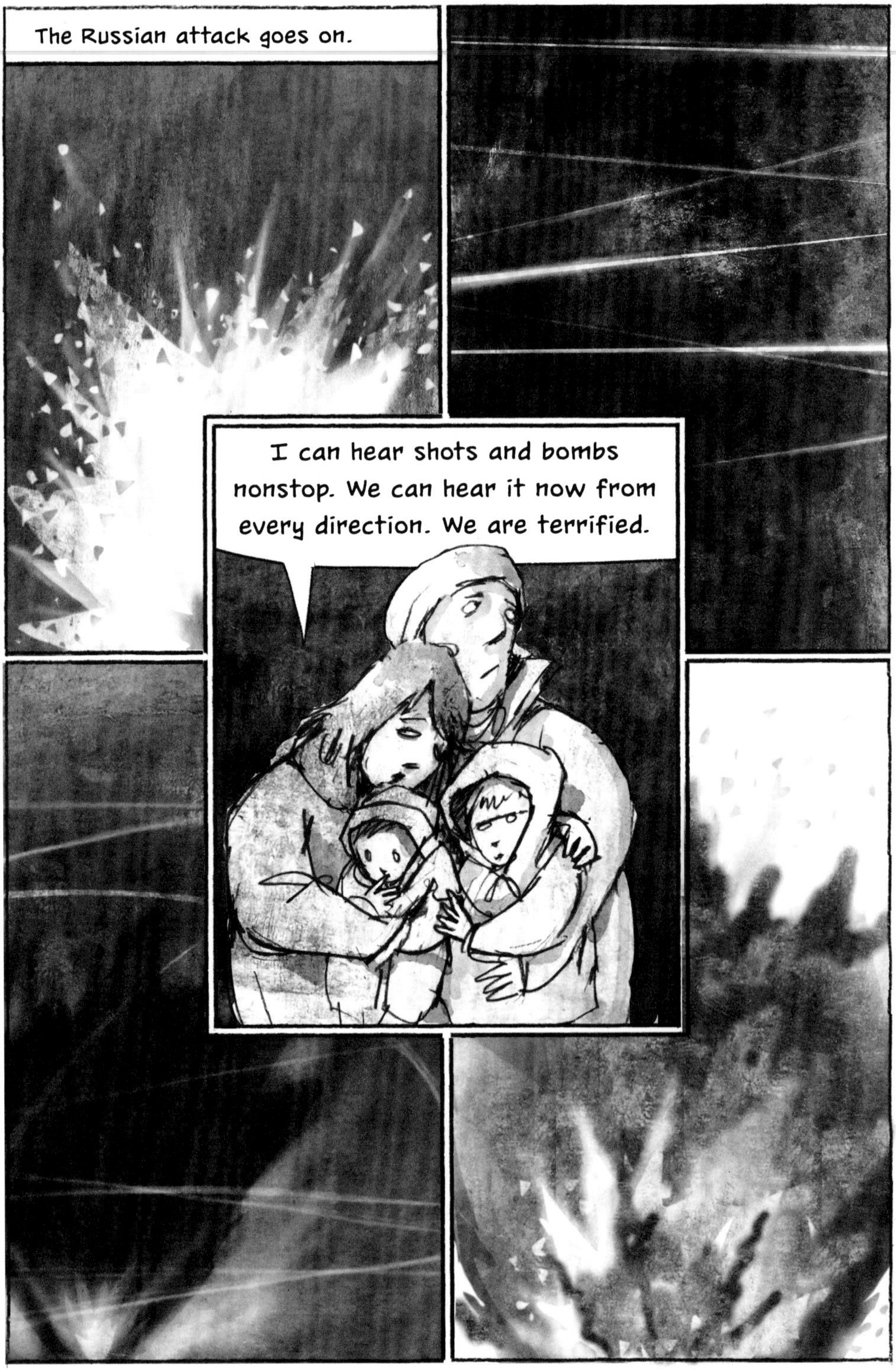
The Russian attack goes on.
I can hear shots and bombs nonstop. We can hear it now from every direction. We are terrified.

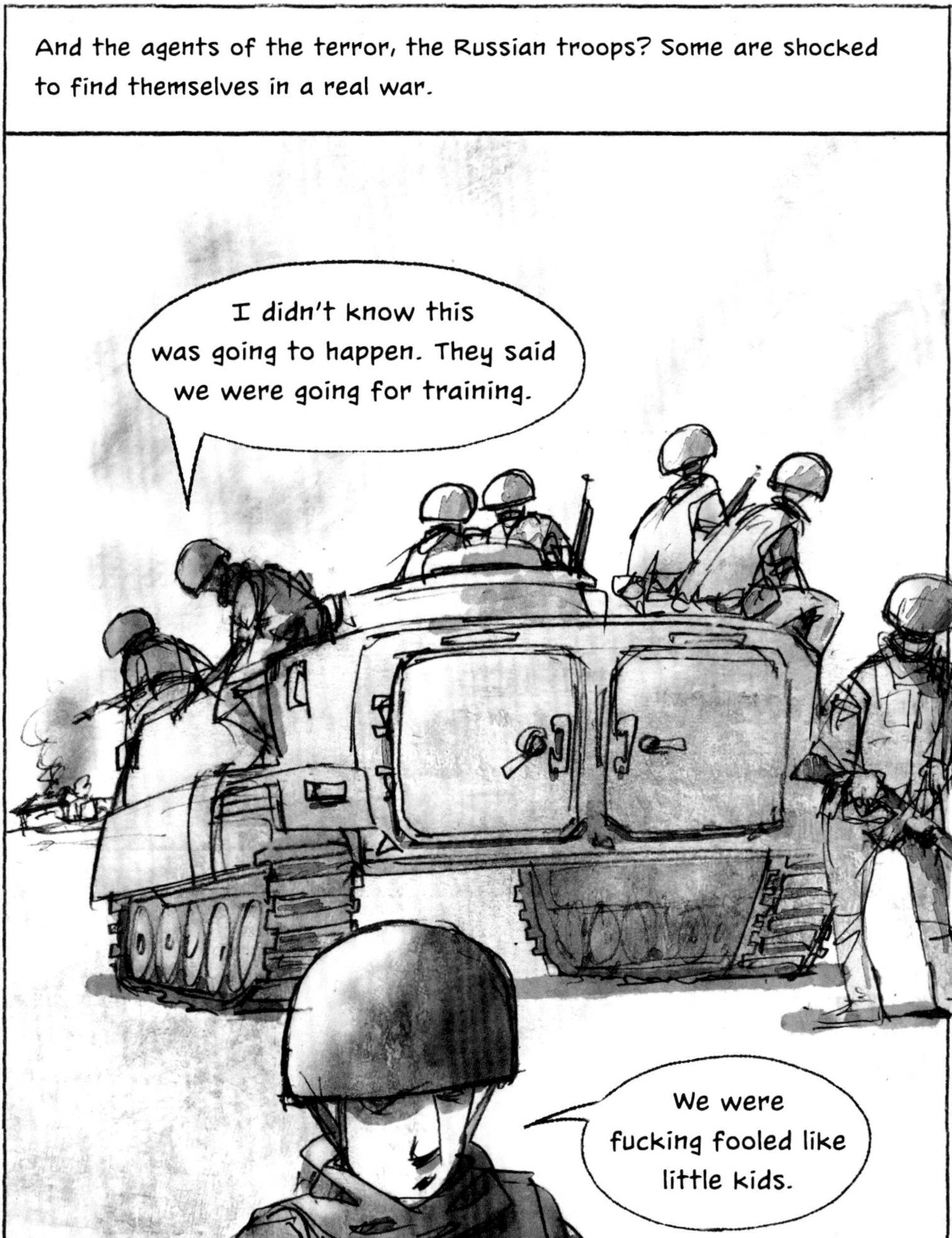
And the agents of the terror, the Russian troops? Some are shocked to find themselves in a real war.
I didn't know this was going to happen. They said we were going for training.
We were fucking fooled like little kids.
Still, the terror goes on.

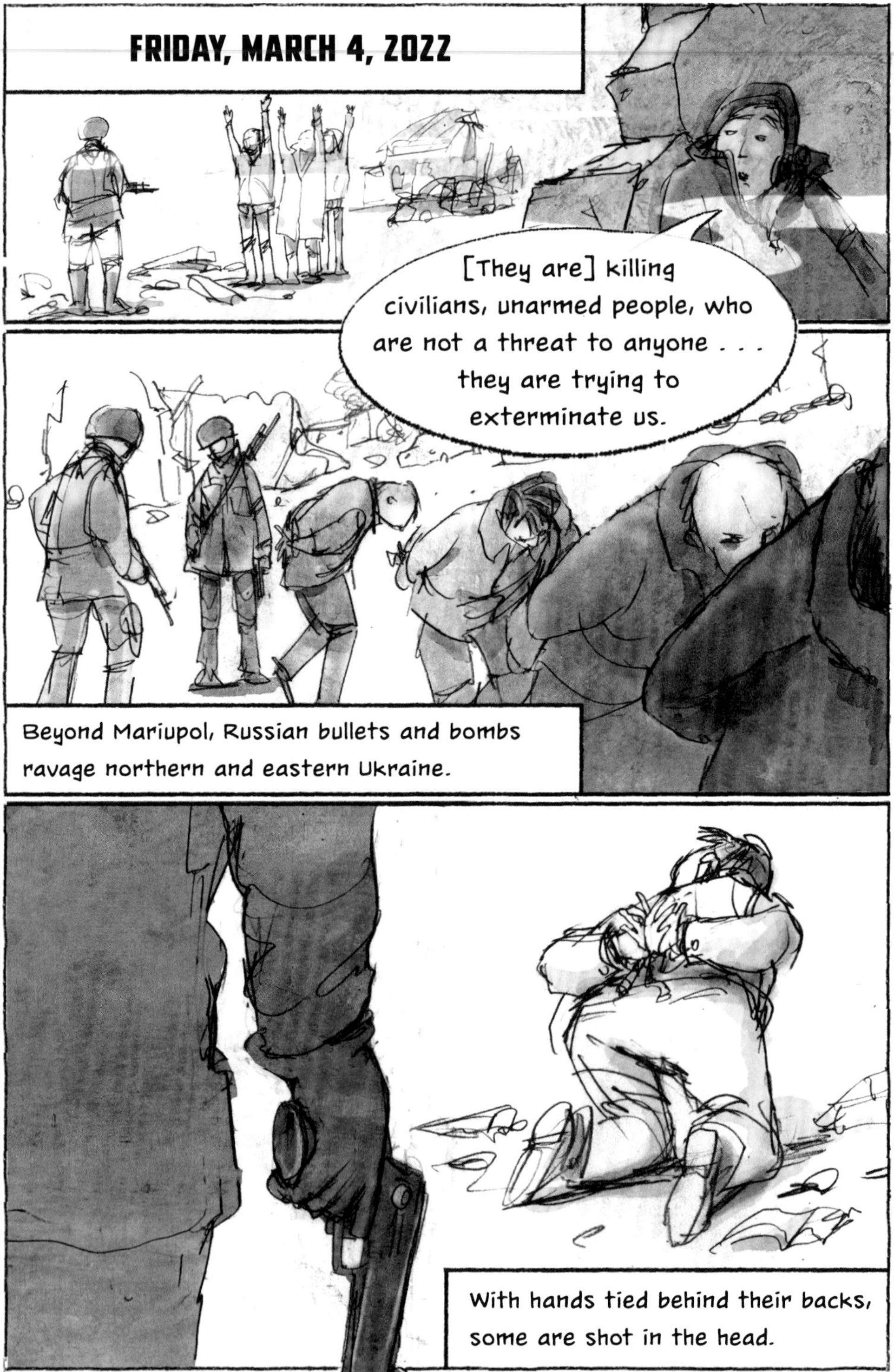
FRIDAY, MARCH 4, 2022
[They are] killing civilians, unarmed people, who are not a threat to anyone . . . they are trying to exterminate us.
Beyond Mariupol, Russian bullets and bombs ravage northern and eastern Ukraine.
With hands tied behind their backs, some are shot in the head.

Bodies are strewn across streets, lying where they were murdered.

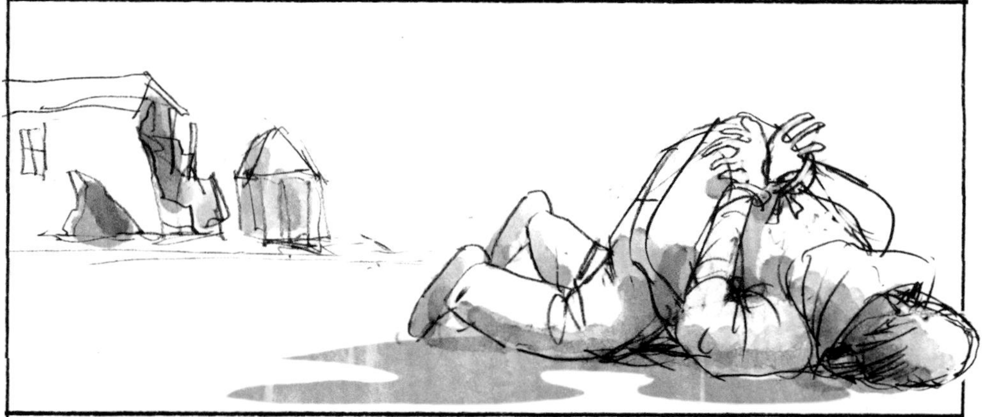

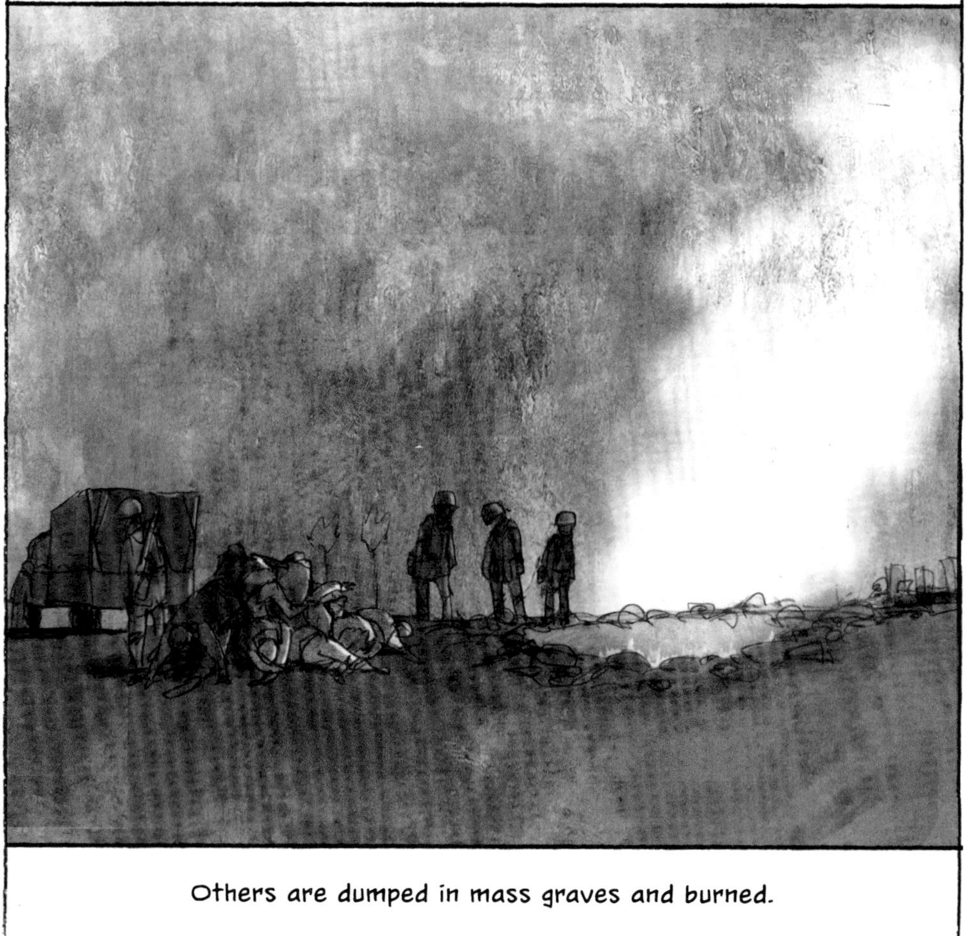

Others are dumped in mass graves and burned.

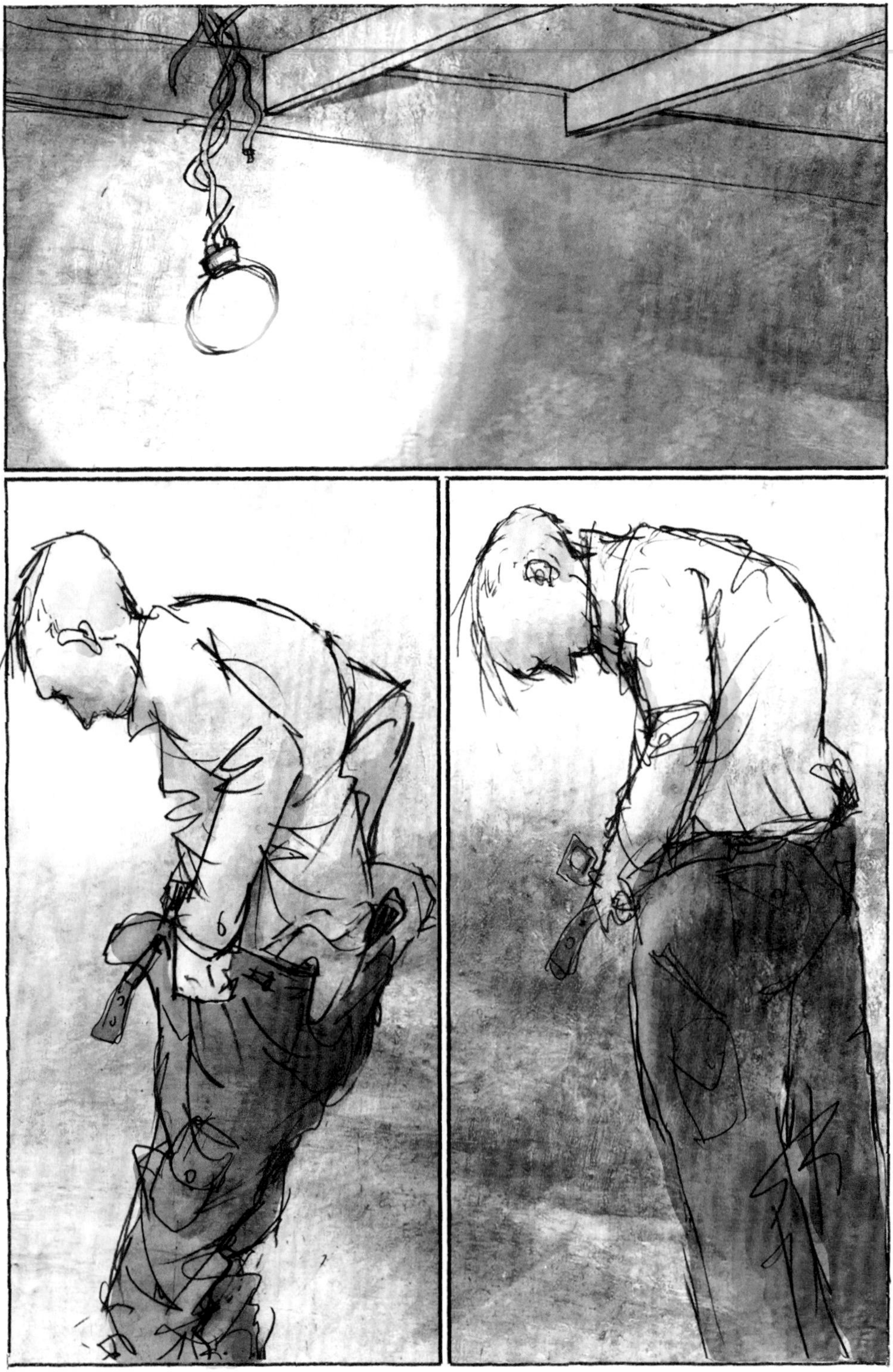

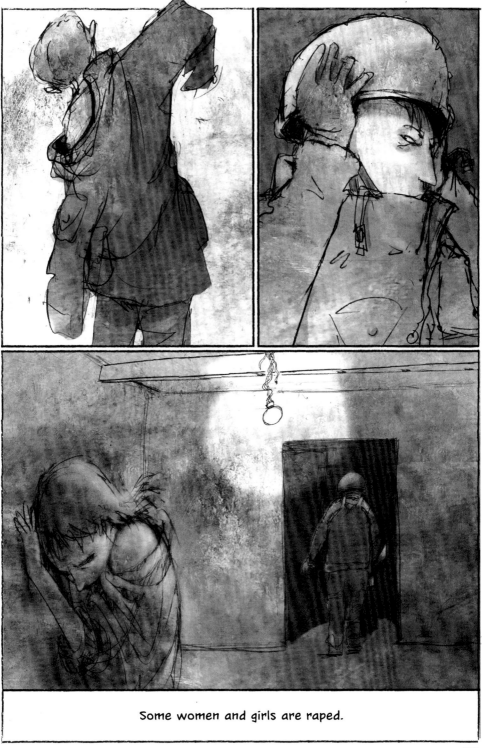

Some women and girls are raped.

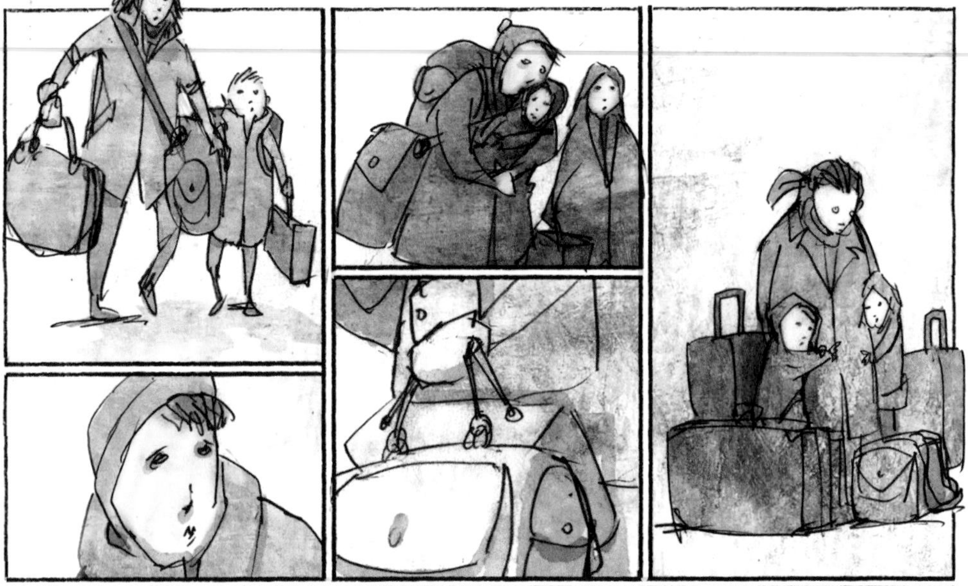

Across Ukraine, rail lines and roads are mobbed with people fleeing west, where it is safer. Many of the refugees leave Ukraine altogether. It is mostly women and children; men ages 18 to 60 are required to remain in the country and be available for the defense of Ukraine. A week after the start of the war, more than a million people have escaped to neighboring countries.

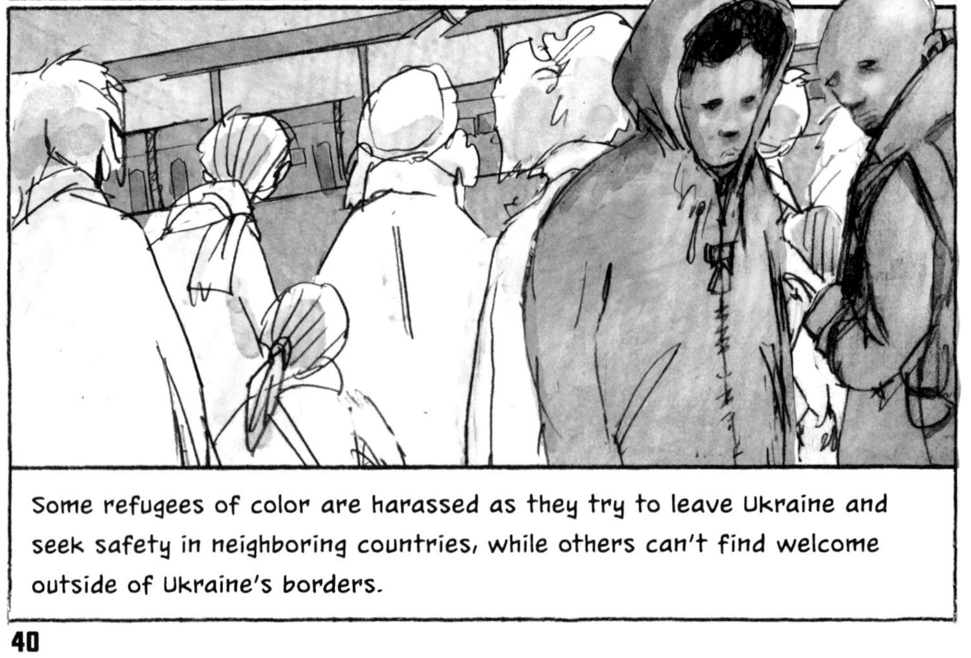

Some refugees of color are harassed as they try to leave Ukraine and seek safety in neighboring countries, while others can't find welcome outside of Ukraine's borders.

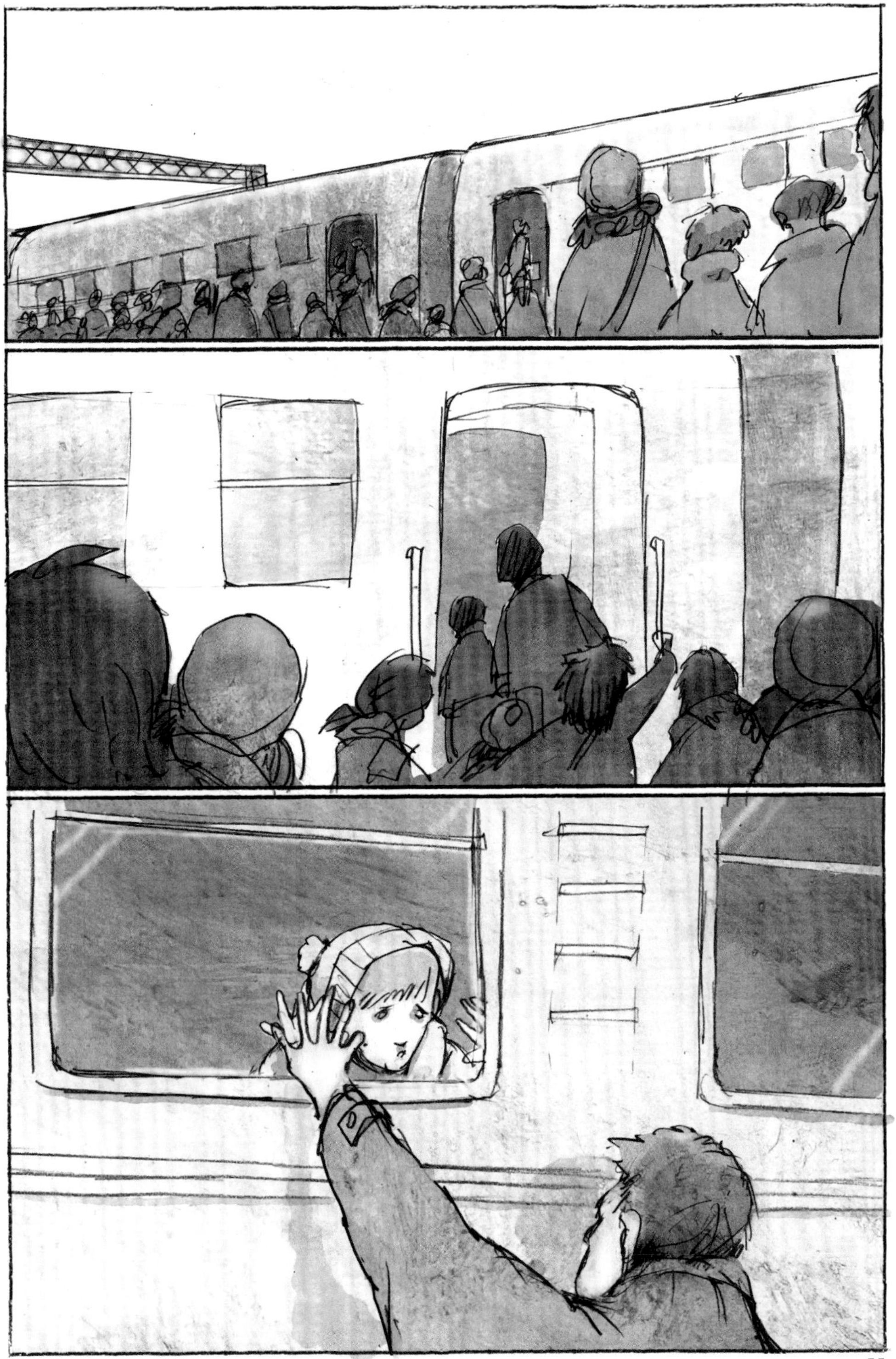

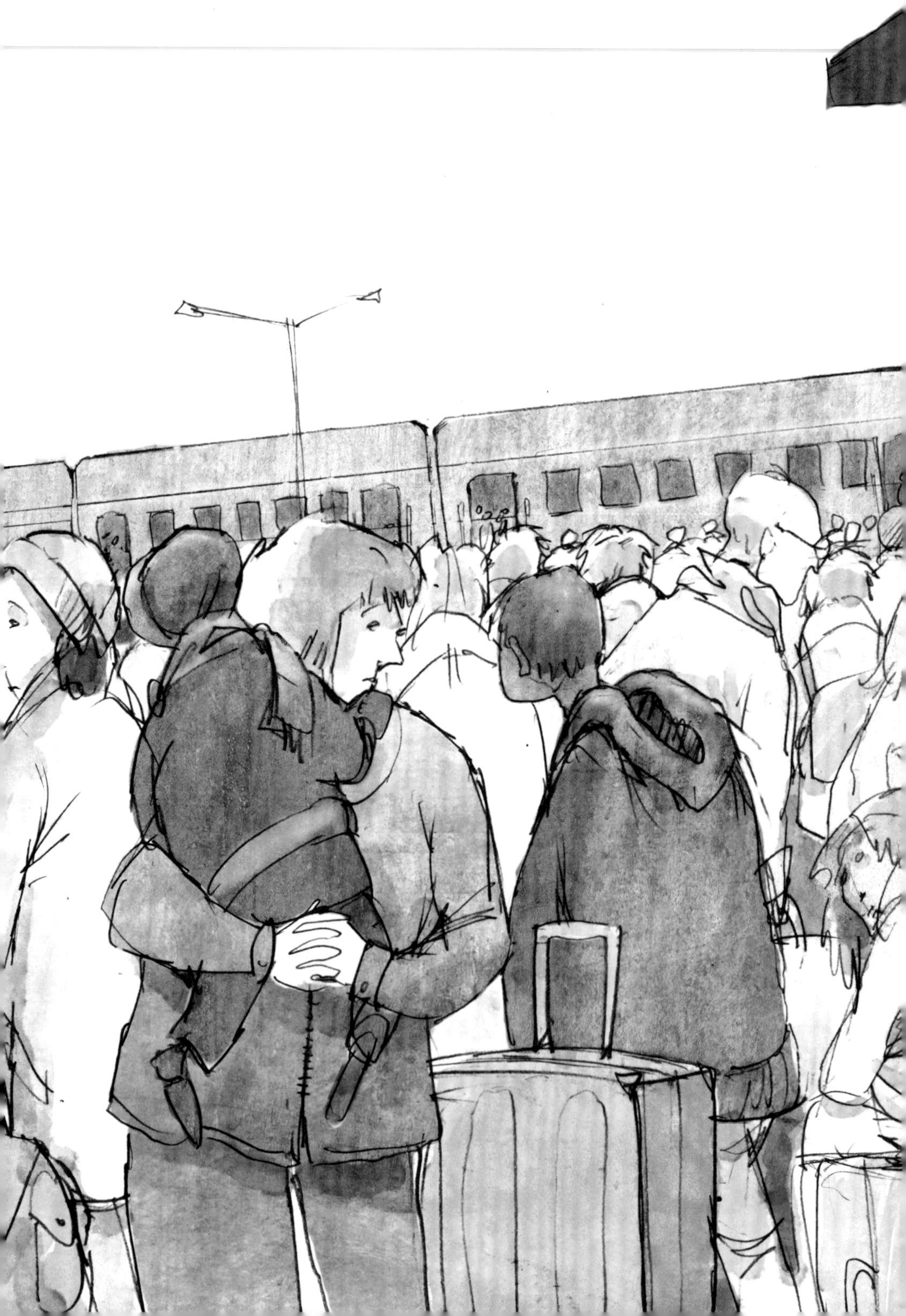

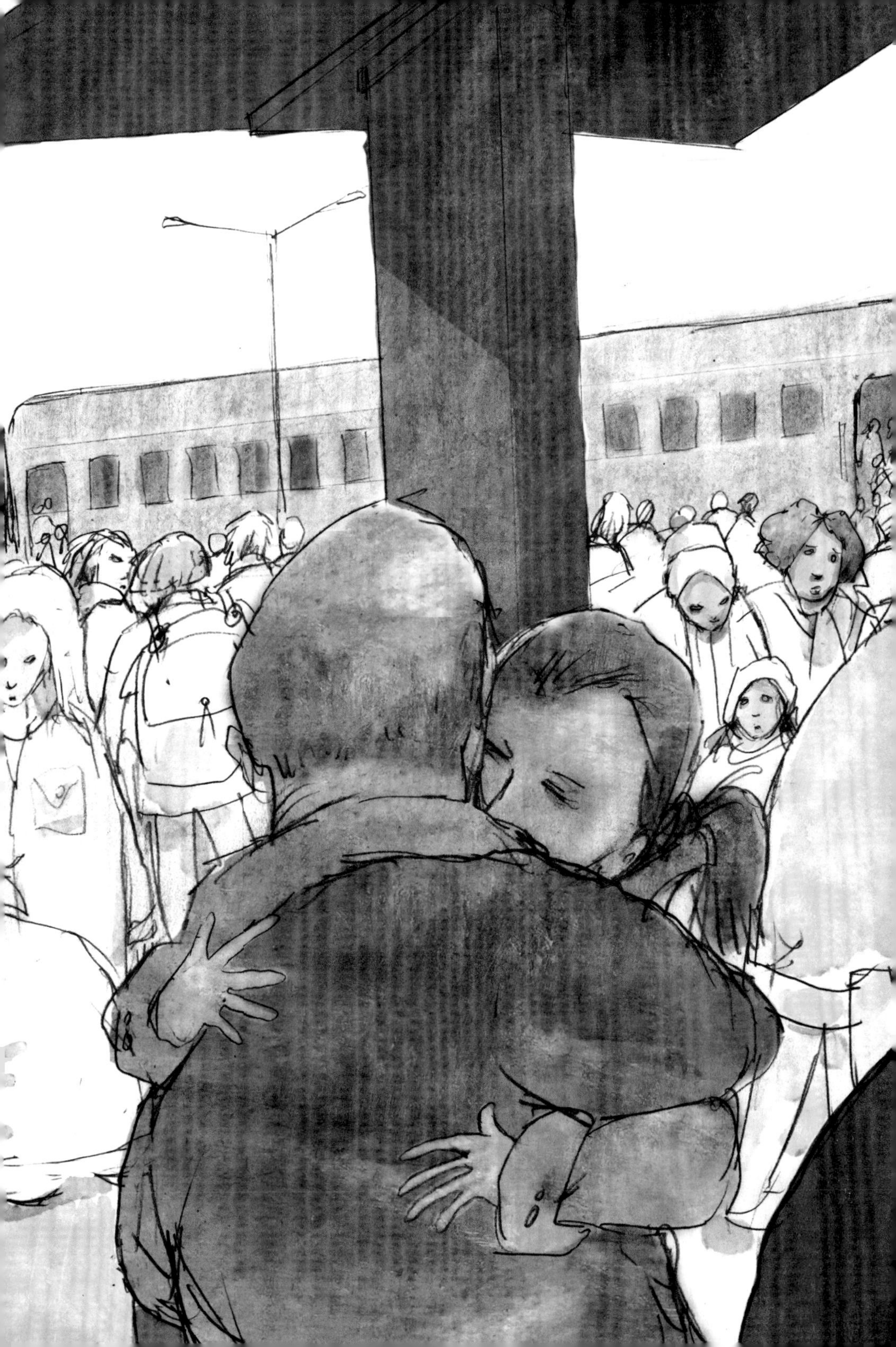

SATURDAY, MARCH 5, 2022

After her house had been shelled four times, a young Mariupol mother gathers her two children and heads to a large theater now acting as a shelter. Already crowded with 1,500 people, she begs to enter and is admitted.

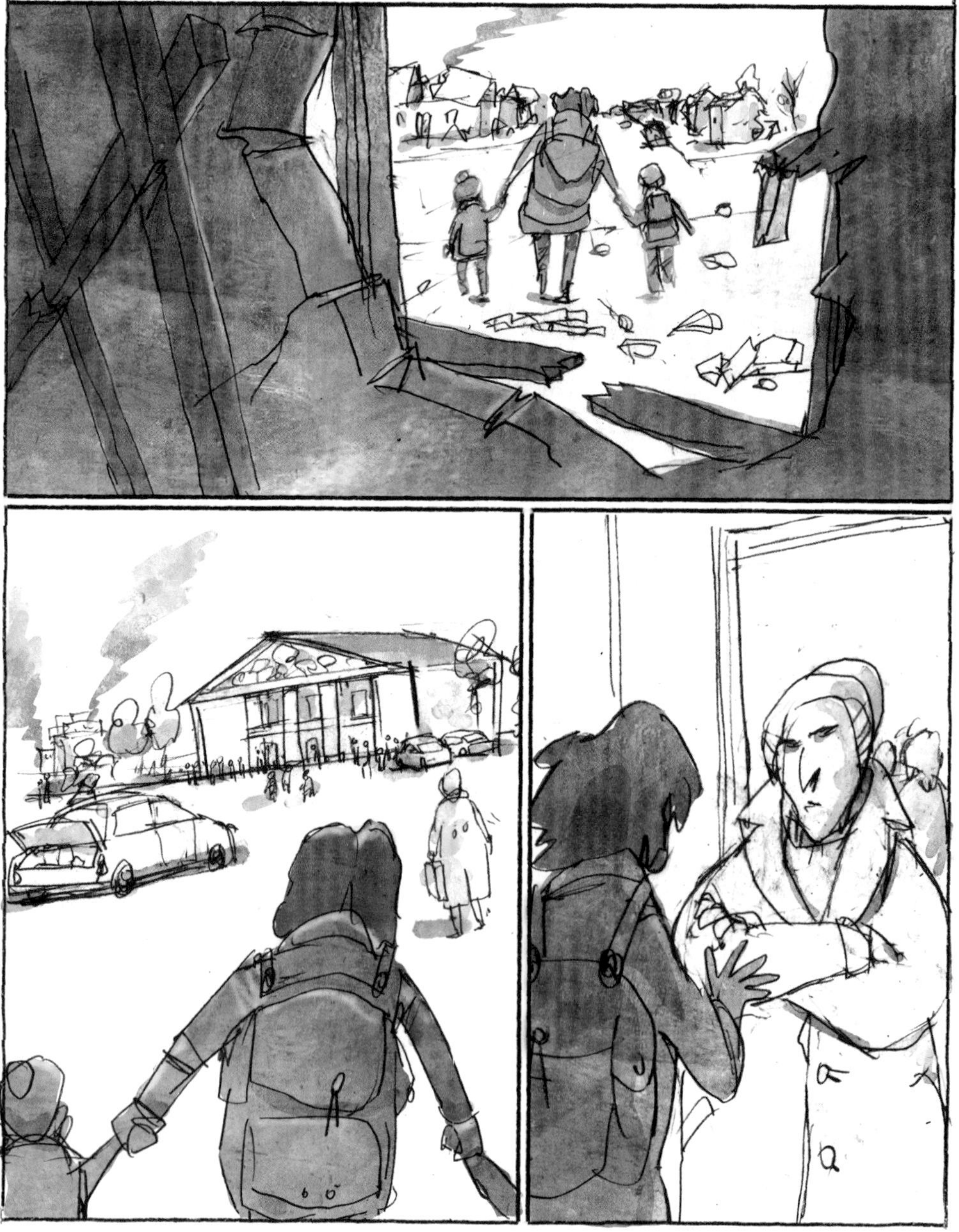

She and her children are given a bowl of soup. There are no beds and they lay sleeping bags on the floor.

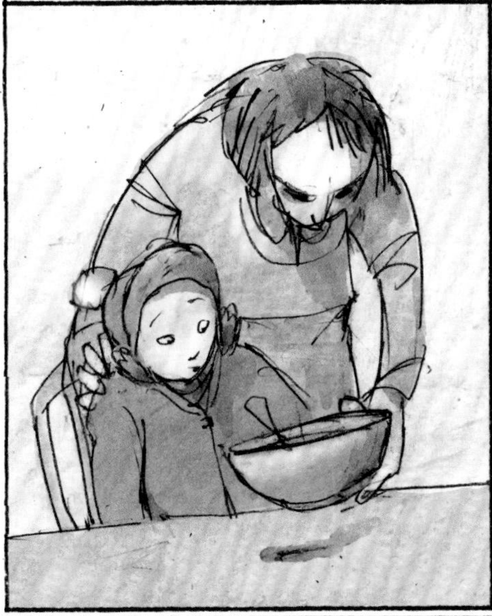

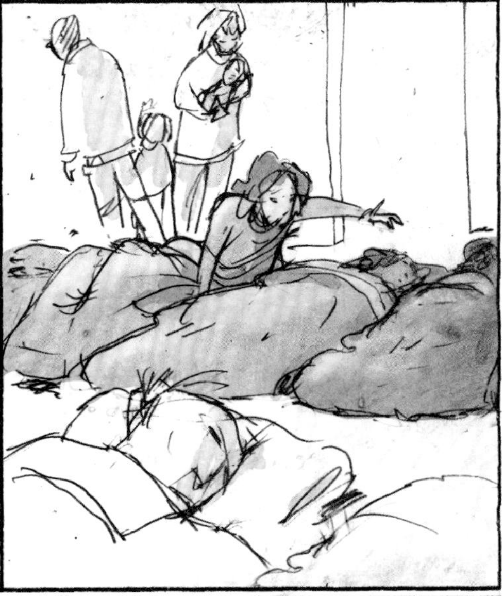

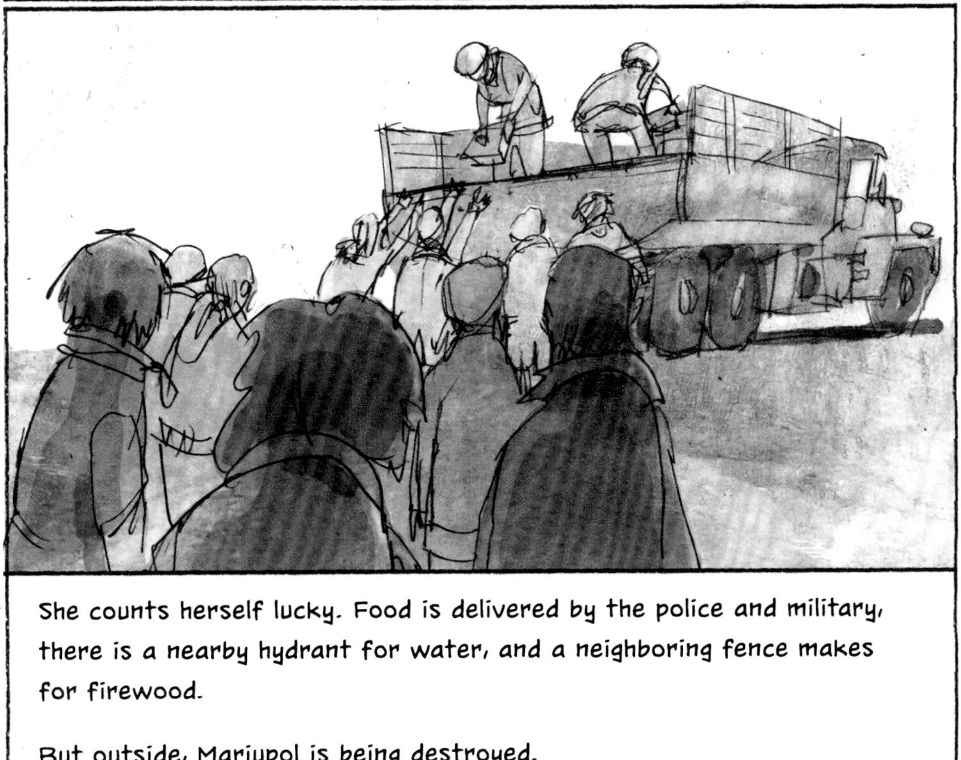

She counts herself lucky. Food is delivered by the police and military, there is a nearby hydrant for water, and a neighboring fence makes for firewood.

But outside, Mariupol is being destroyed.

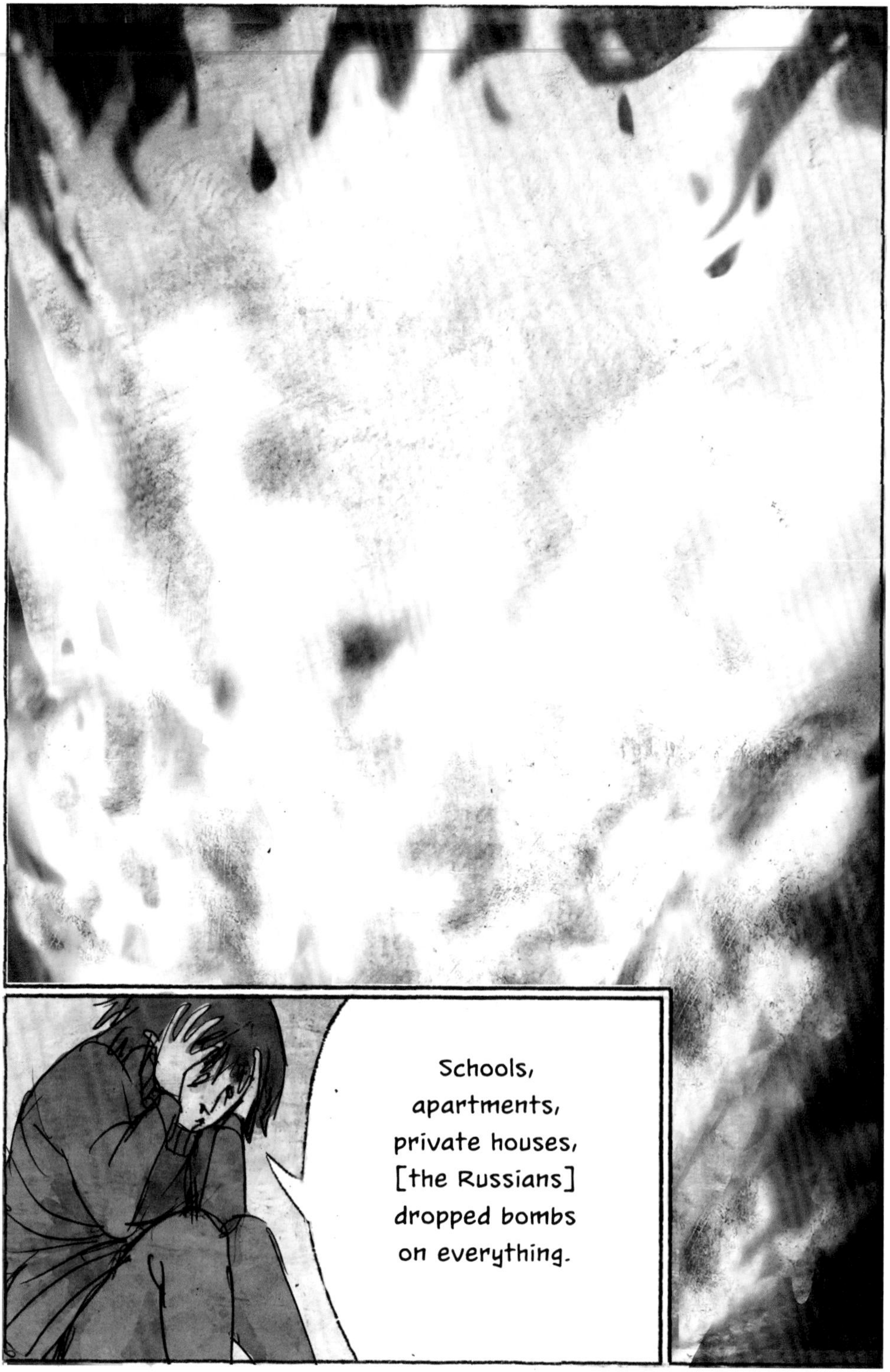
Schools, apartments, private houses, [the Russians] dropped bombs on everything.

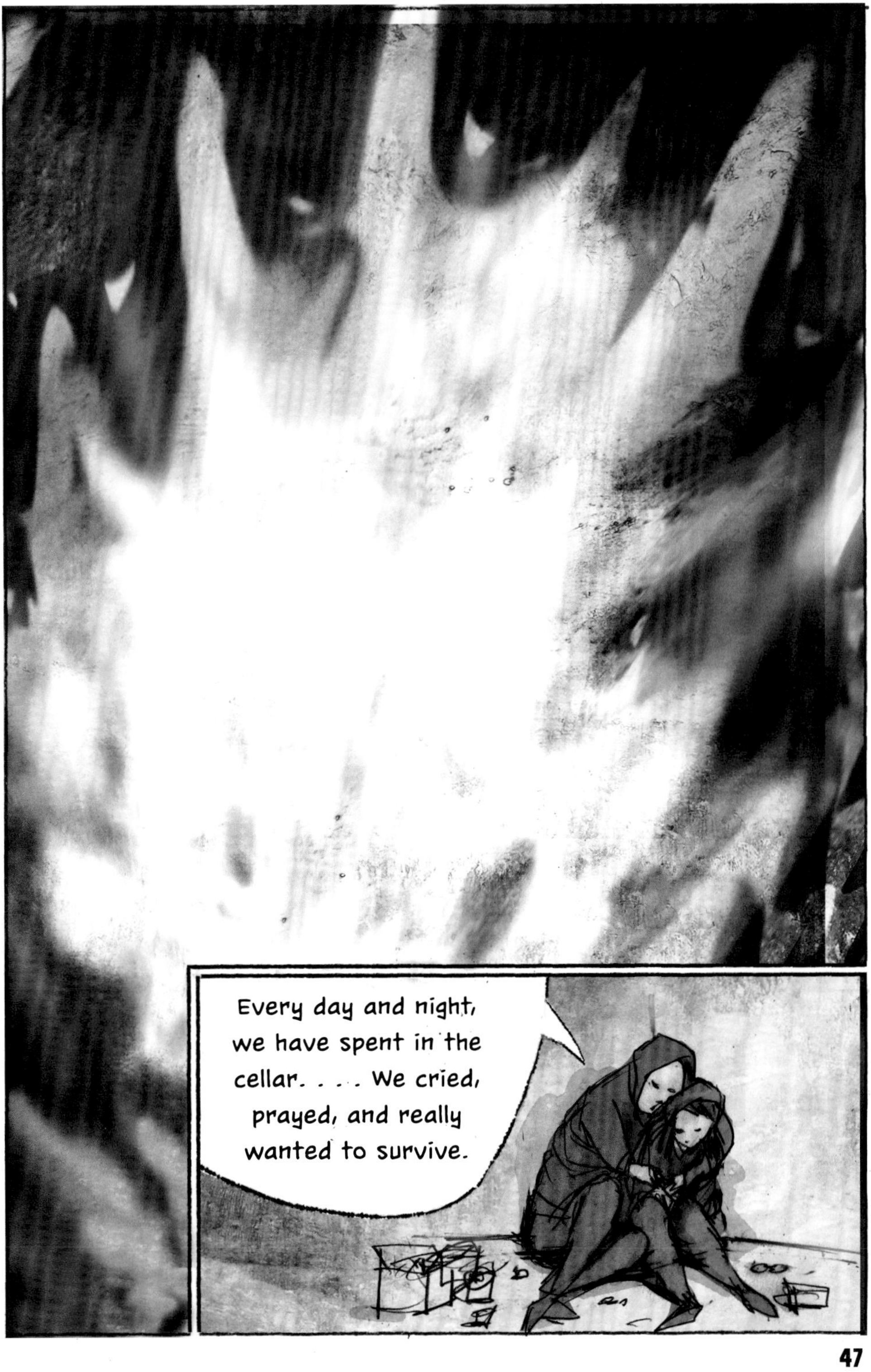
Every day and night, we have spent in the cellar. . . . We cried, prayed, and really wanted to survive.

Russian and Ukrainian officials agree to allow civilians to escape. One convoy of about 120 cars sets out.

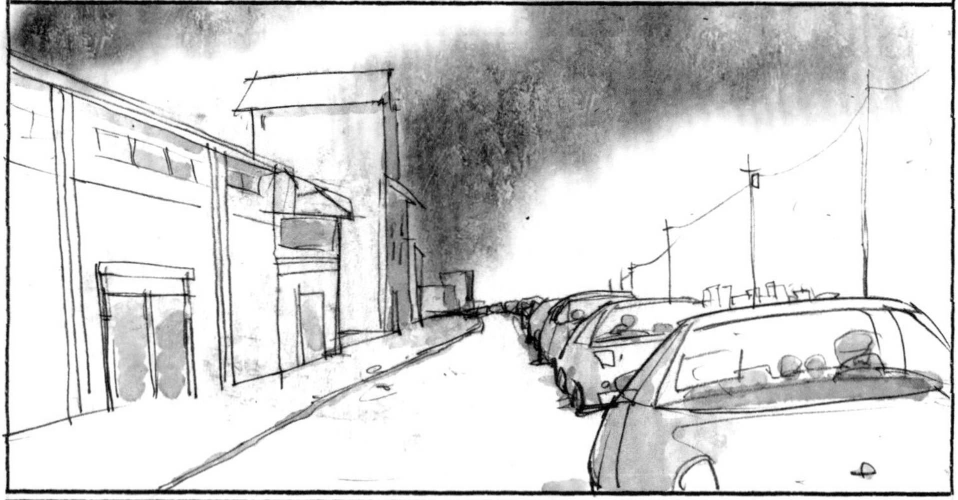

They pass six Russian checkpoints but are stopped at the seventh. The enemy soldiers have no orders to allow them to pass and have no way to contact their superiors. The convoy spends the night in the homes of helpful villagers.

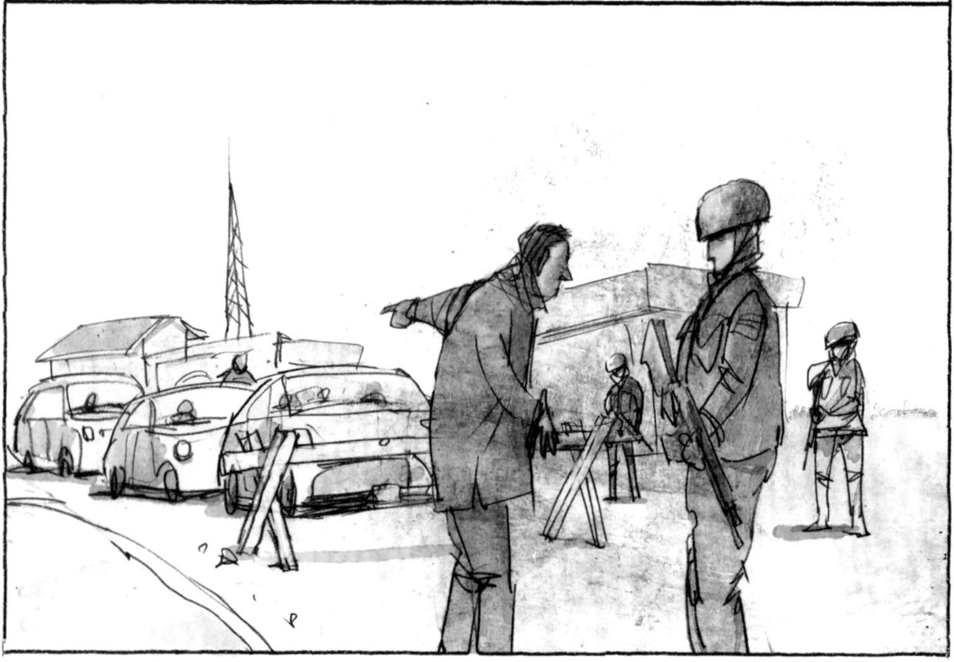

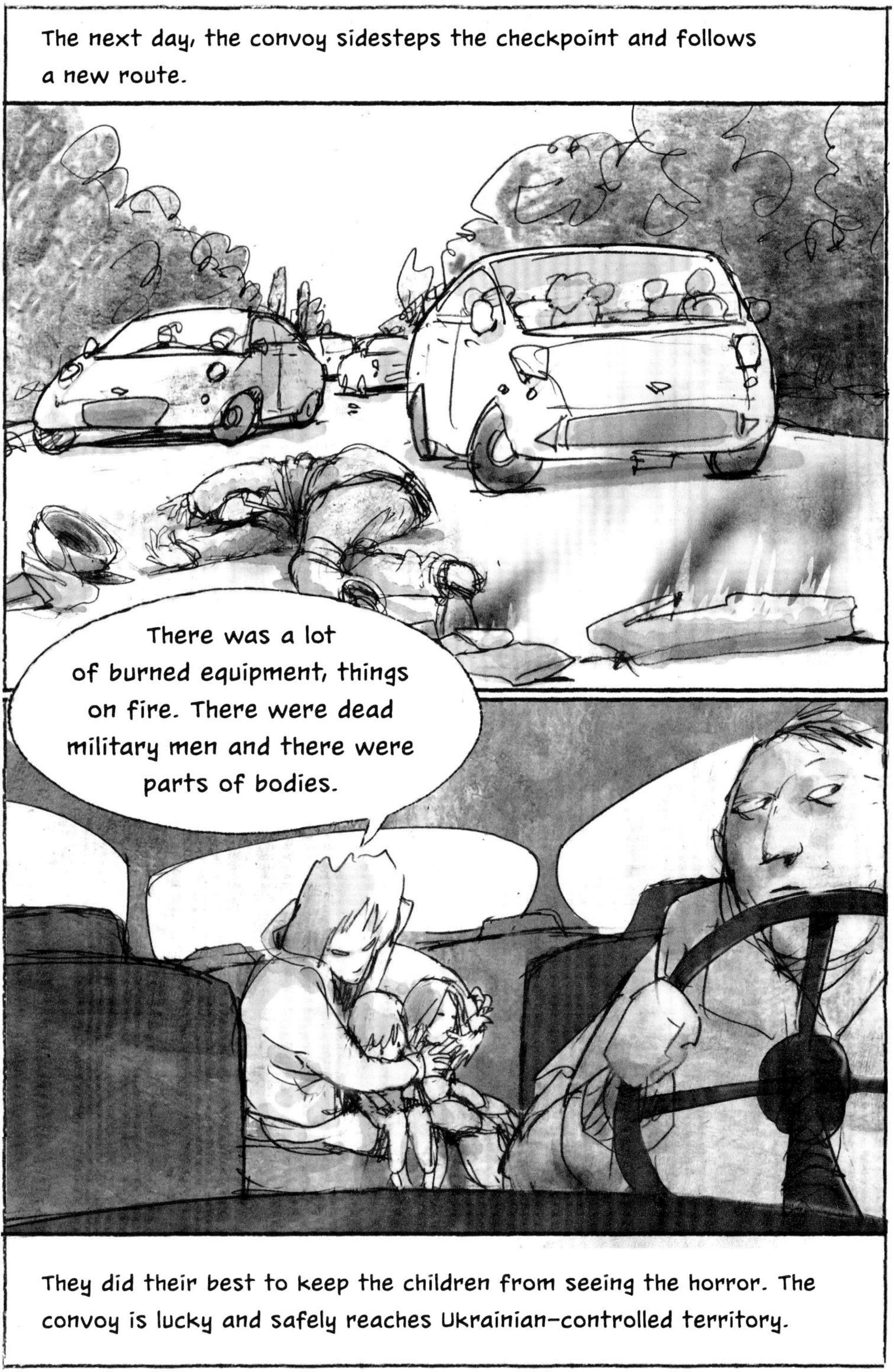
The next day, the convoy sidesteps the checkpoint and follows a new route.
There was a lot of burned equipment, things on fire. There were dead military men and there were parts of bodies.
They did their best to keep the children from seeing the horror. The convoy is lucky and safely reaches Ukrainian-controlled territory.

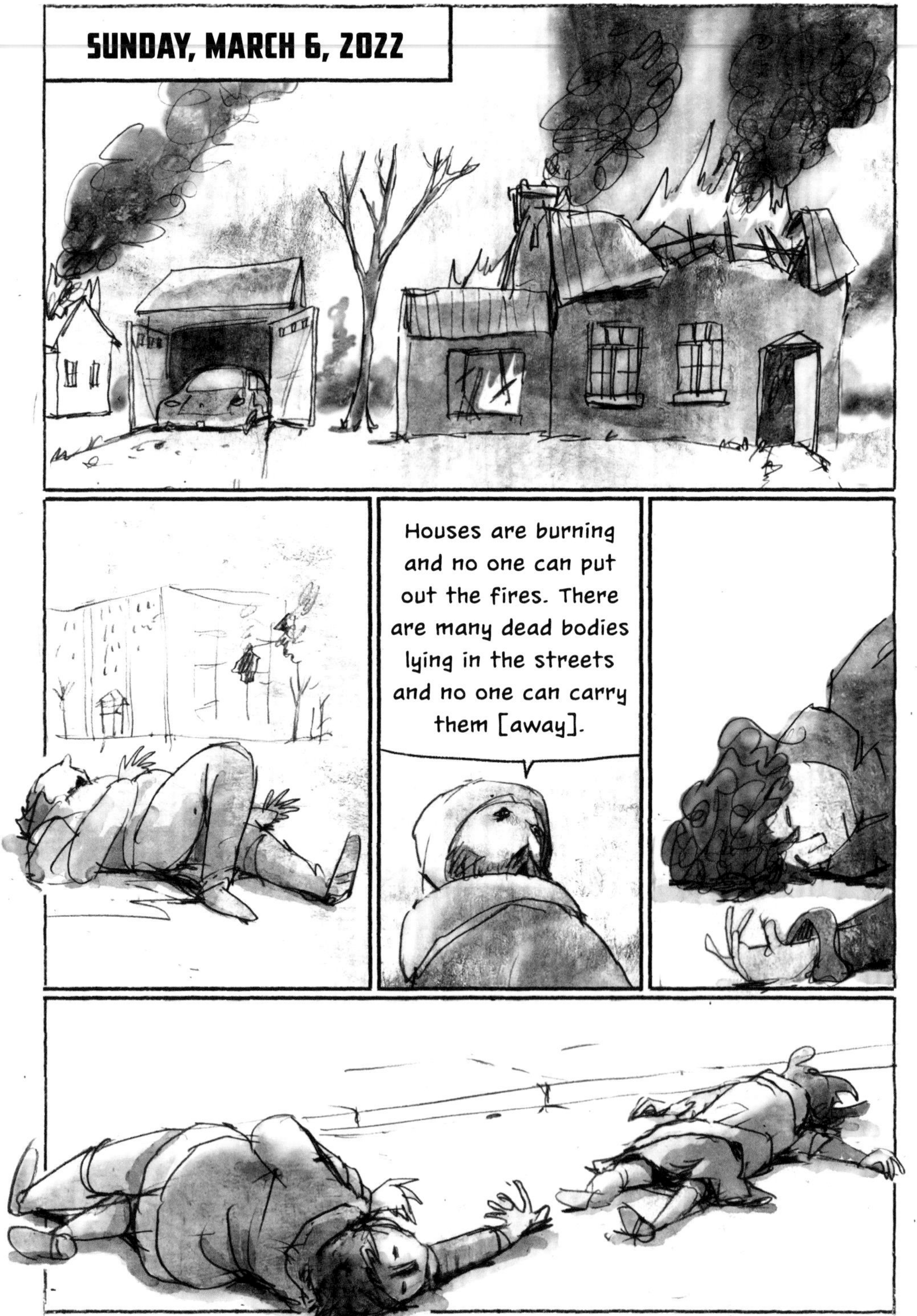
SUNDAY, MARCH 6, 2022
Houses are burning and no one can put out the fires. There are many dead bodies lying in the streets and no one can carry them [away].

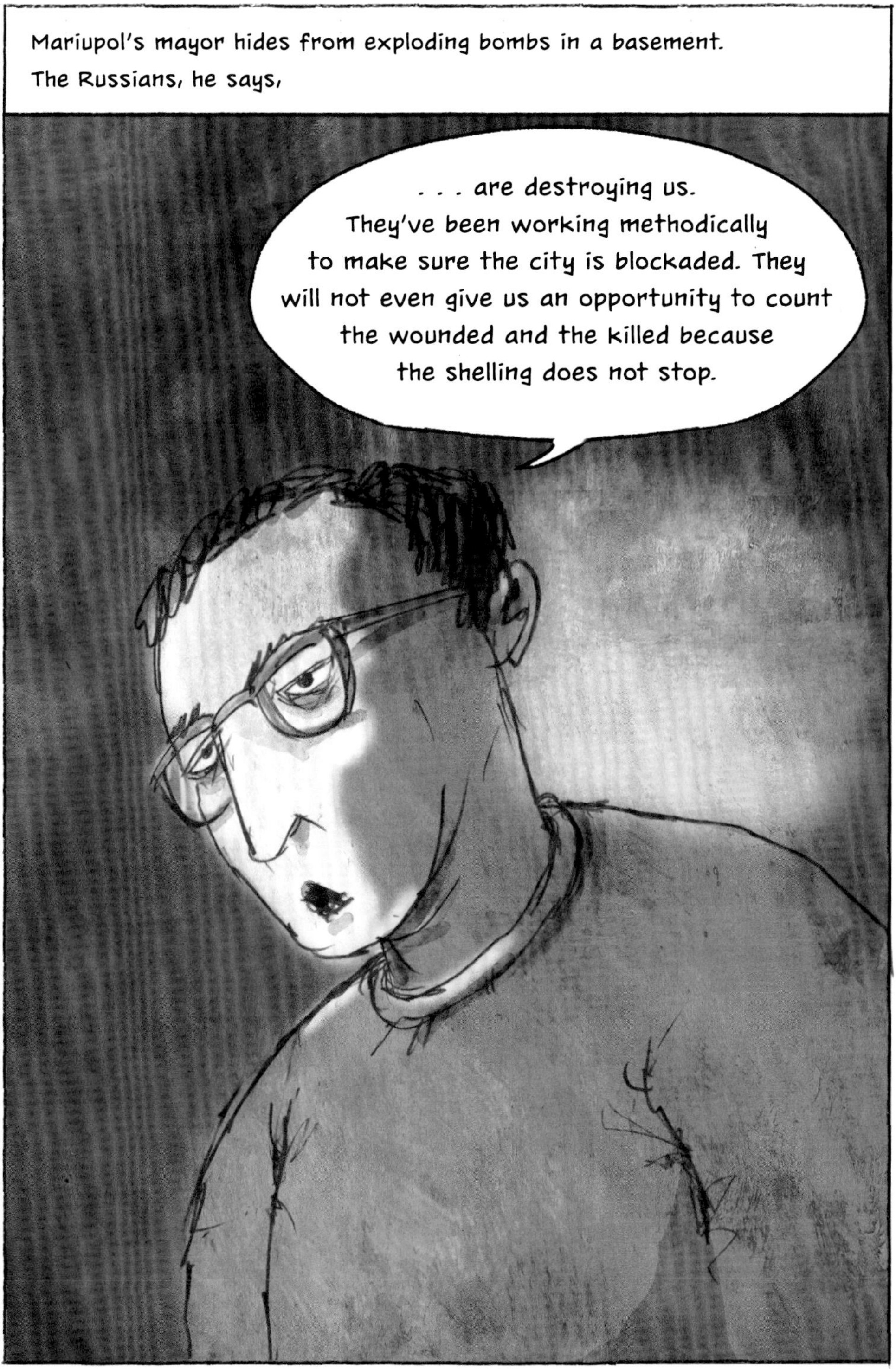
Mariupol's mayor hides from exploding bombs in a basement.
The Russians, he says,
. . . are destroying us. They've been working methodically to make sure the city is blockaded. They will not even give us an opportunity to count the wounded and the killed because the shelling does not stop.

WEDNESDAY, MARCH 9, 2022

A Russian airstrike blasts a Mariupol maternity and children's hospital, tearing off the front of a building, setting on fire nearby cars, scorching trees, and leaving a smoking crater.

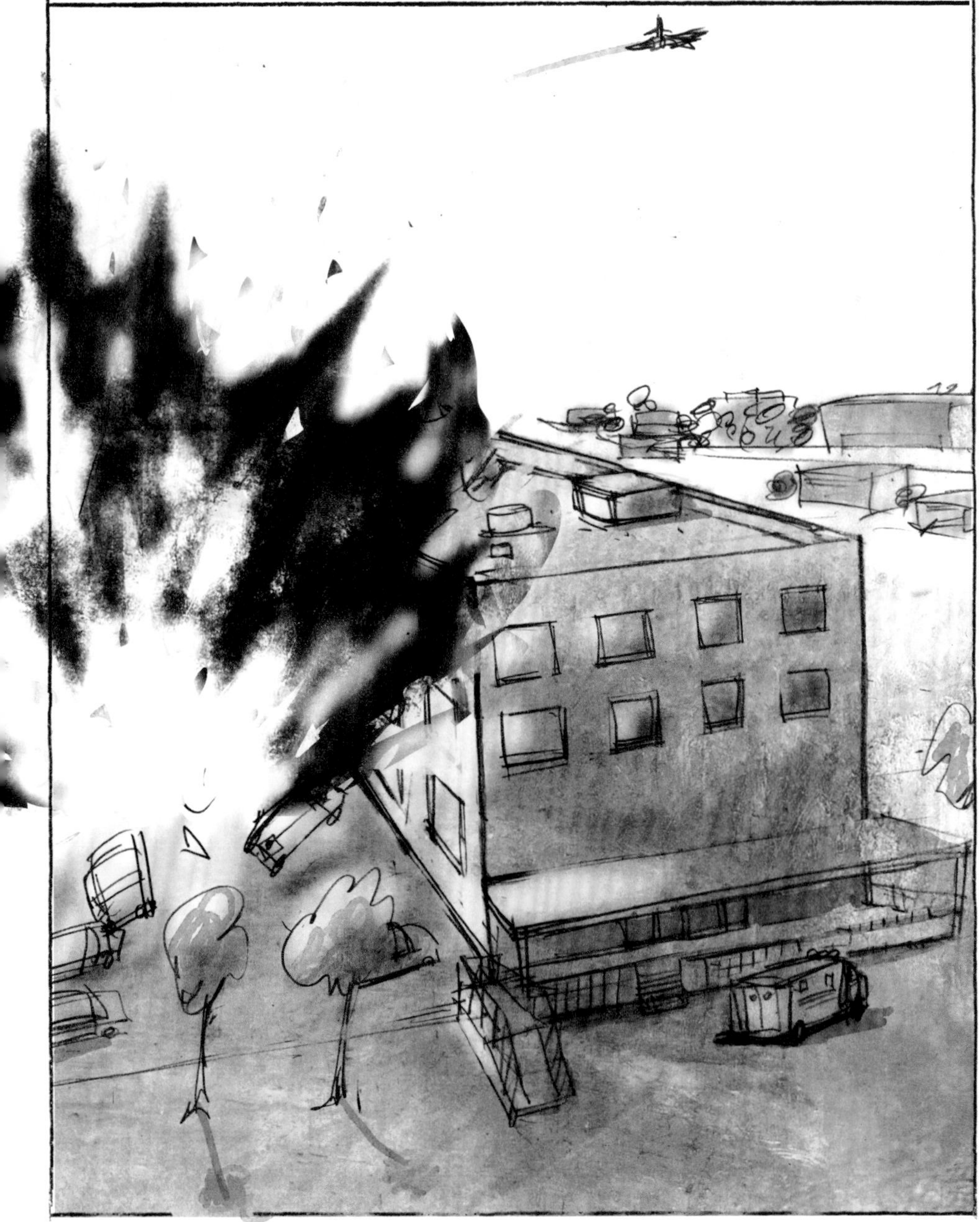

Three people are killed, including a child. Injured people stream out of the wreckage. A wounded pregnant woman is carried away. She and her unborn child don't survive their injuries.

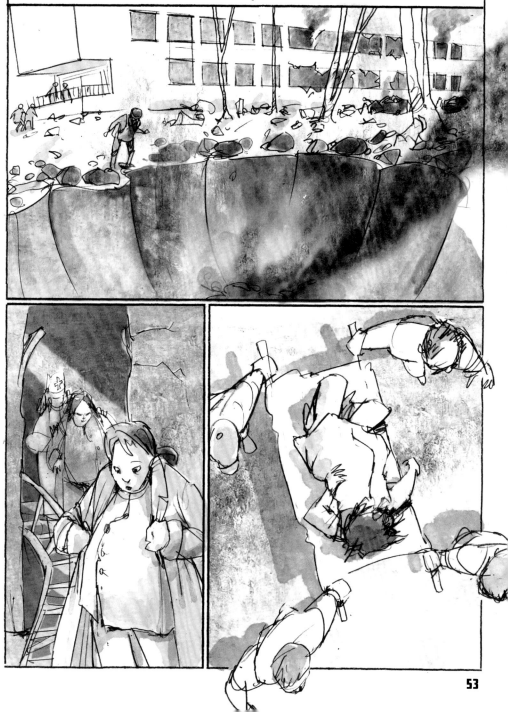

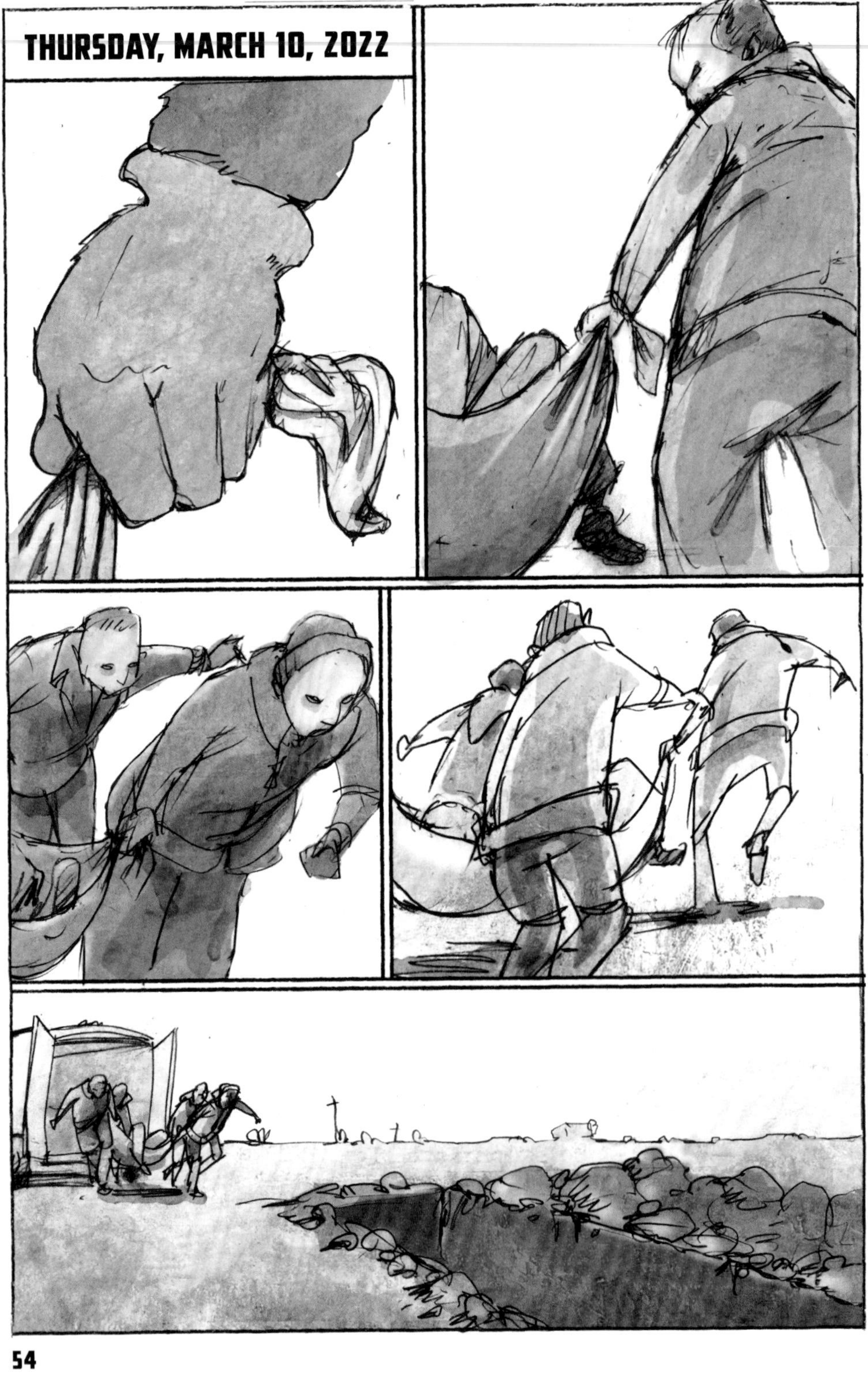
THURSDAY, MARCH 10, 2022

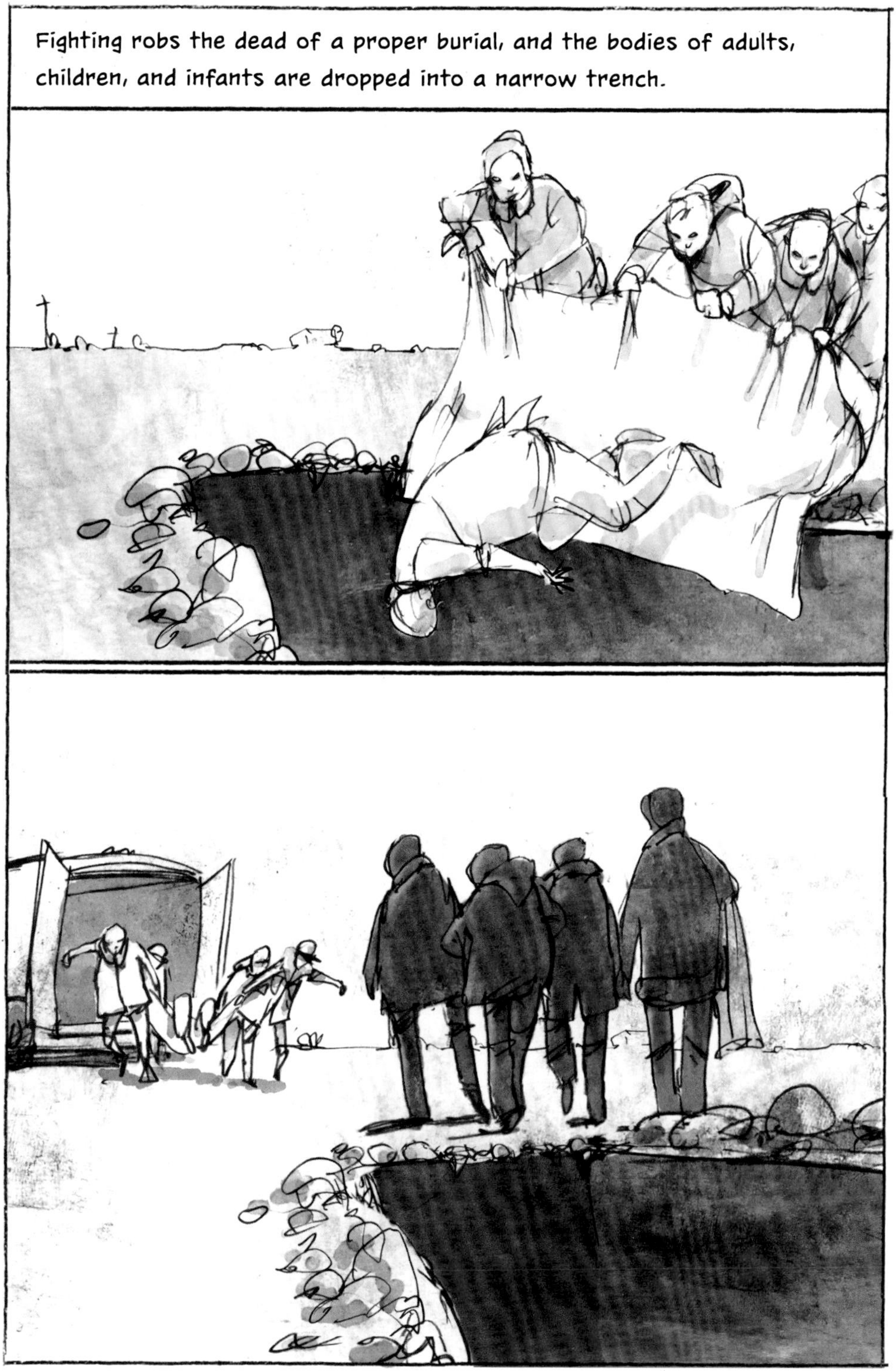
Fighting robs the dead of a proper burial, and the bodies of adults, children, and infants are dropped into a narrow trench.

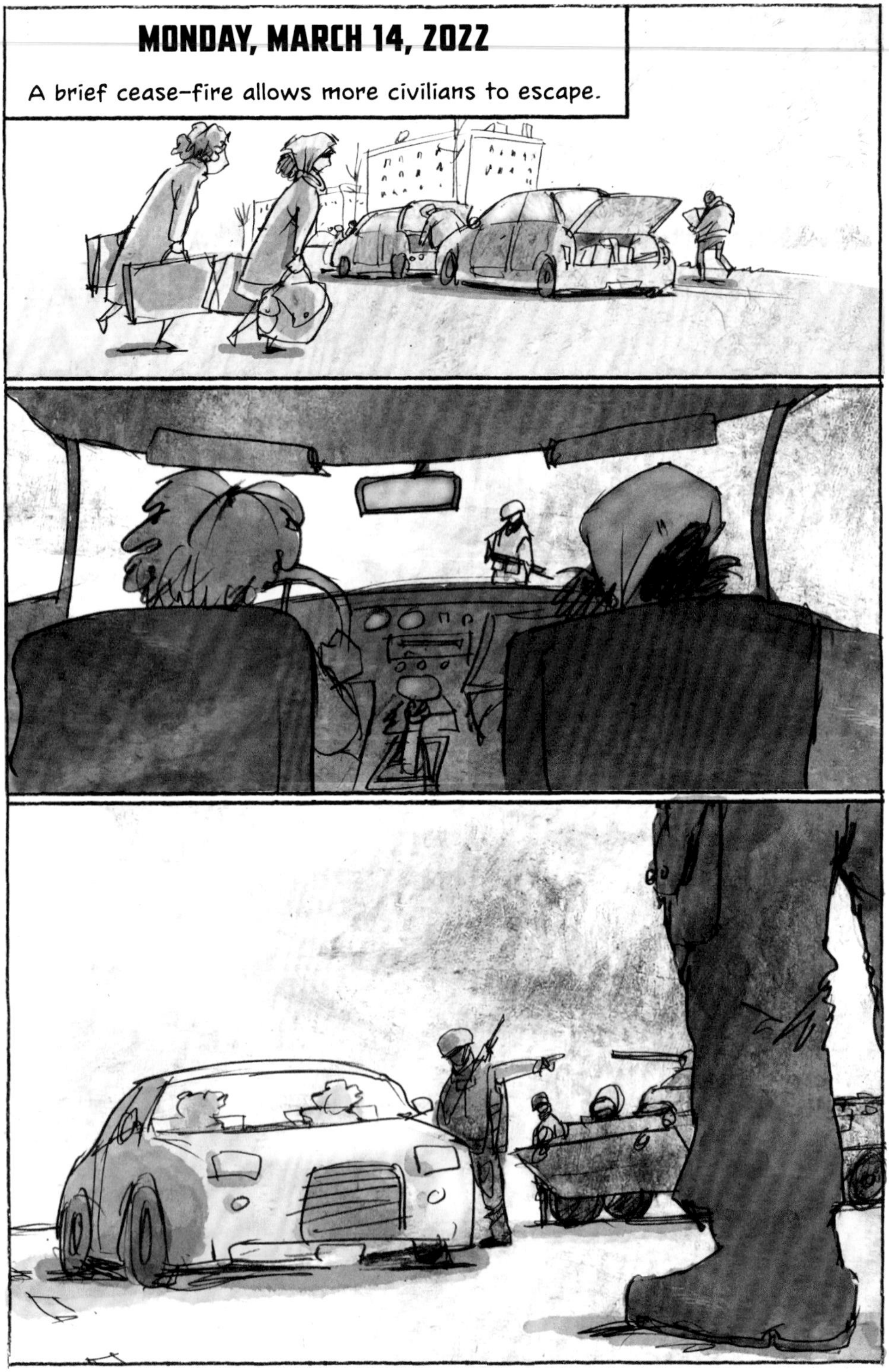
MONDAY, MARCH 14, 2022
A brief cease-fire allows more civilians to escape.

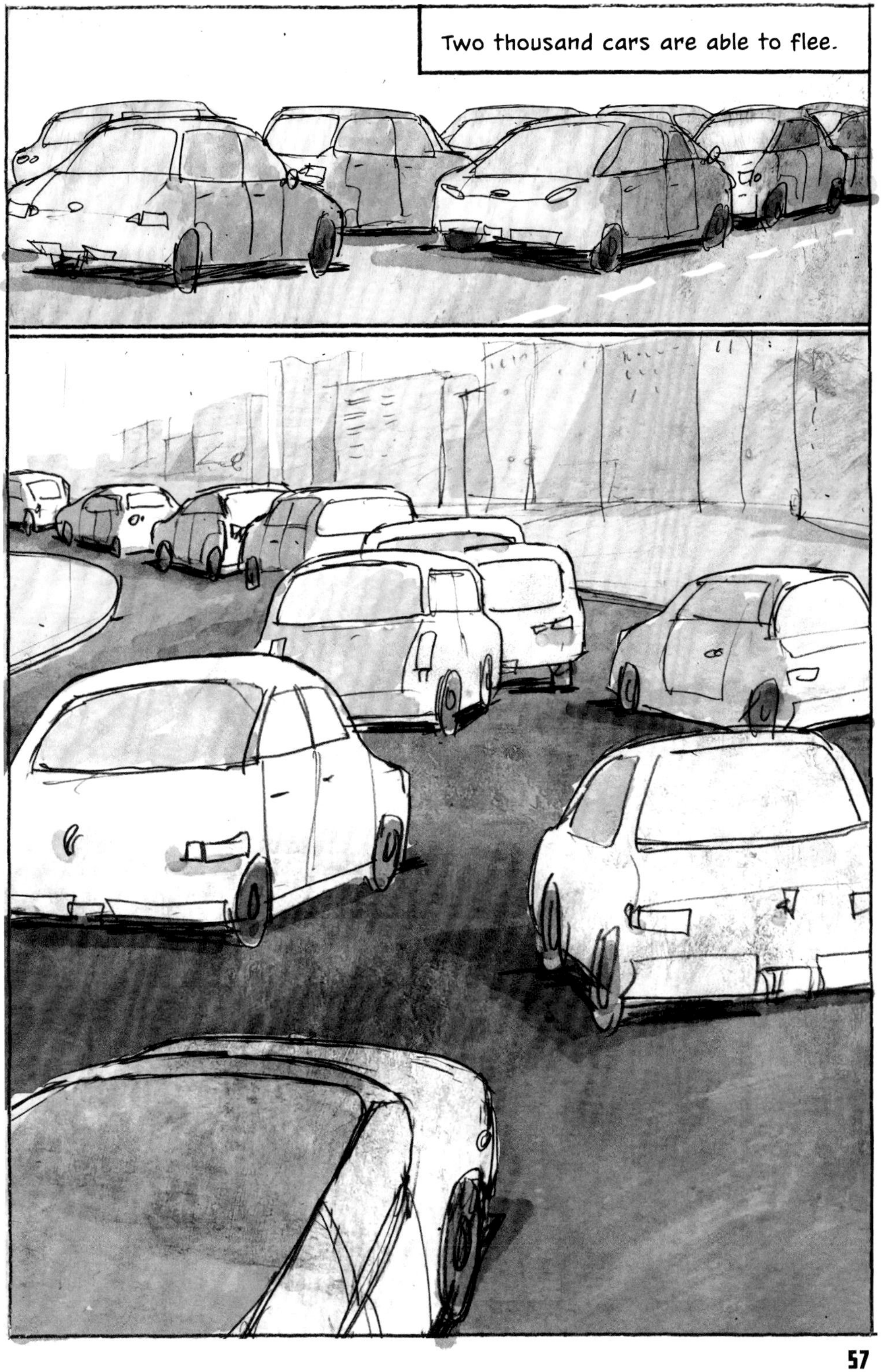
Two thousand cars are able to flee.

WEDNESDAY, MARCH 16, 2022

A white flag flies atop the theater now sheltering more than a thousand people. ДЕТИ, the Russian word for "children," is painted on the concrete beside it to alert the Russians that it is not a military building.

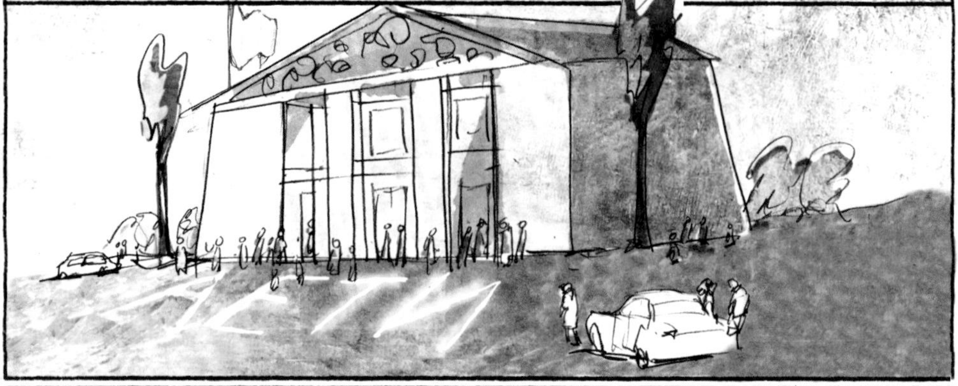

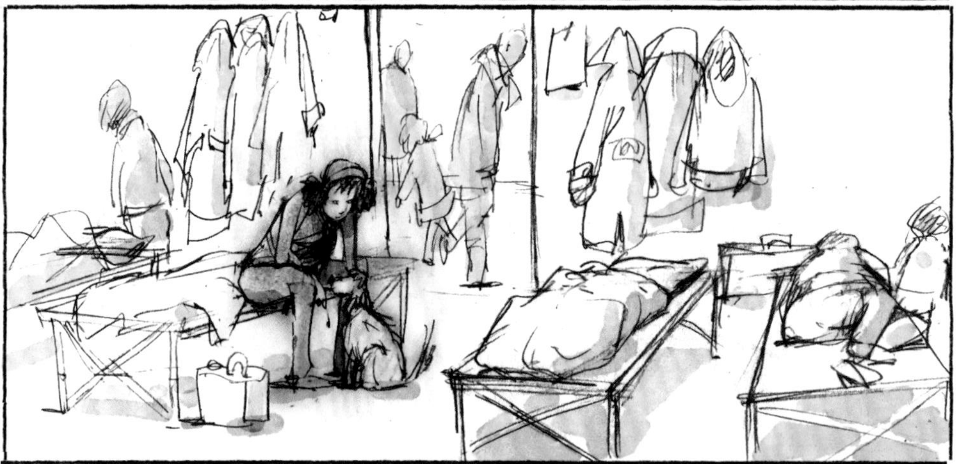

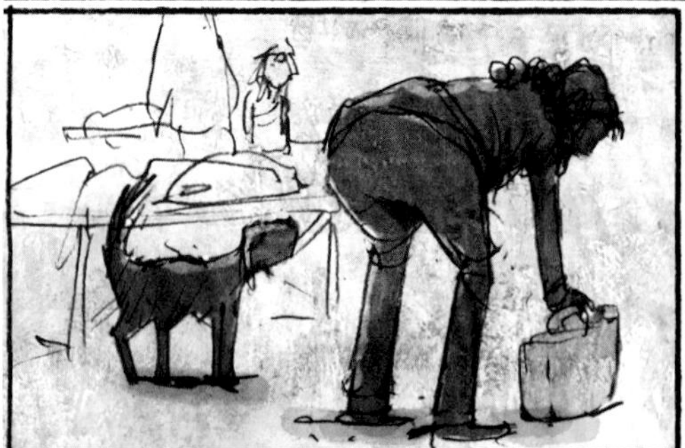

At 10:00 a.m., a woman leaves the building to get water for her dog.

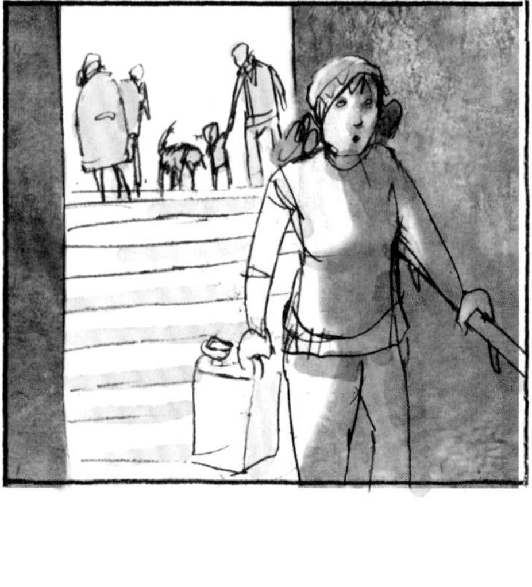

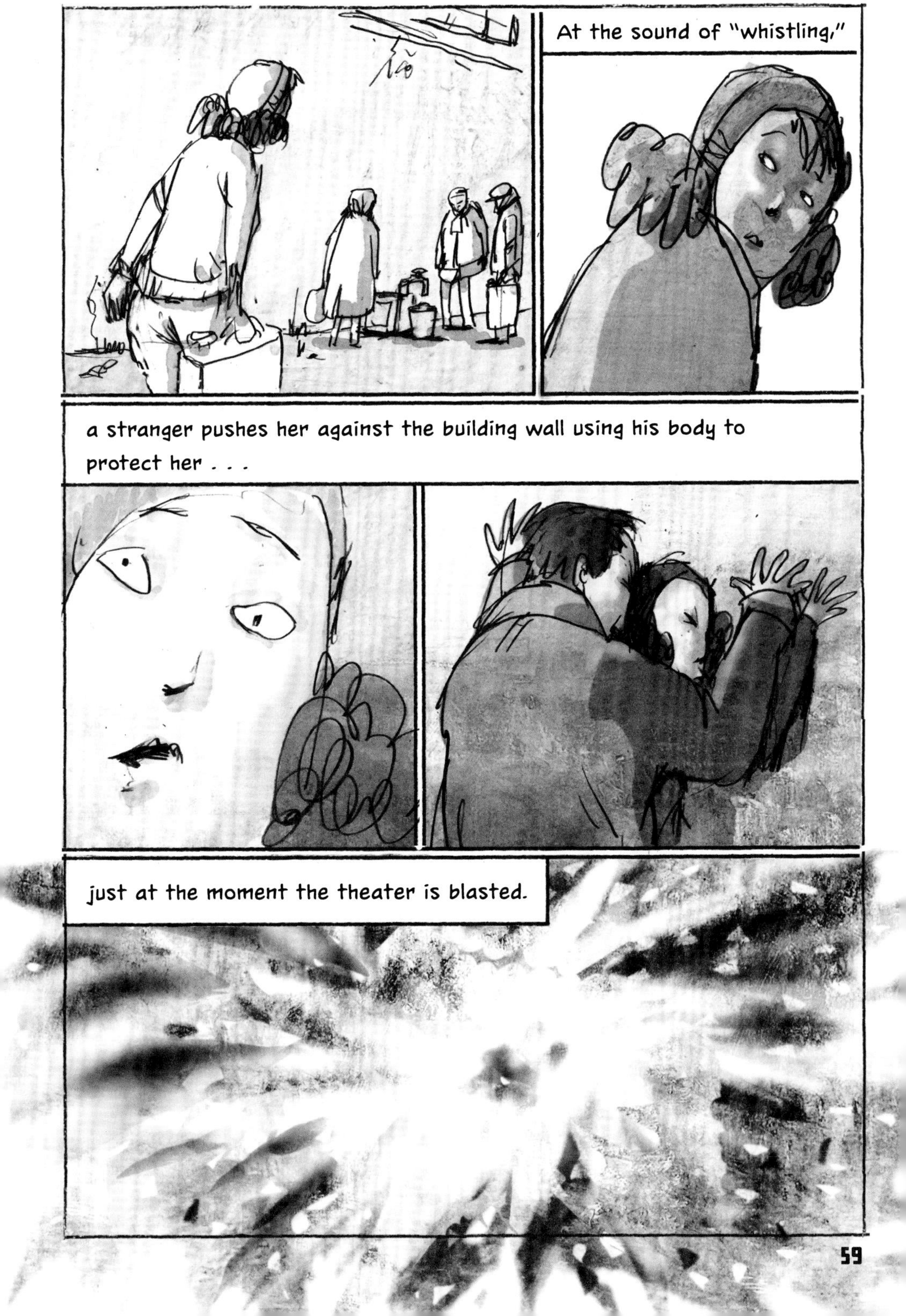
At the sound of "whistling,"
a stranger pushes her against the building wall using his body to protect her . . .
just at the moment the theater is blasted.

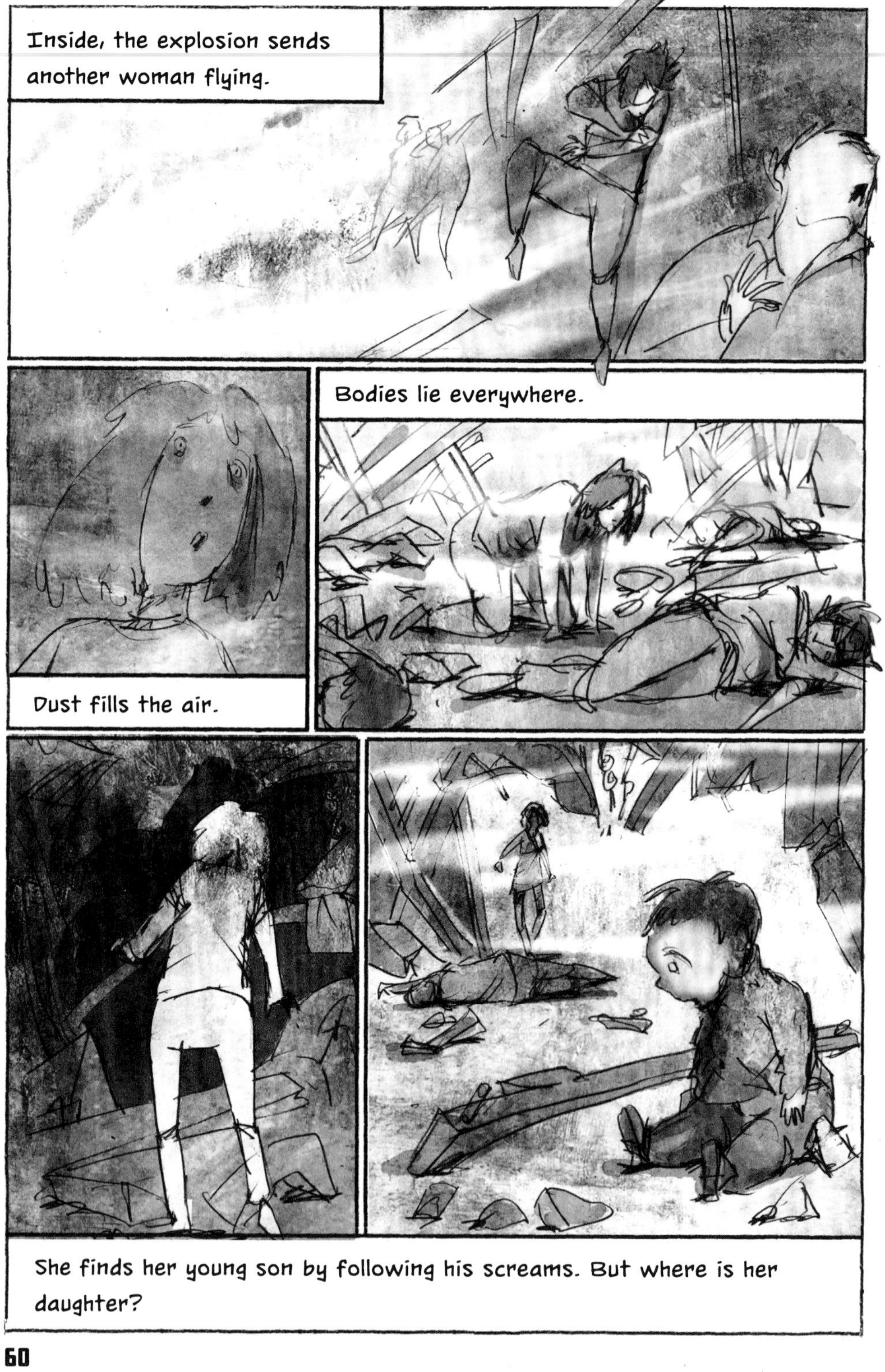
Inside, the explosion sends another woman flying.
Dust fills the air.
Bodies lie everywhere.
She finds her young son by following his screams. But where is her daughter?

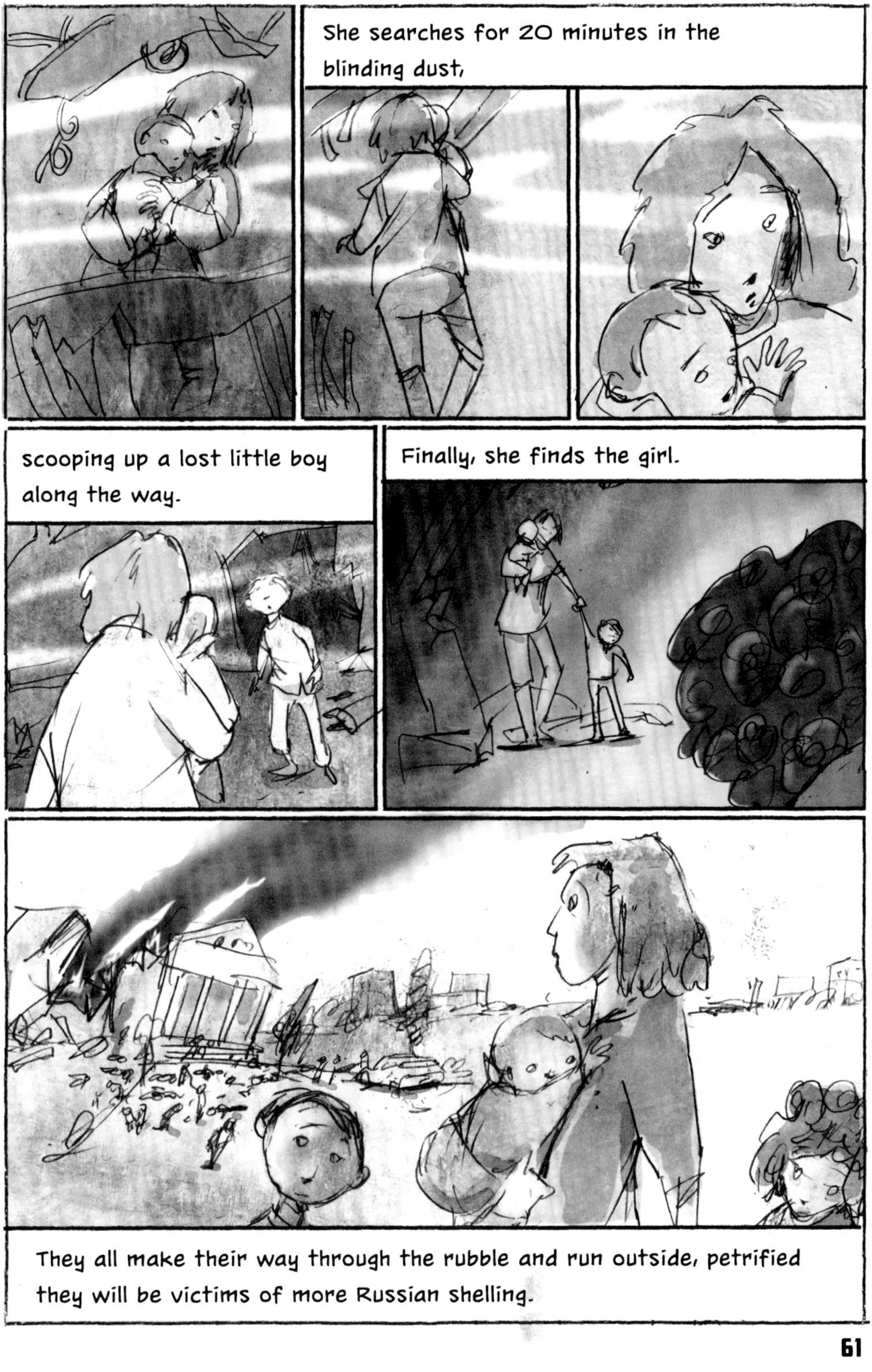
She searches for 20 minutes in the blinding dust,
scooping up a lost little boy along the way.
Finally, she finds the girl.
They all make their way through the rubble and run outside, petrified they will be victims of more Russian shelling.

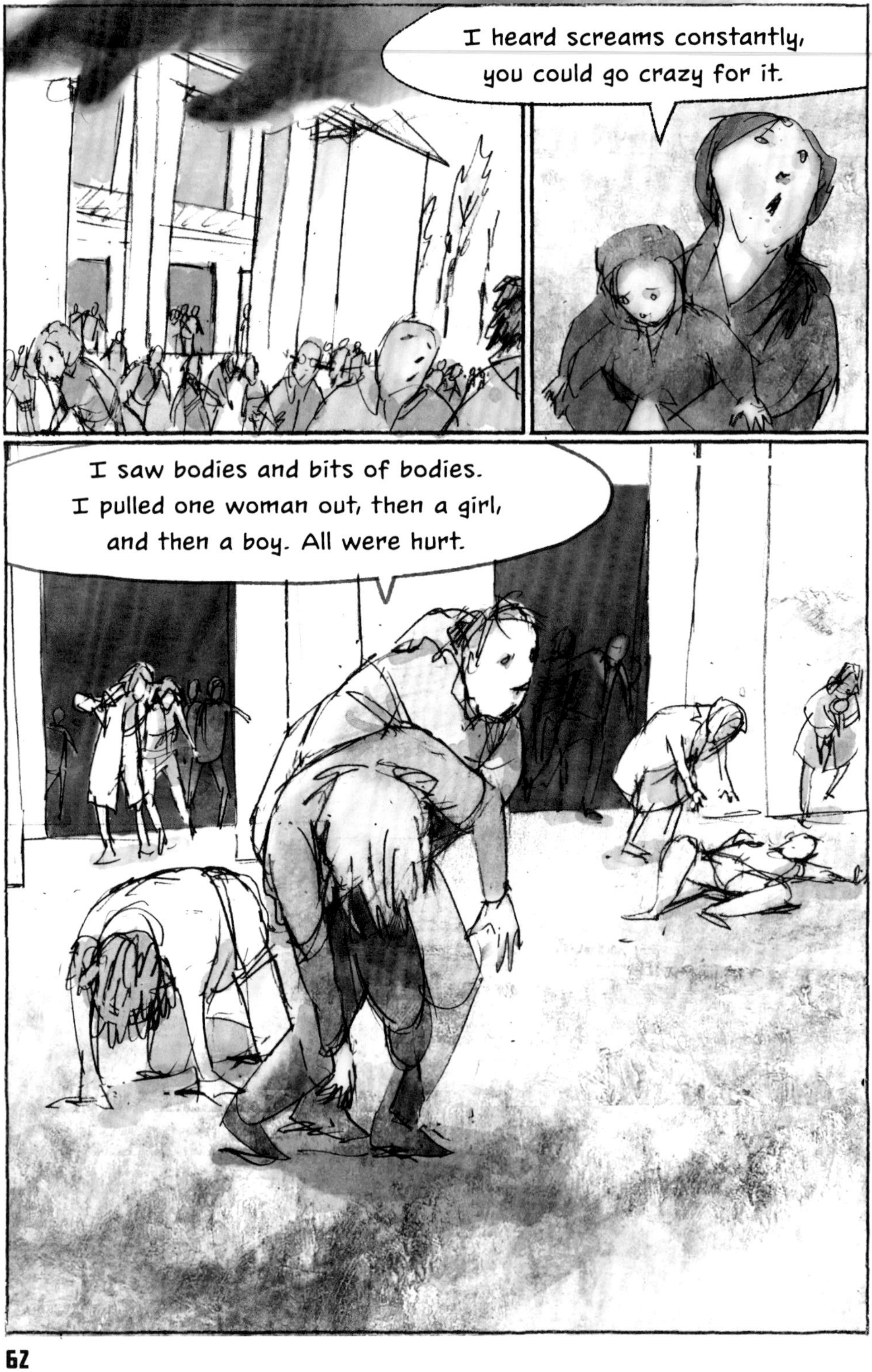
I heard screams constantly, you could go crazy for it.
I saw bodies and bits of bodies. I pulled one woman out, then a girl, and then a boy. All were hurt.

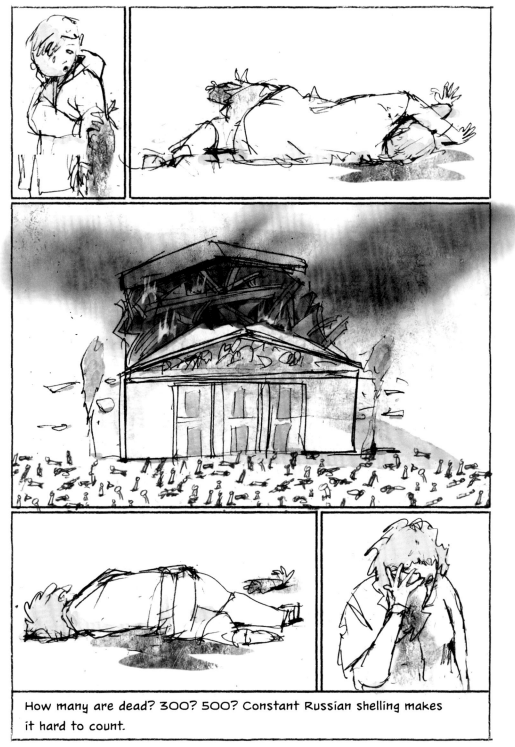

How many are dead? 300? 500? Constant Russian shelling makes it hard to count.

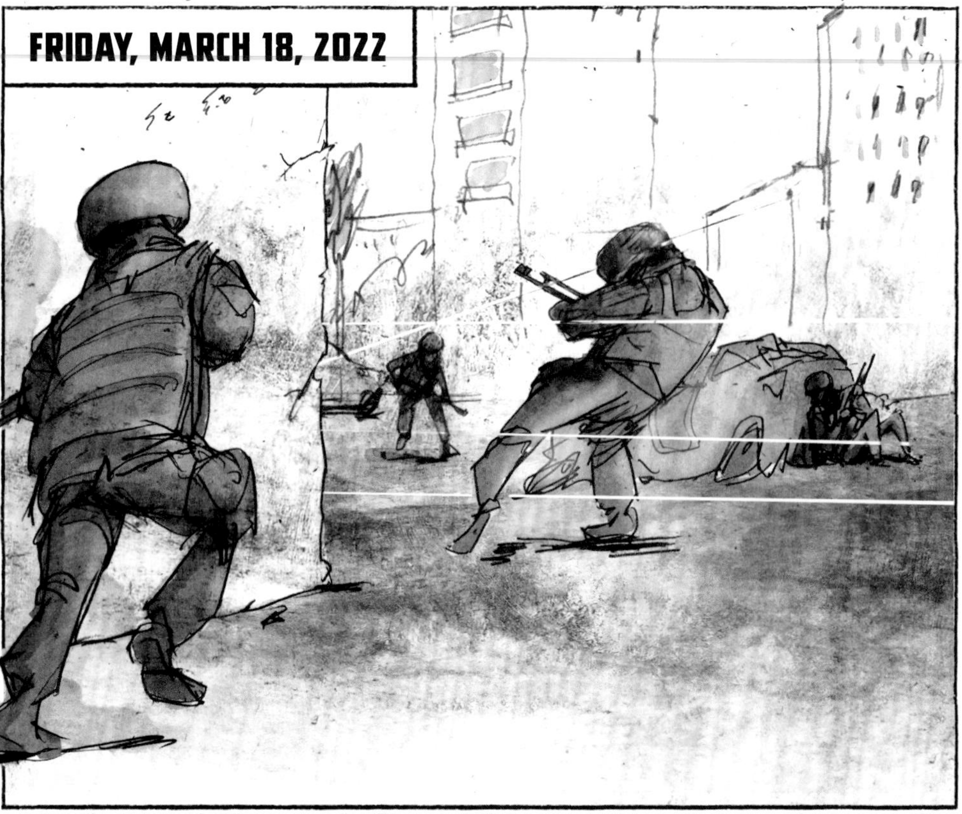
FRIDAY, MARCH 18, 2022

Ukrainian soldiers defend Mariupol's center.

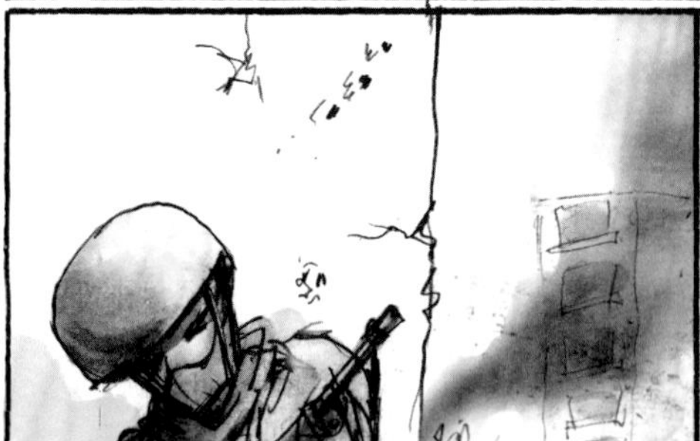

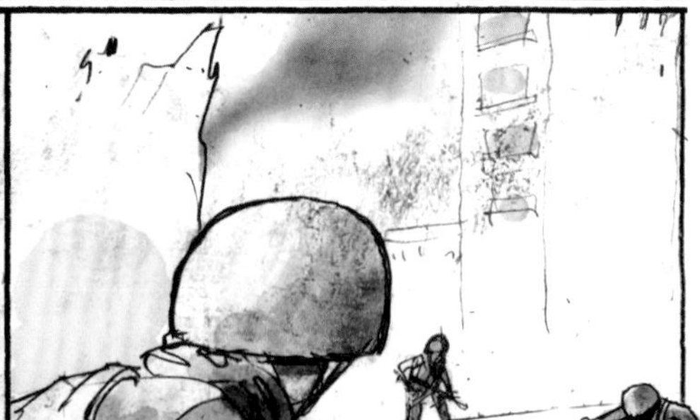

A hospital overflows with patients. Medical supplies are low. The hospital basement fills with the dead.

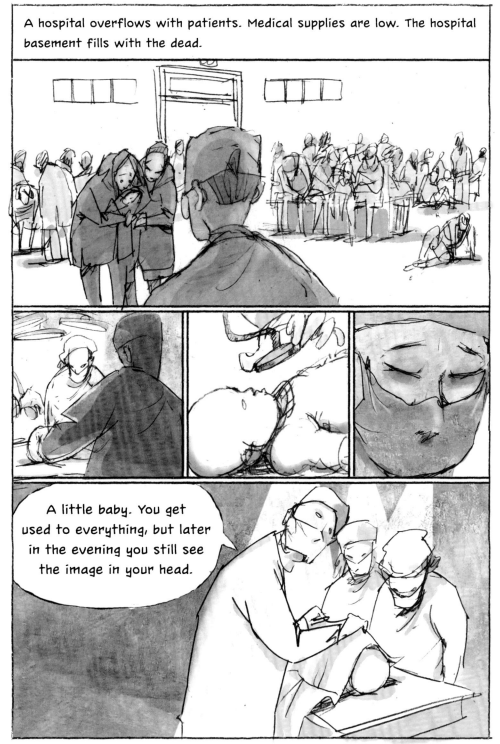

A little baby. You get used to everything, but later in the evening you still see the image in your head.

SATURDAY, MARCH 19, 2022

Russian soldiers deport some Mariupol residents to Russia, removing possibly restive opponents.

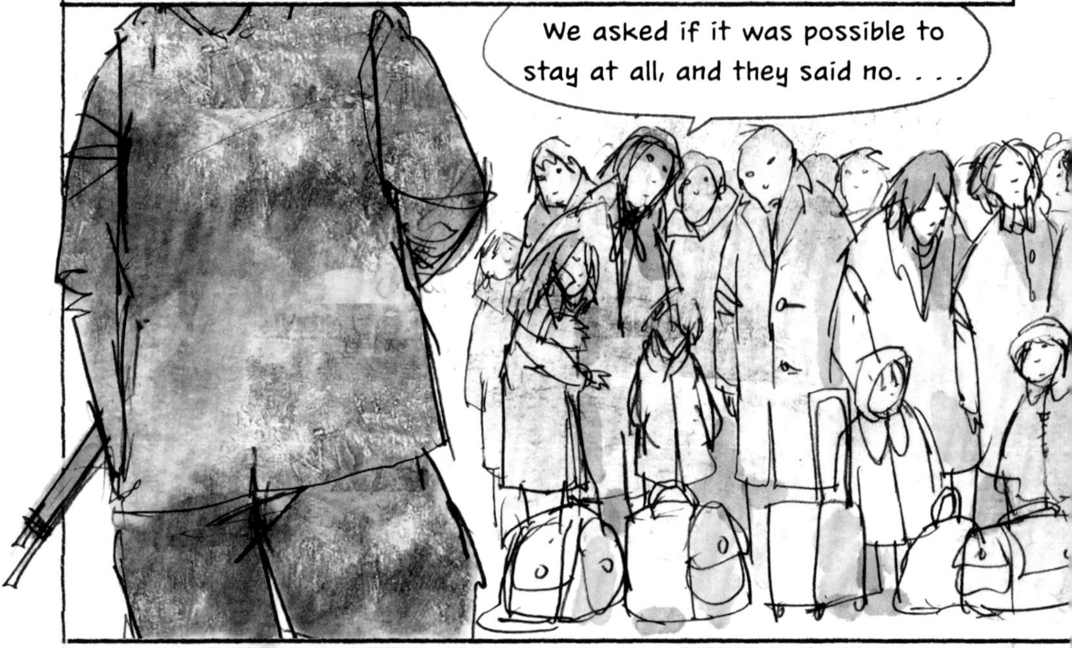
We asked if it was possible to stay at all, and they said no. . . .

They are taken to "filtration camps" where phones are taken and contacts downloaded.

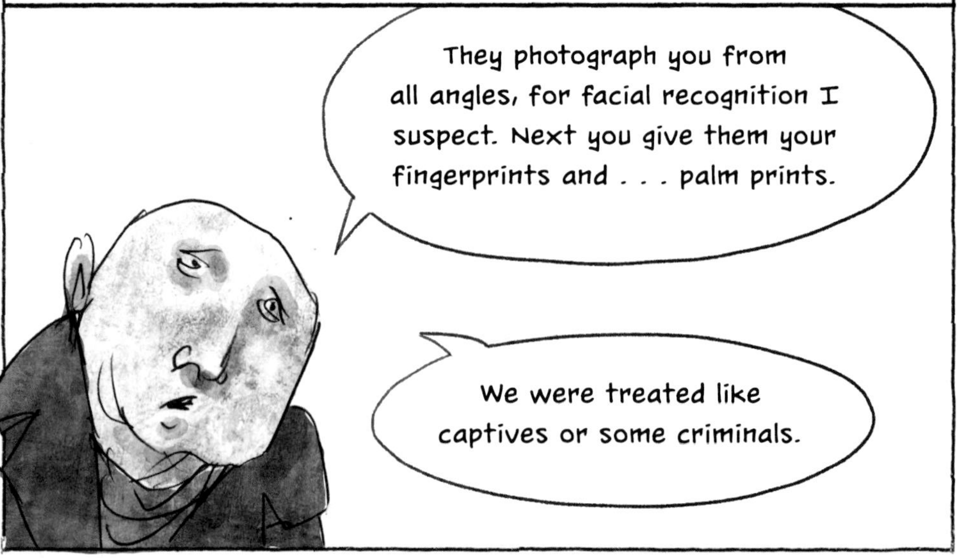
They photograph you from all angles, for facial recognition I suspect. Next you give them your fingerprints and . . . palm prints.
We were treated like captives or some criminals.

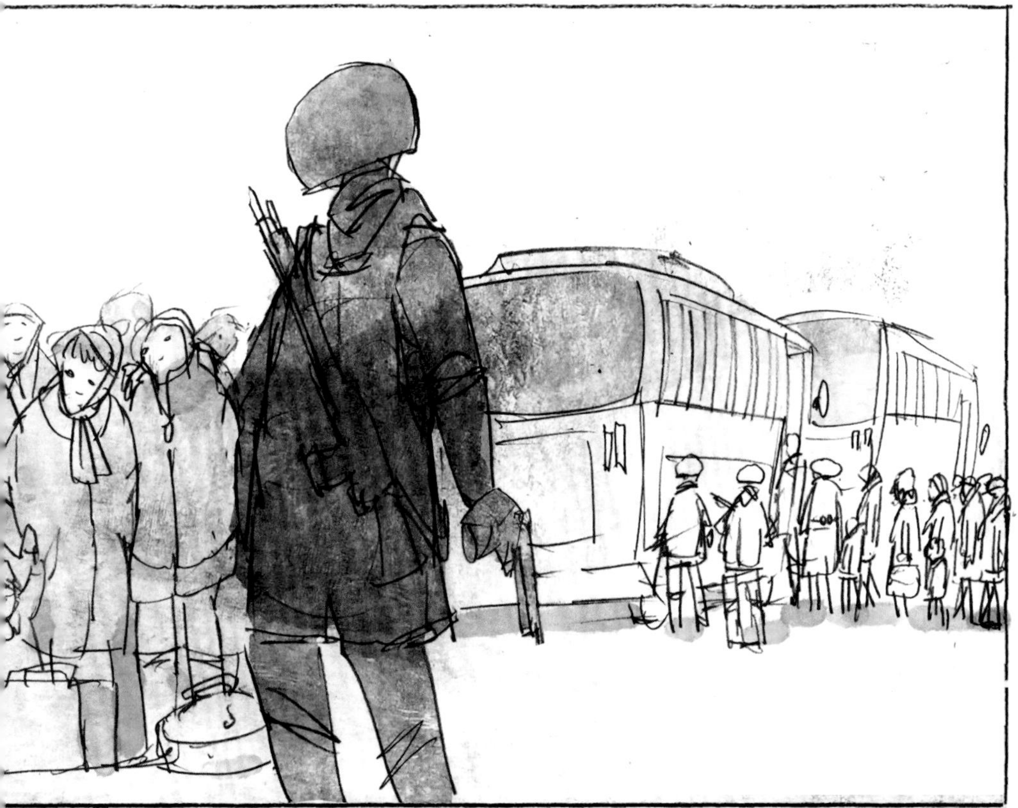

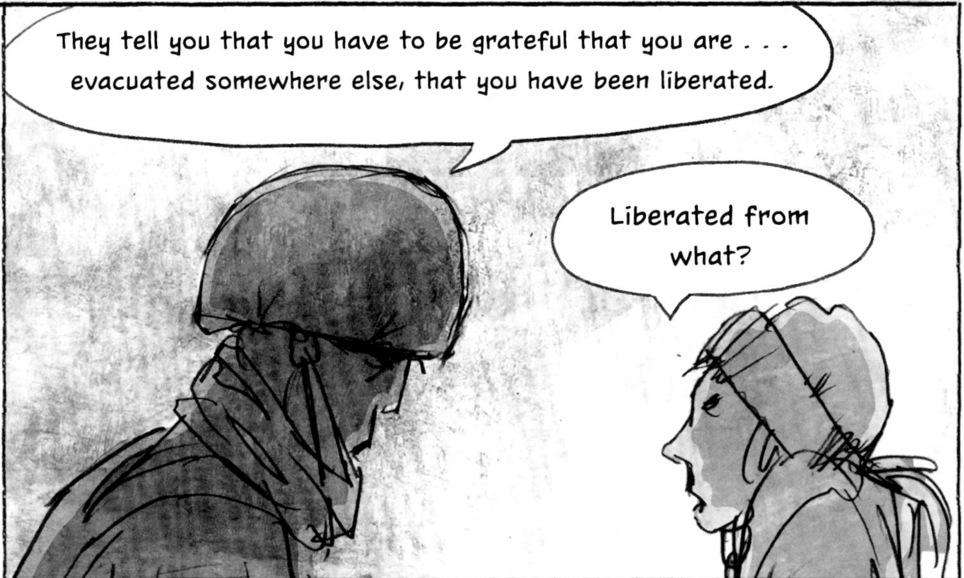
They tell you that you have to be grateful that you are . . . evacuated somewhere else, that you have been liberated.
Liberated from what?

There are reports of terrible abuse.

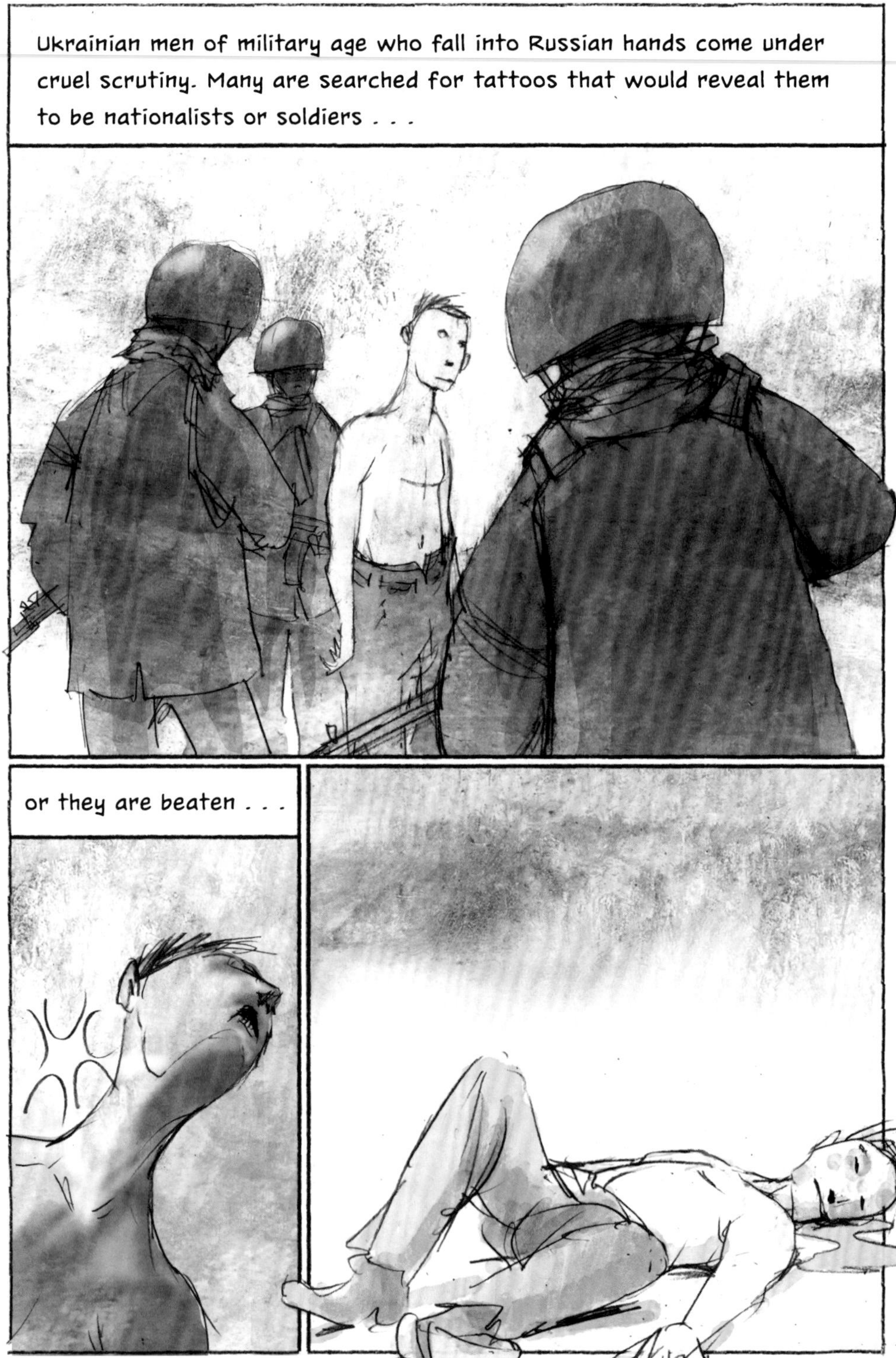
Ukrainian men of military age who fall into Russian hands come under cruel scrutiny. Many are searched for tattoos that would reveal them to be nationalists or soldiers . . .
or they are beaten . . .

. . . and tortured with electric shocks to divulge information they don't possess.

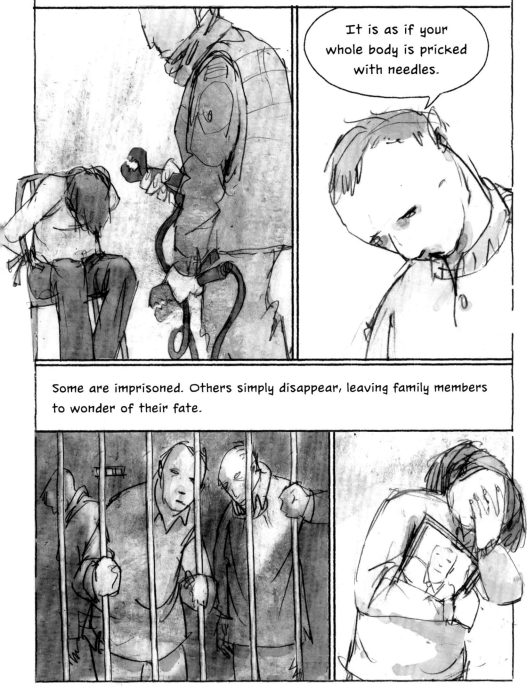

It is as if your whole body is pricked with needles.

Some are imprisoned. Others simply disappear, leaving family members to wonder of their fate.

SUNDAY, MARCH 20, 2022

At the Azovstal steel plant, people endure ceaseless bombardment, surviving on a bowl of soup a day and living mostly by candlelight.

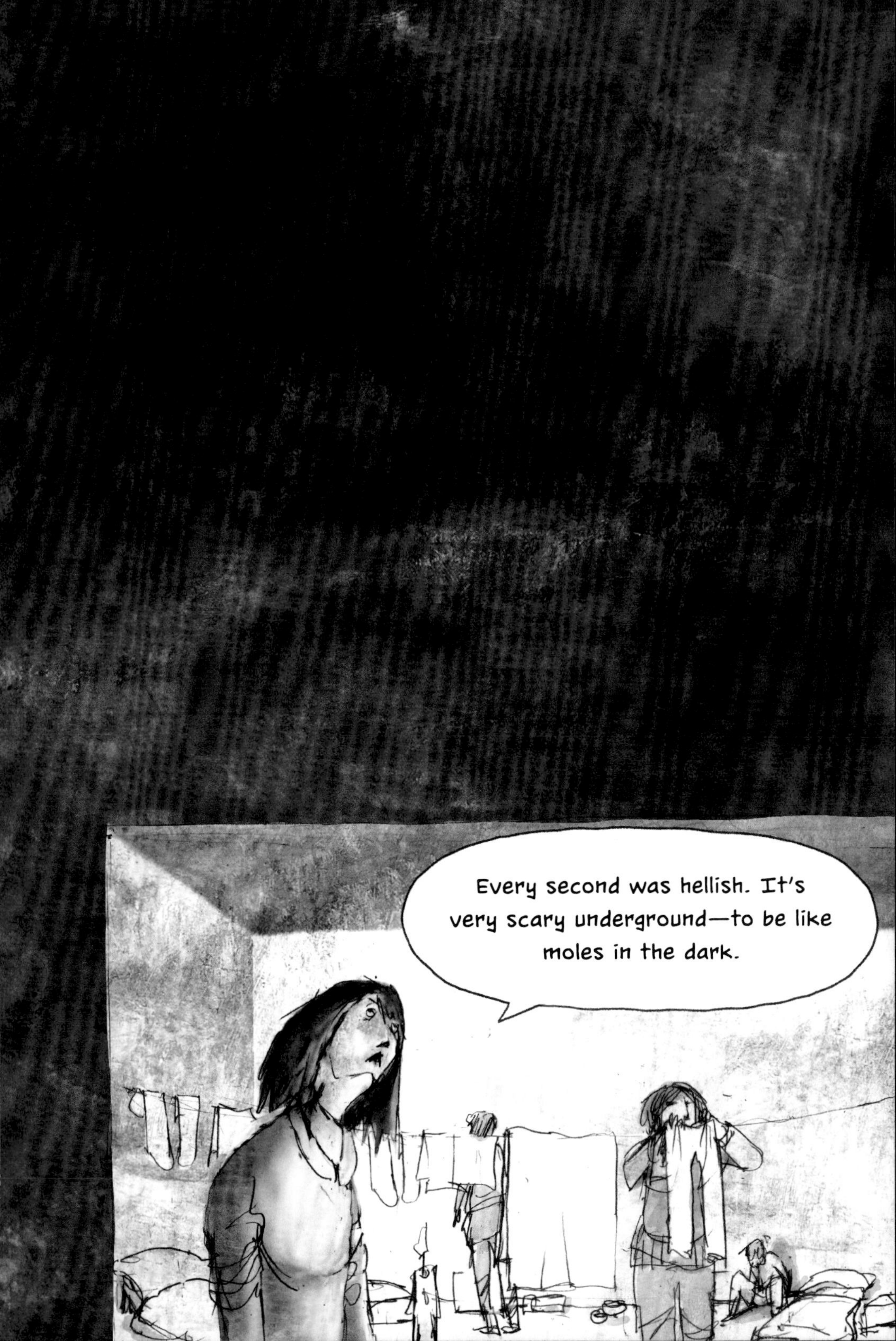
Every second was hellish. It's very scary underground—to be like moles in the dark.

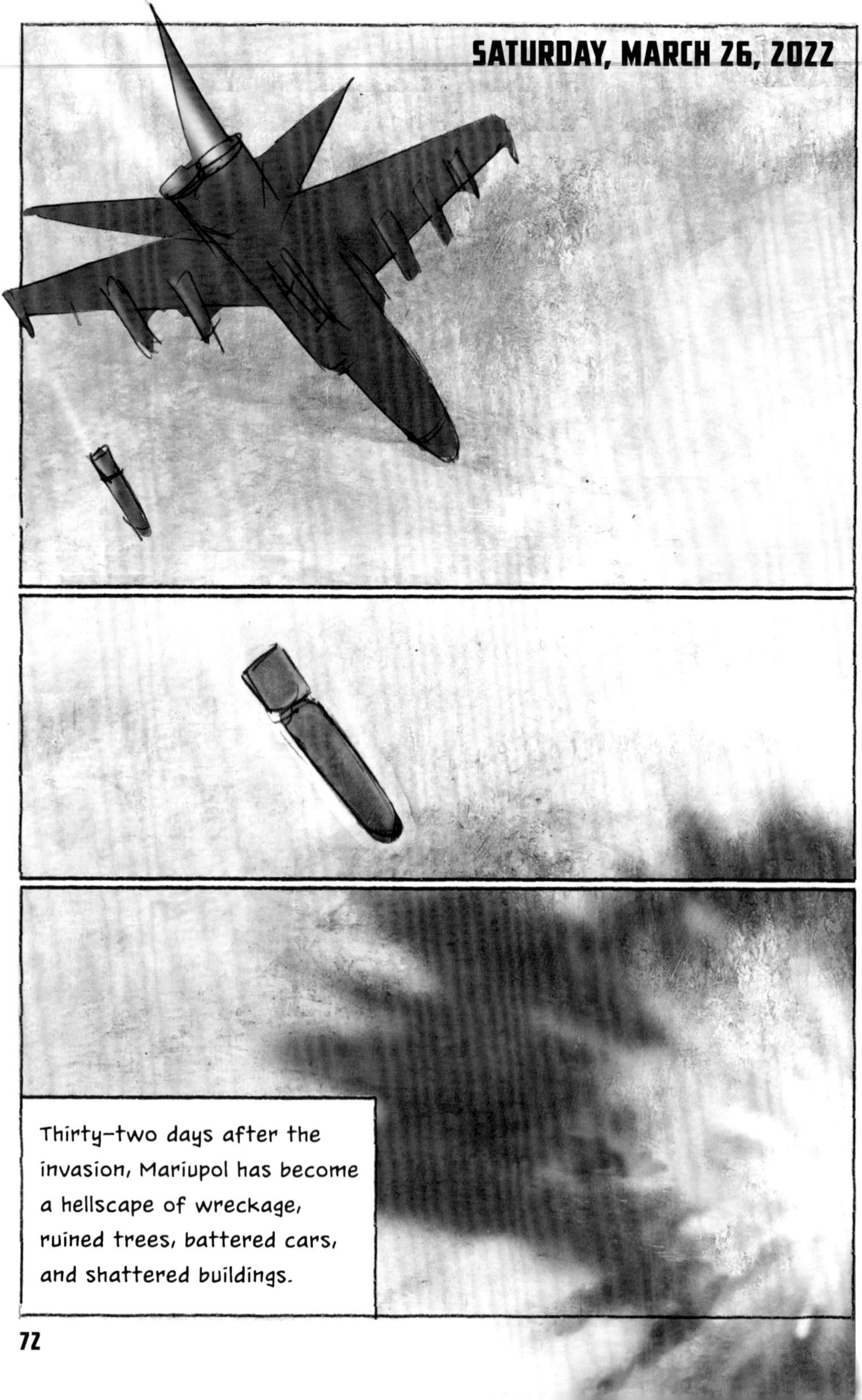
SATURDAY, MARCH 26, 2022
Thirty-two days after the invasion, Mariupol has become a hellscape of wreckage, ruined trees, battered cars, and shattered buildings.

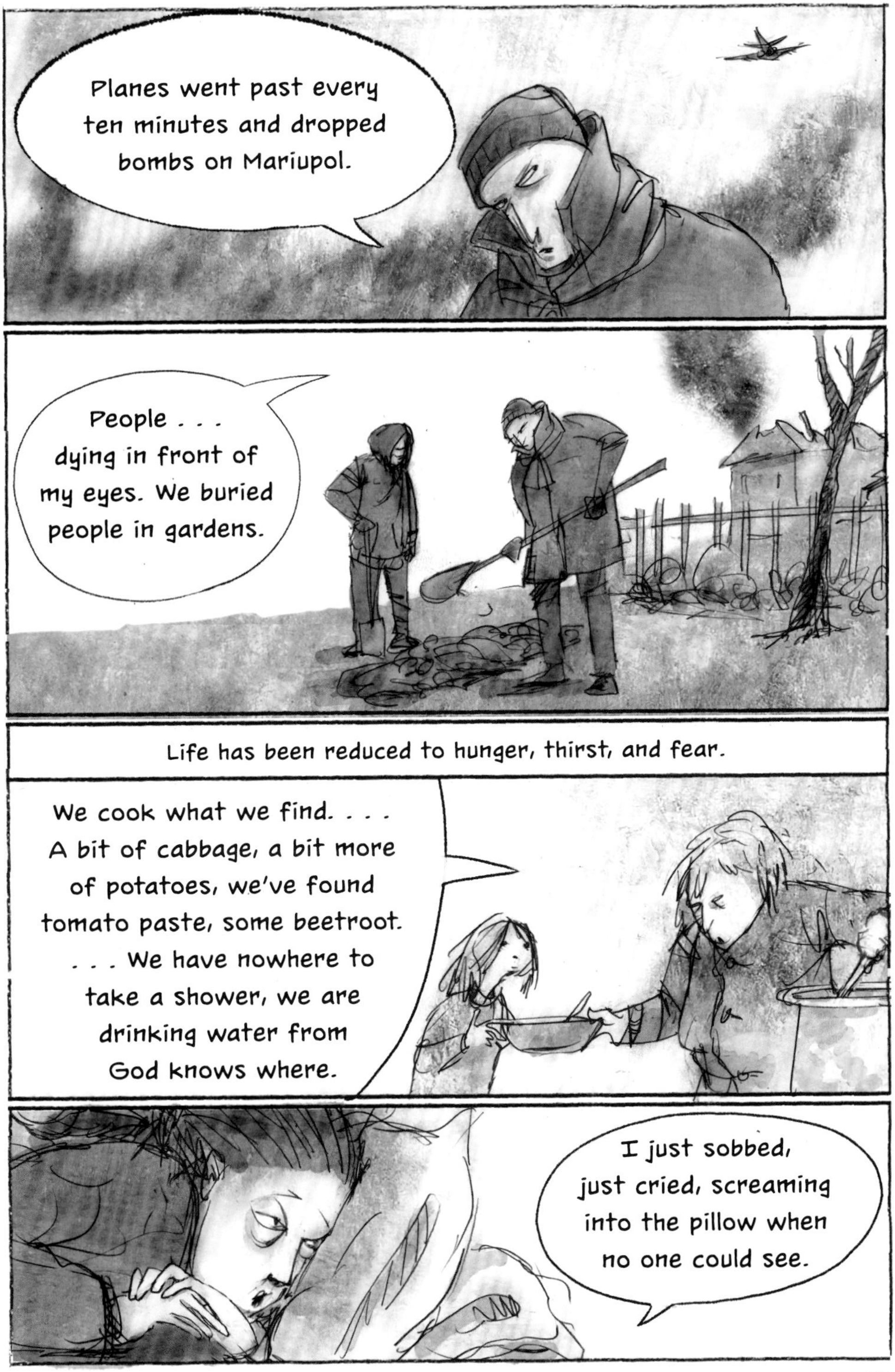
Planes went past every ten minutes and dropped bombs on Mariupol.
People . . . dying in front of my eyes. We buried people in gardens.
Life has been reduced to hunger, thirst, and fear.
We cook what we find. . . . A bit of cabbage, a bit more of potatoes, we've found tomato paste, some beetroot. . . . We have nowhere to take a shower, we are drinking water from God knows where.
I just sobbed, just cried, screaming into the pillow when no one could see.

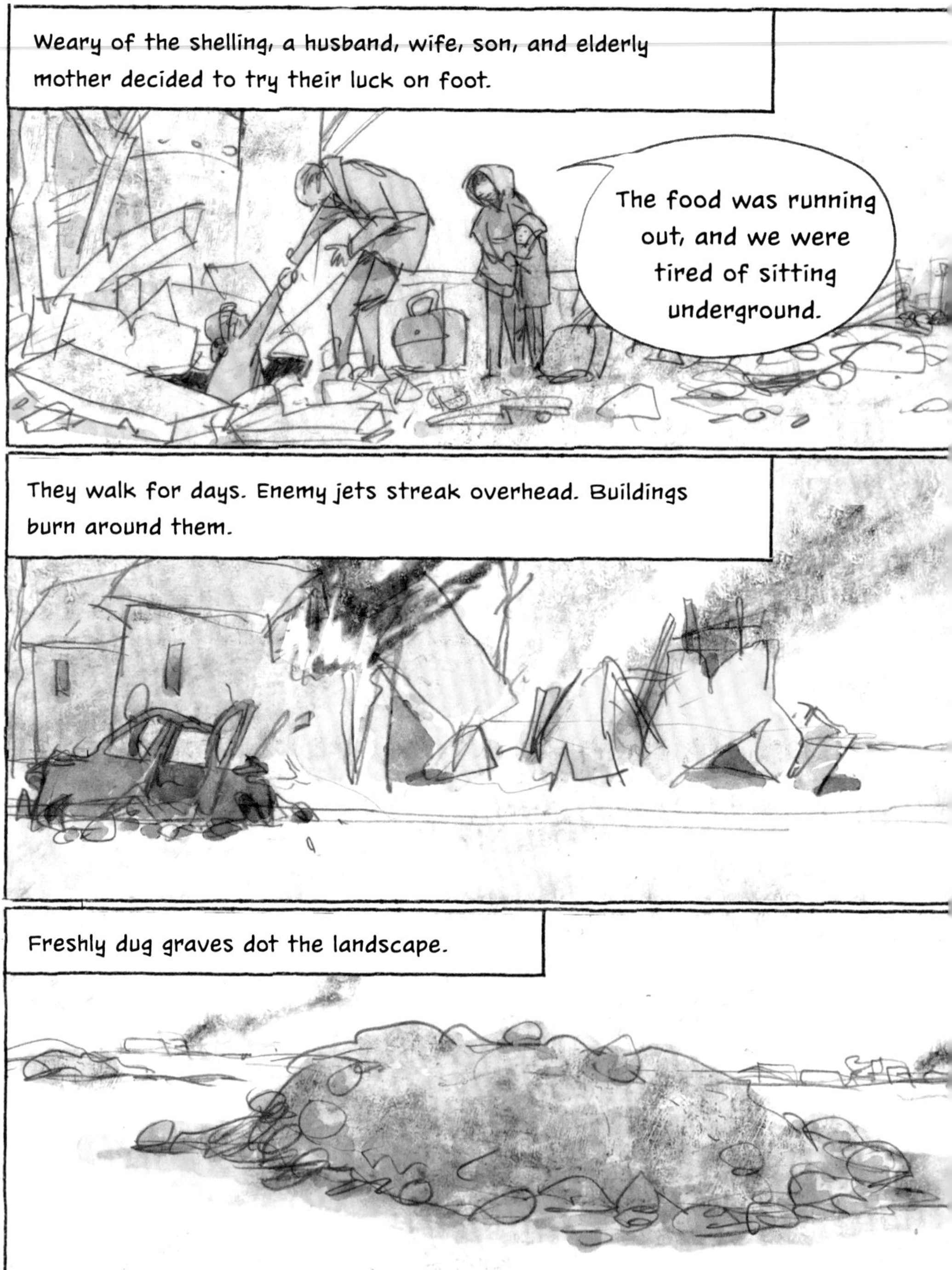
Weary of the shelling, a husband, wife, son, and elderly mother decided to try their luck on foot.
The food was running out, and we were tired of sitting underground.
They walk for days. Enemy jets streak overhead. Buildings burn around them.
Freshly dug graves dot the landscape.

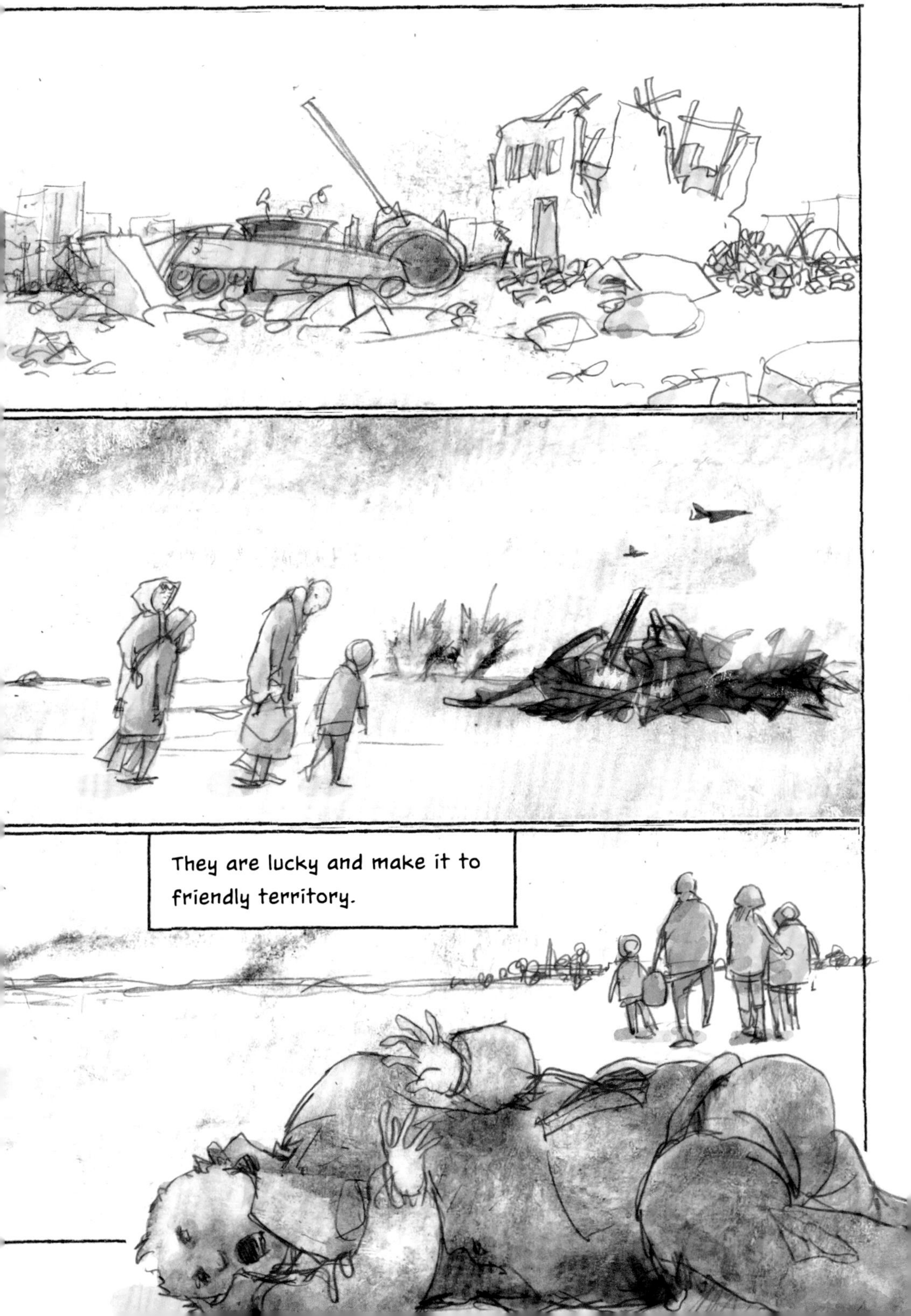
They are lucky and make it to friendly territory.

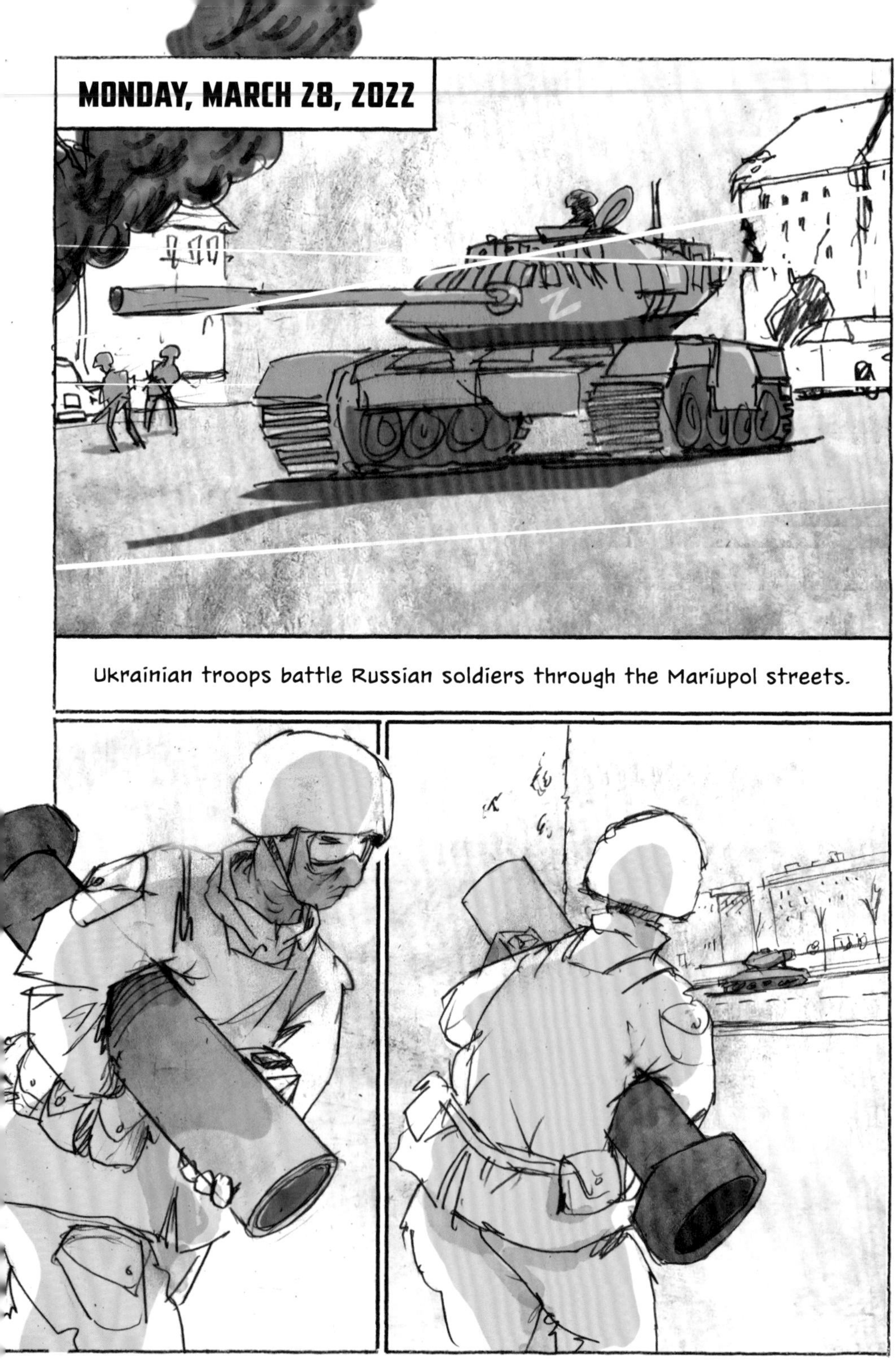
MONDAY, MARCH 28, 2022
Z
Ukrainian troops battle Russian soldiers through the Mariupol streets.

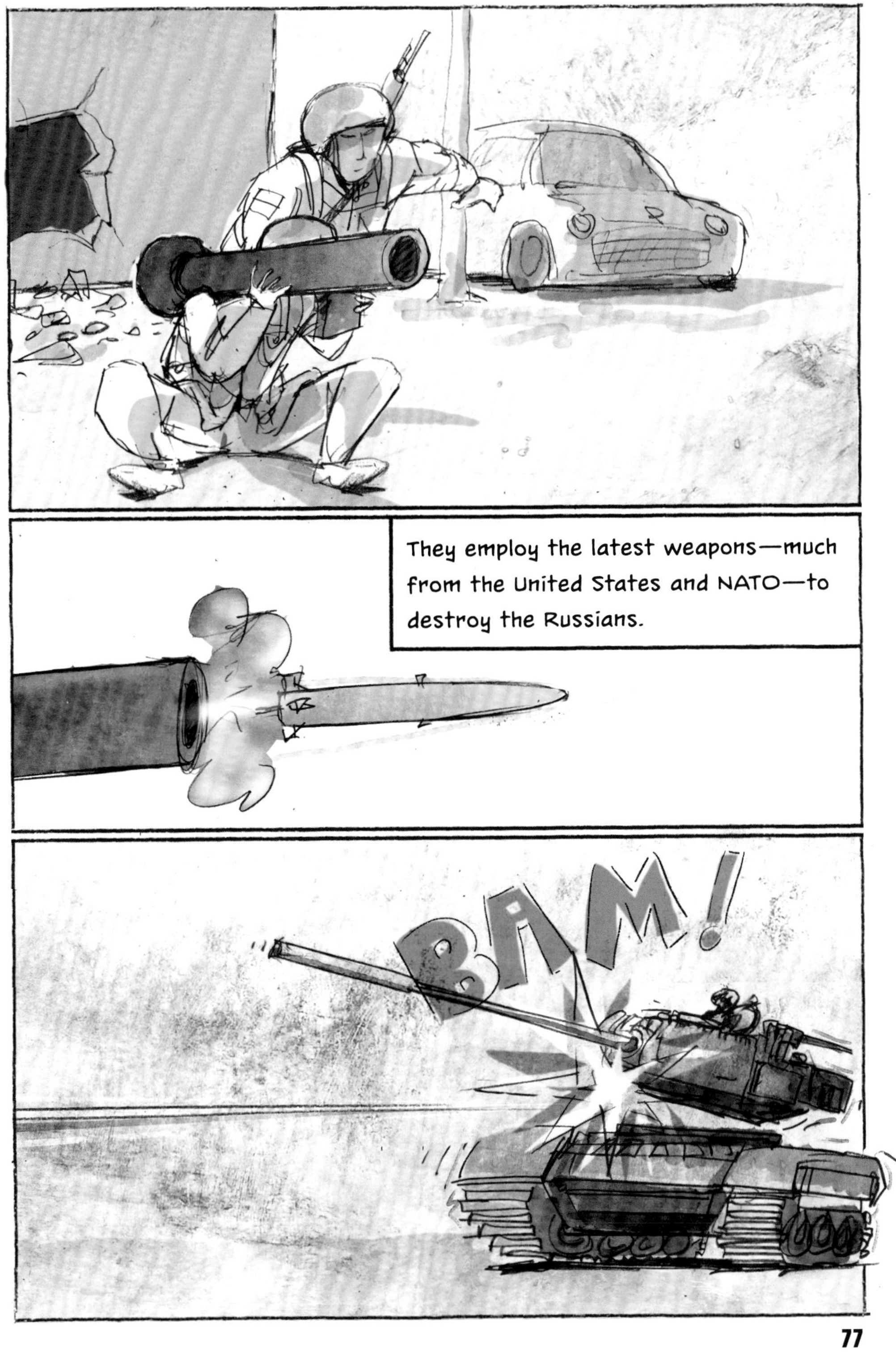
They employ the latest weapons—much from the United States and NATO—to destroy the Russians.
BAM!

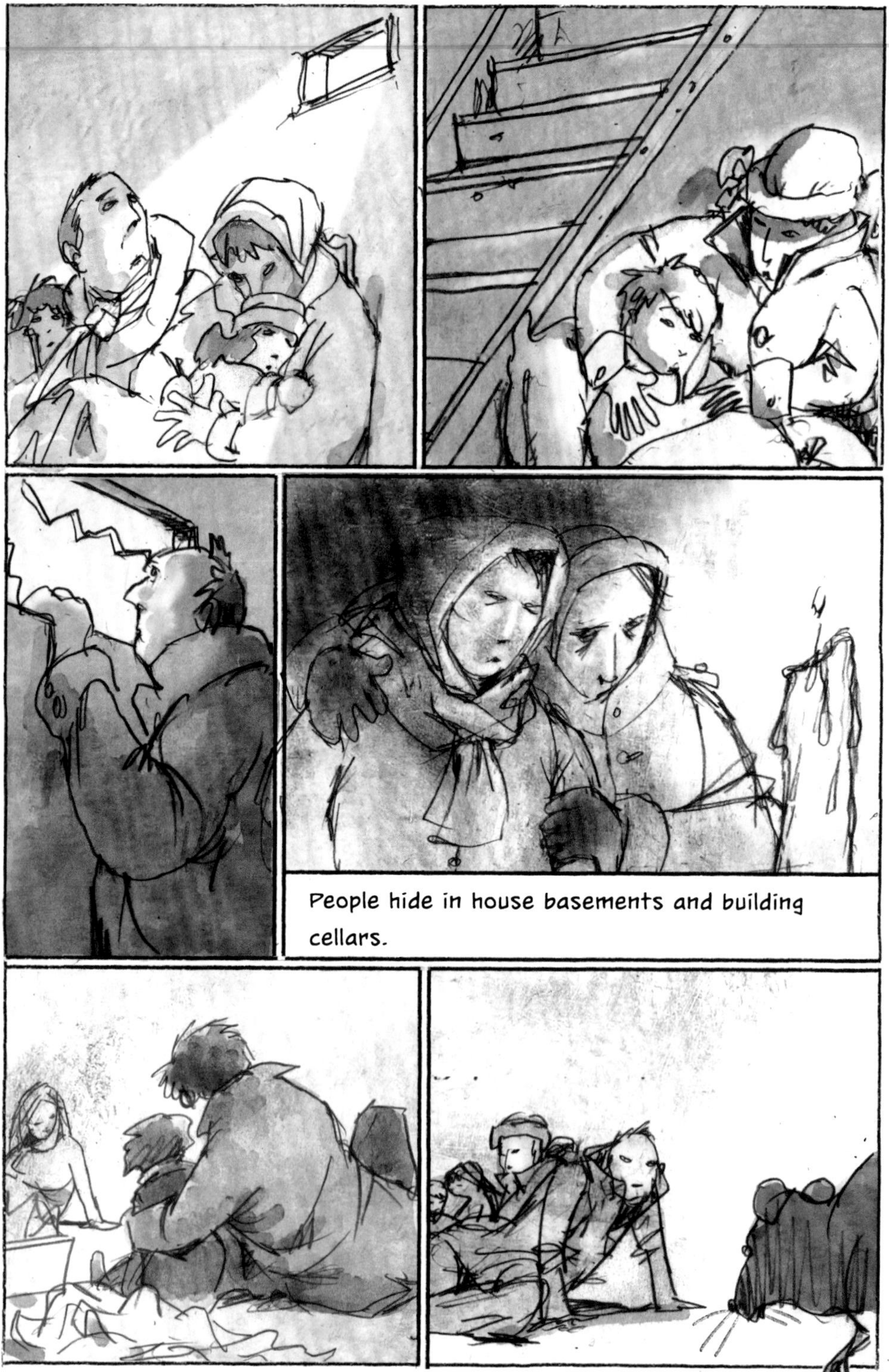
People hide in house basements and building cellars.

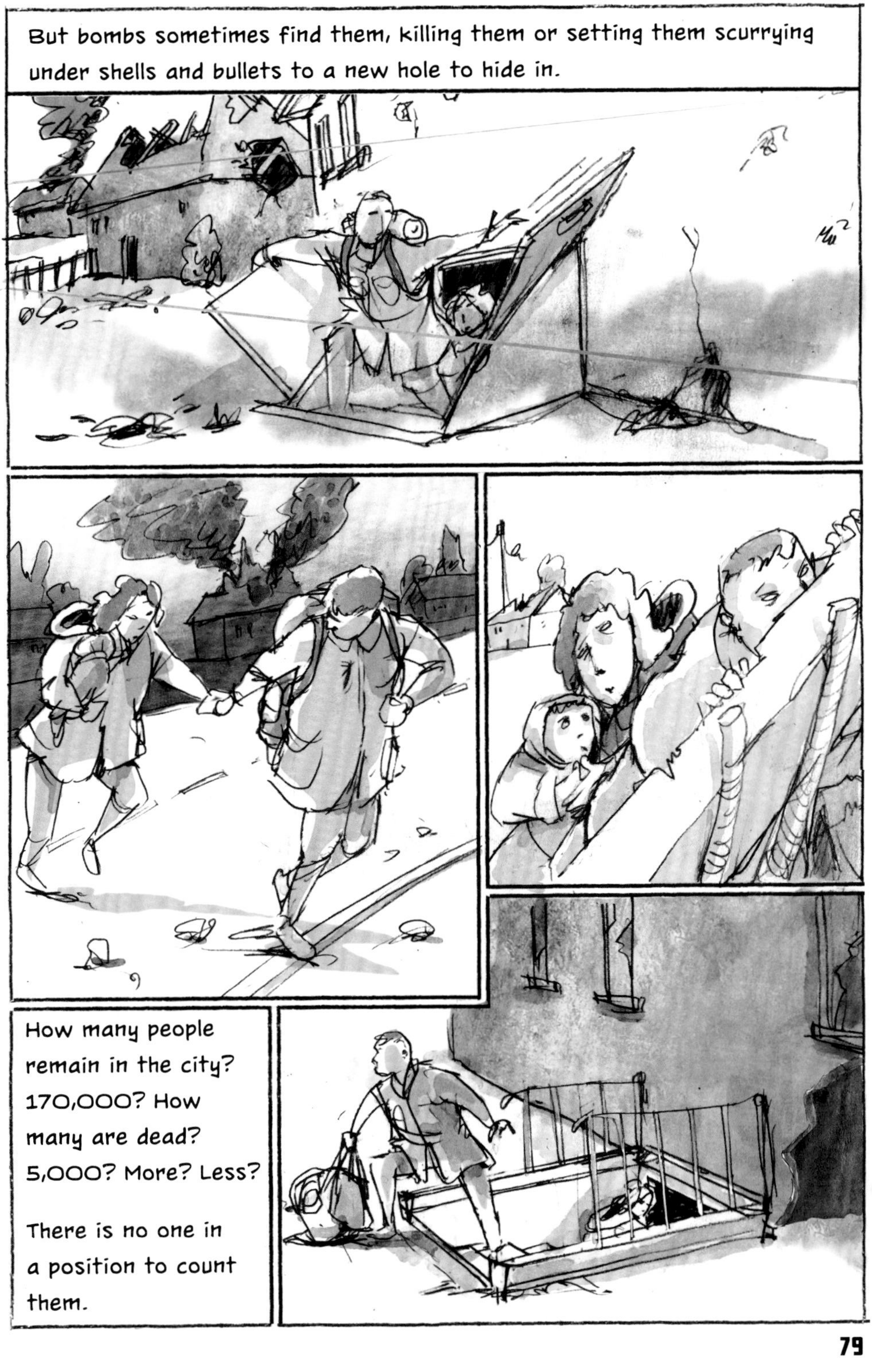
But bombs sometimes find them, killing them or setting them scurrying under shells and bullets to a new hole to hide in.
How many people remain in the city? 170,000? How many are dead? 5,000? More? Less?
There is no one in a position to count them.

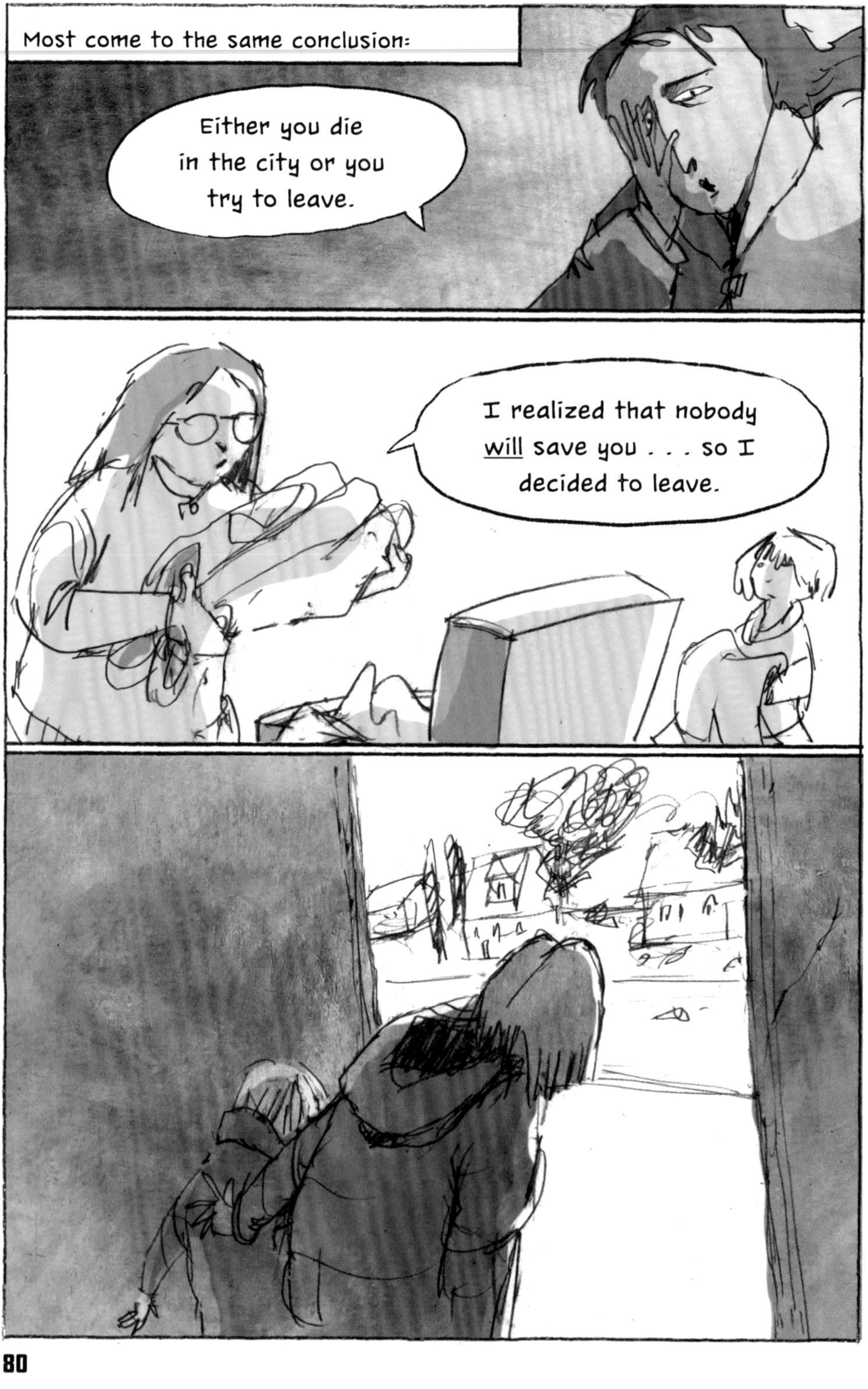
Most come to the same conclusion:
Either you die in the city or you try to leave.
I realized that nobody will save you . . . so I decided to leave.

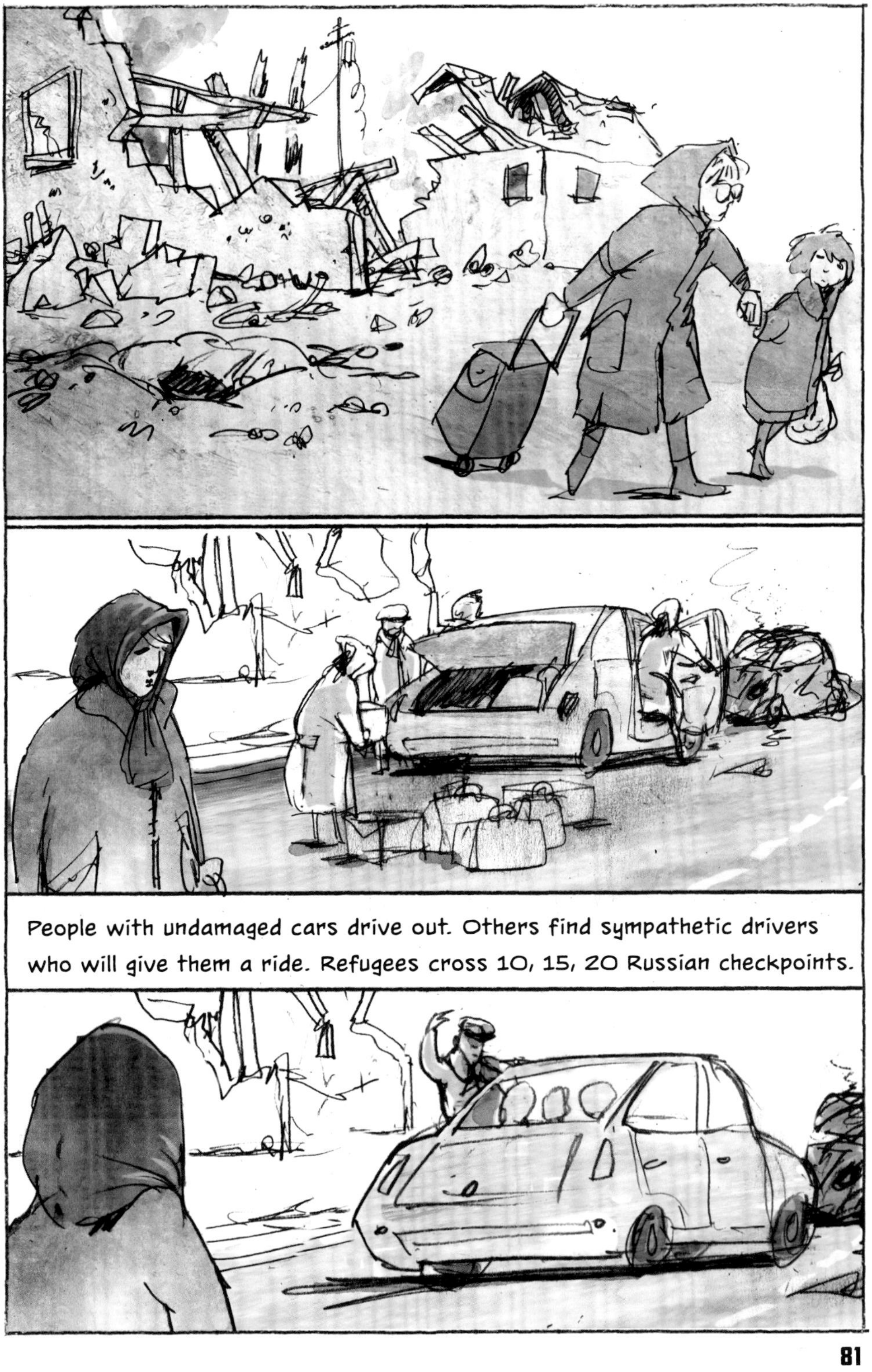
People with undamaged cars drive out. Others find sympathetic drivers who will give them a ride. Refugees cross 10, 15, 20 Russian checkpoints.

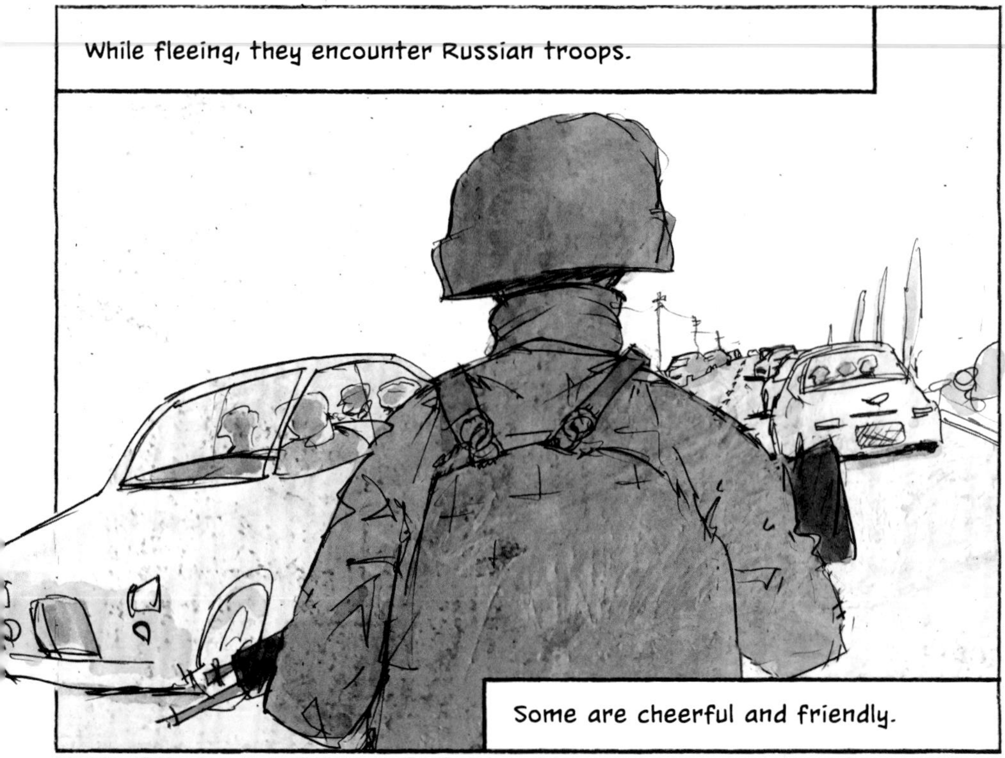
While fleeing, they encounter Russian troops.
Some are cheerful and friendly.

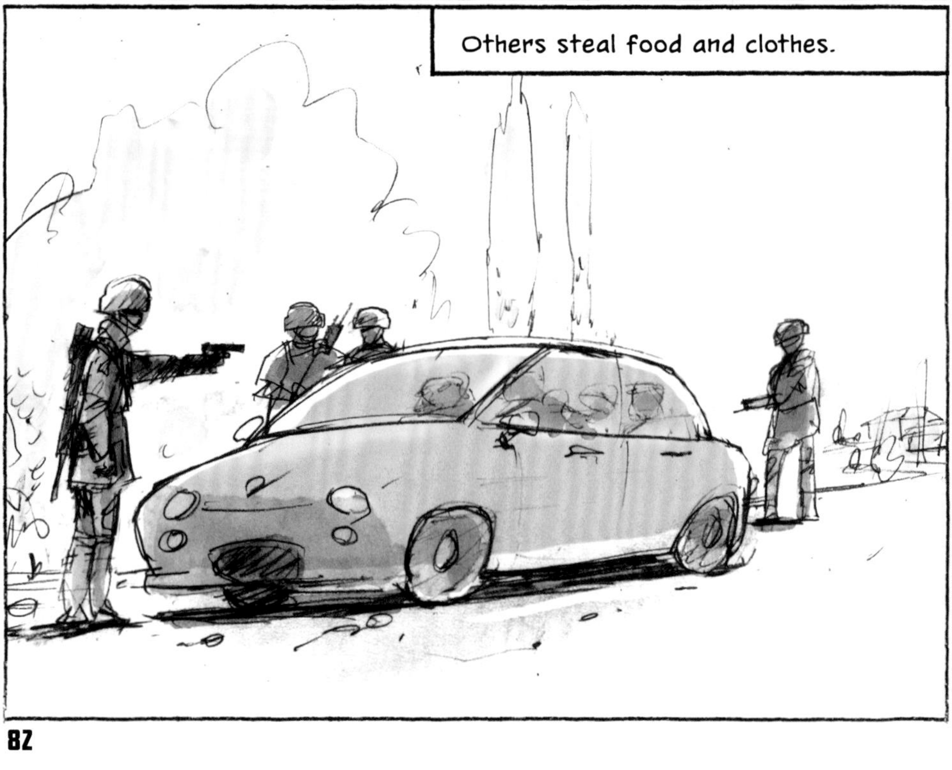
Others steal food and clothes.

Or they may beat travelers.

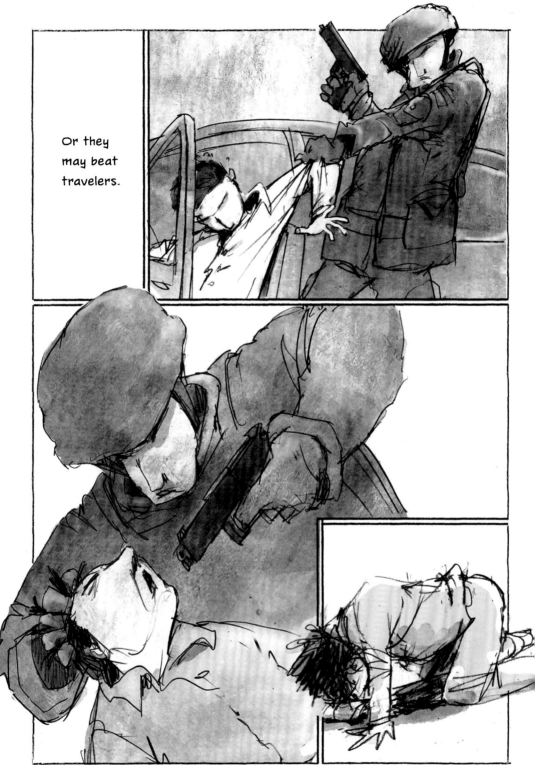

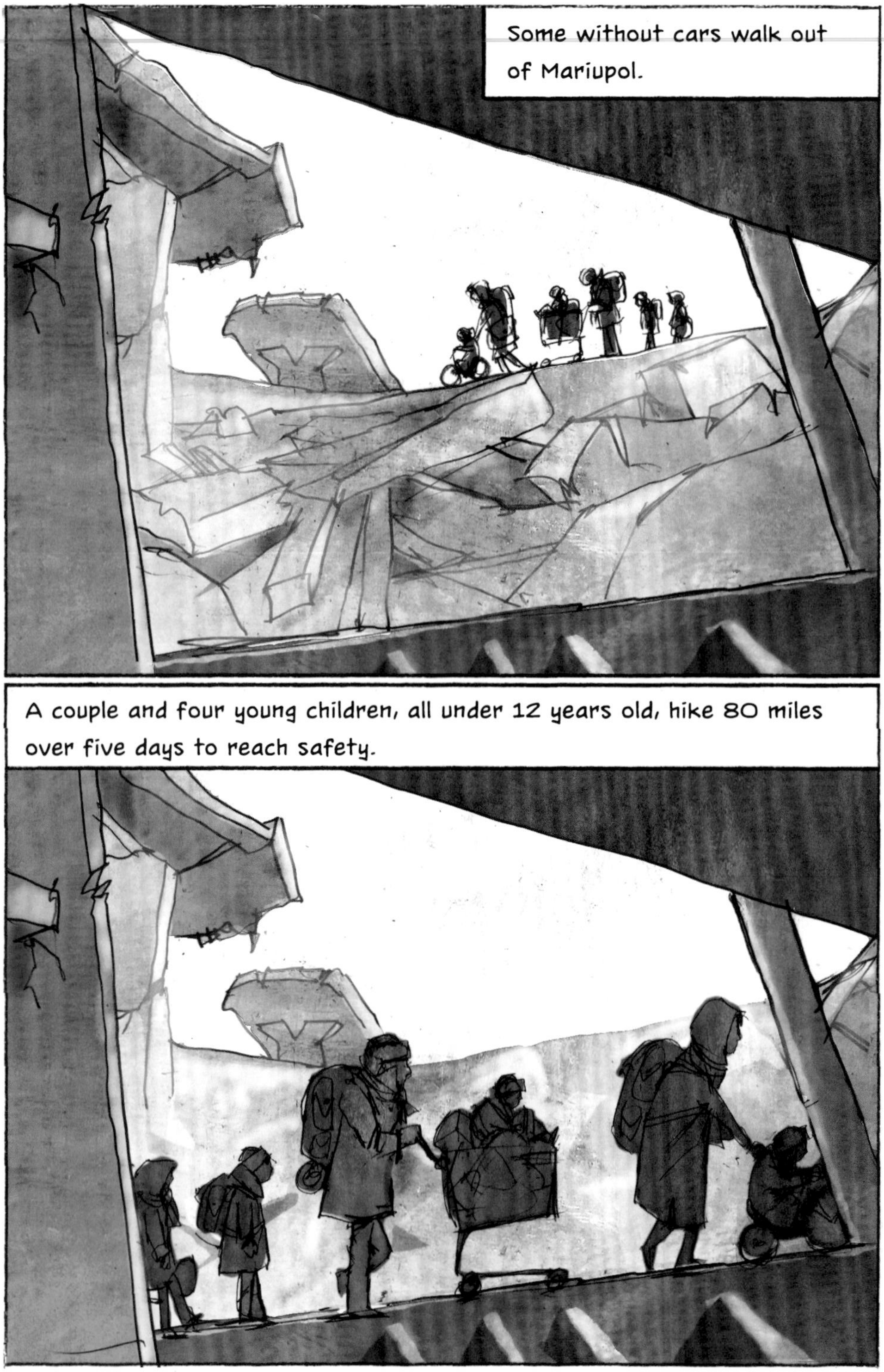
Some without cars walk out of Mariupol.
A couple and four young children, all under 12 years old, hike 80 miles over five days to reach safety.

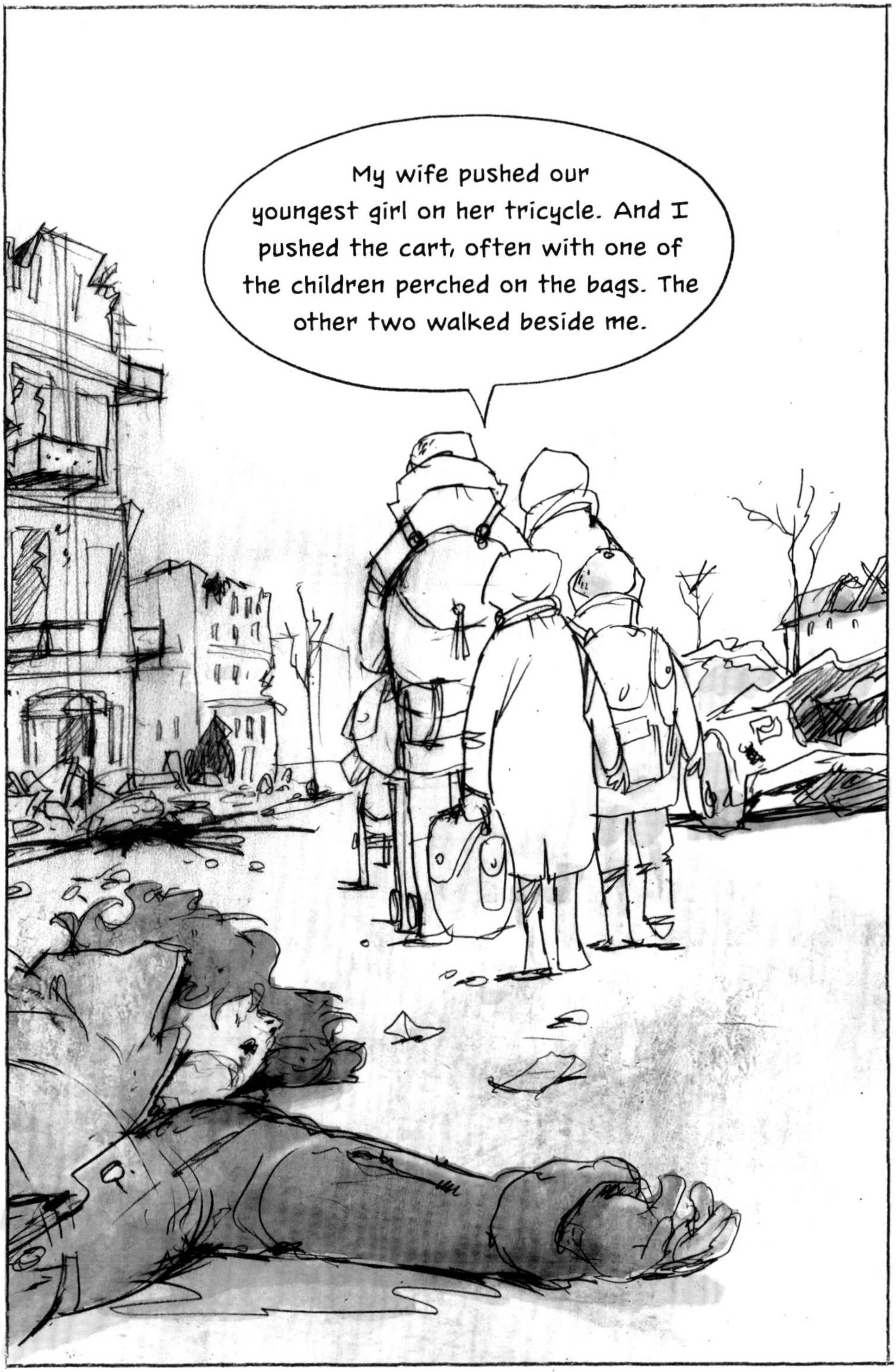
My wife pushed our youngest girl on her tricycle. And I pushed the cart, often with one of the children perched on the bags. The other two walked beside me.

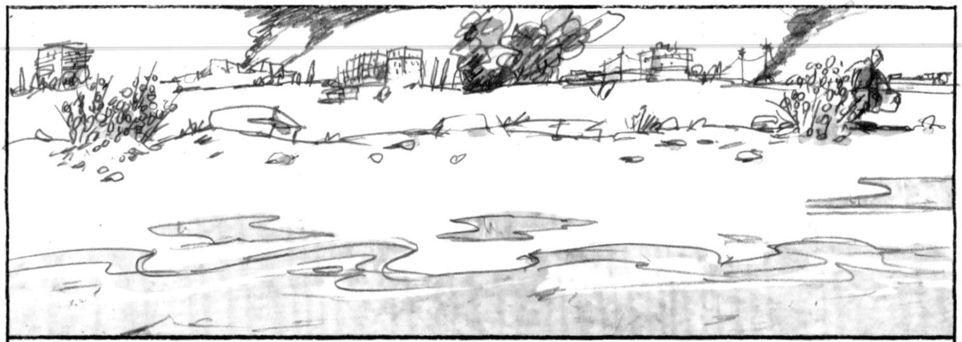

One man swims out of Mariupol using big plastic bottles to help him float. He swims two and half hours in frigid water to skirt Russian positions.

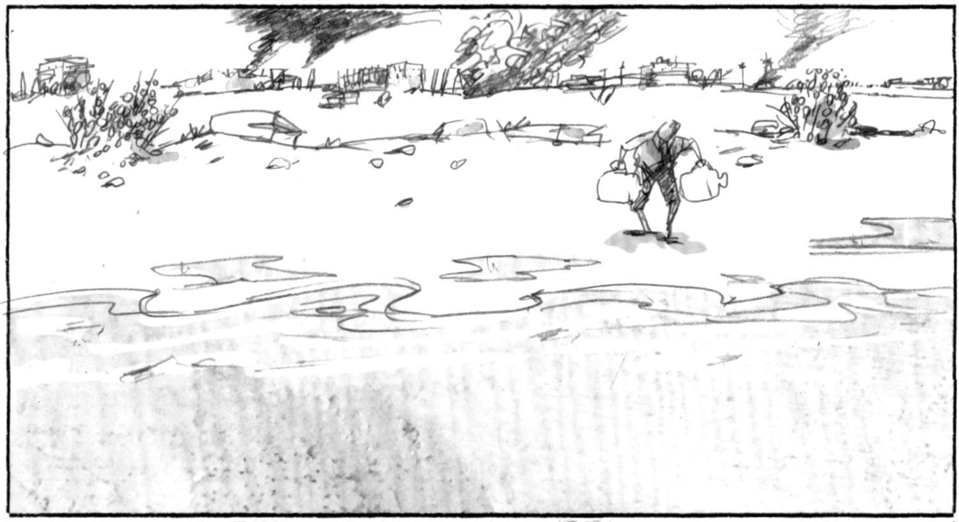

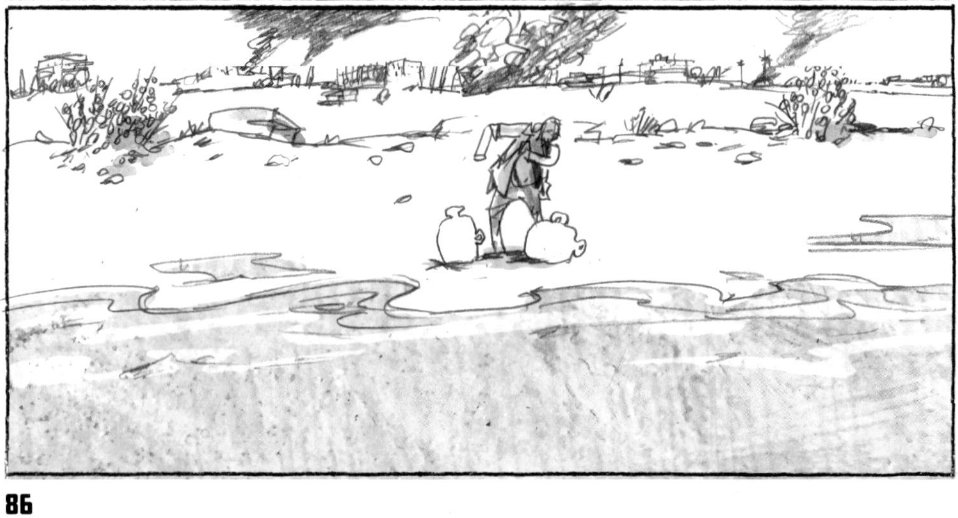

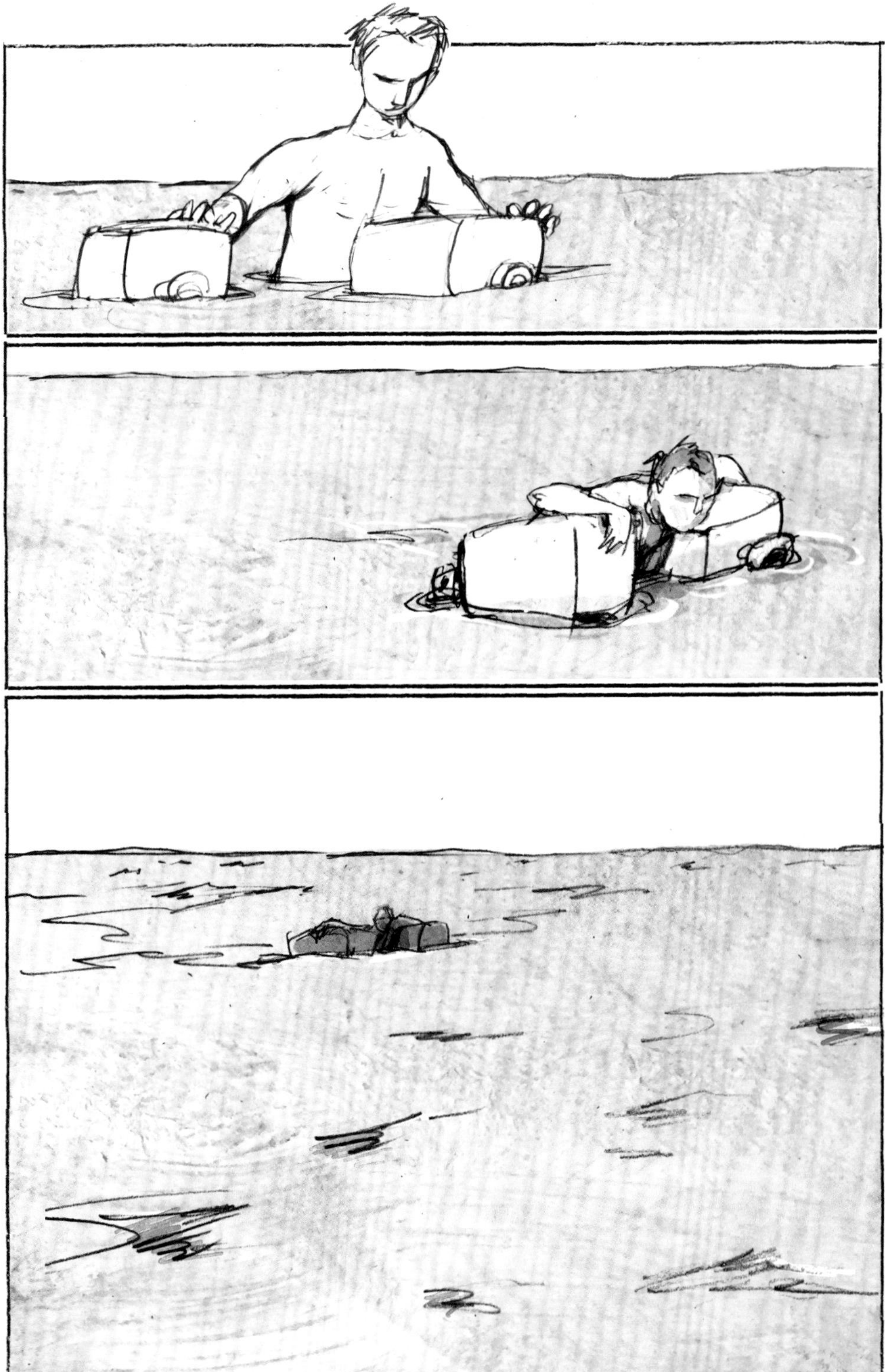

SUNDAY, APRIL 3

Thirty-nine days into a war most everyone thought would be over in three days, the defenders of Ukraine fight on.

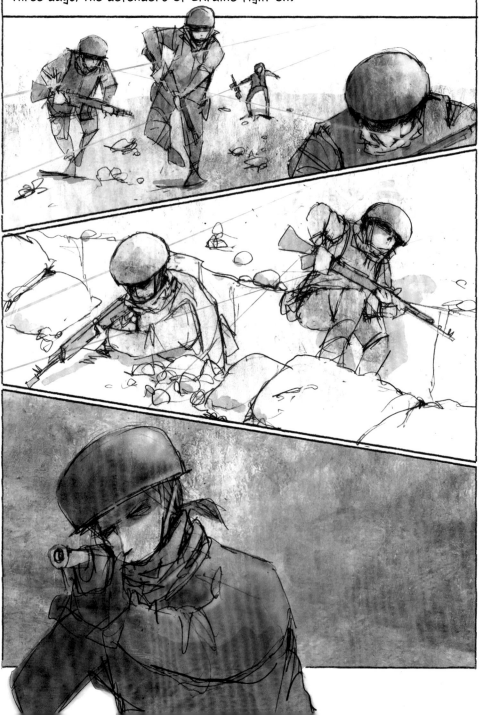

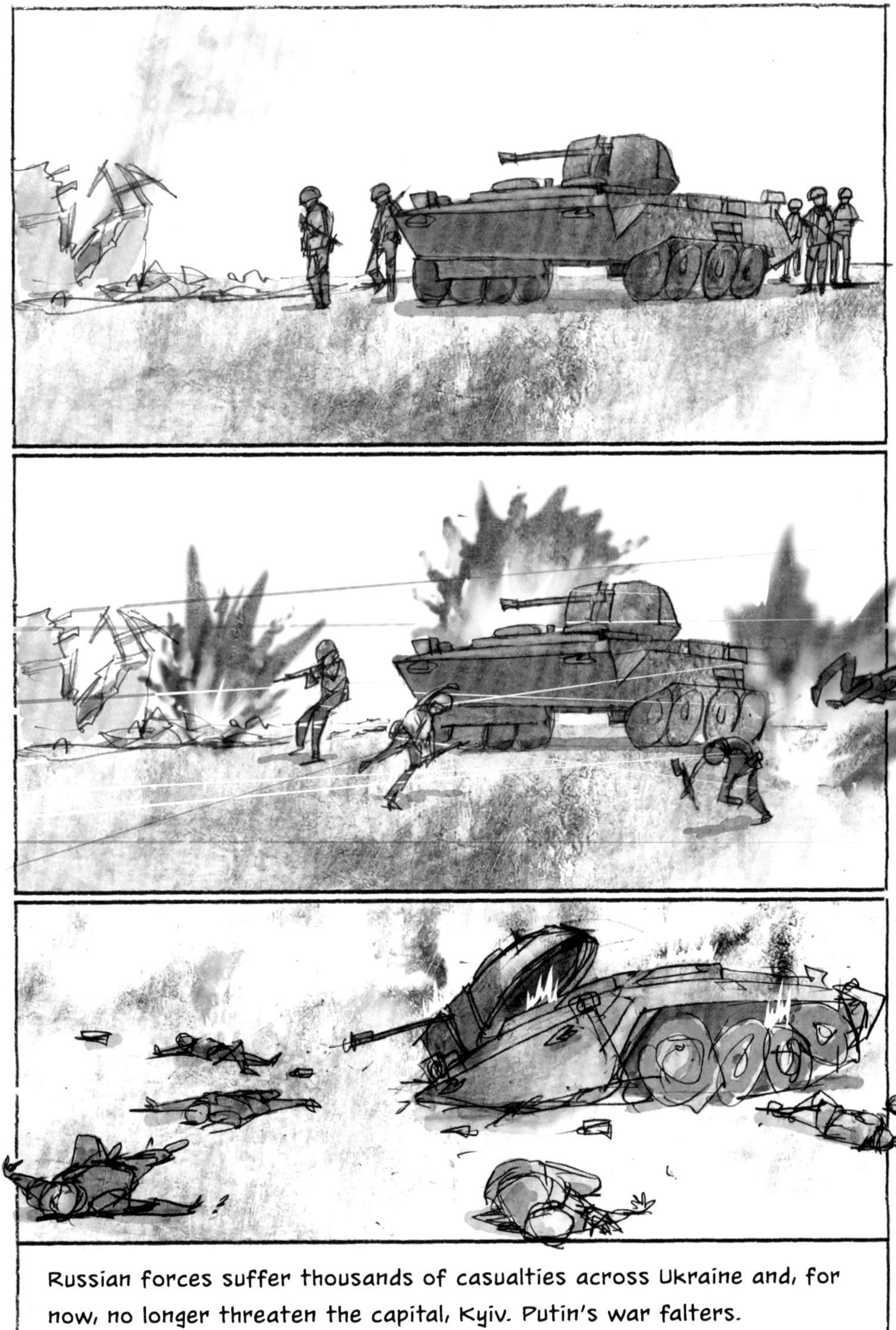
Russian forces suffer thousands of casualties across Ukraine and, for now, no longer threaten the capital, Kyiv. Putin's war falters.

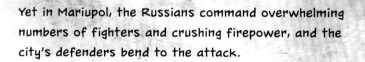

Yet in Mariupol, the Russians command overwhelming numbers of fighters and crushing firepower, and the city's defenders bend to the attack.

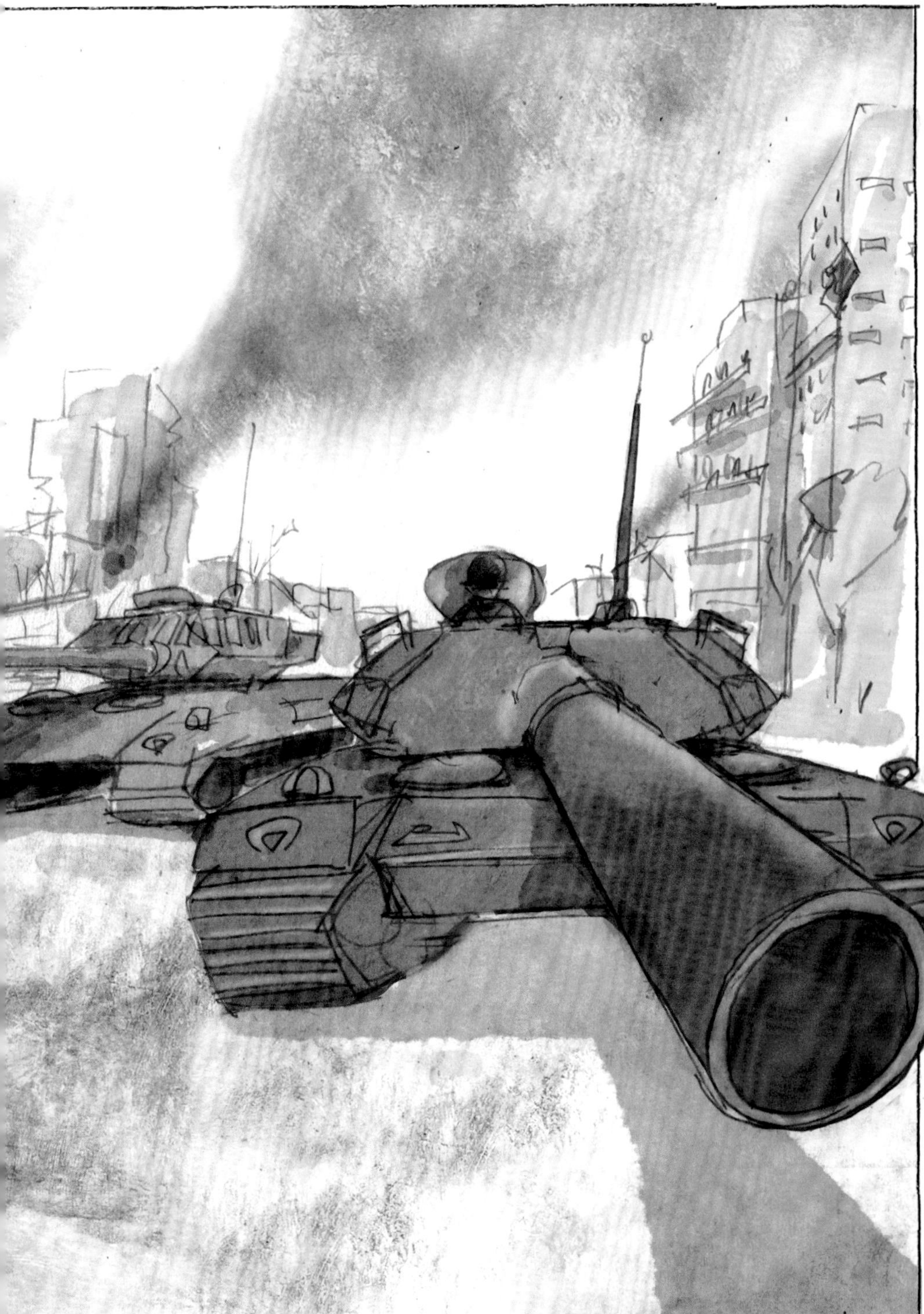

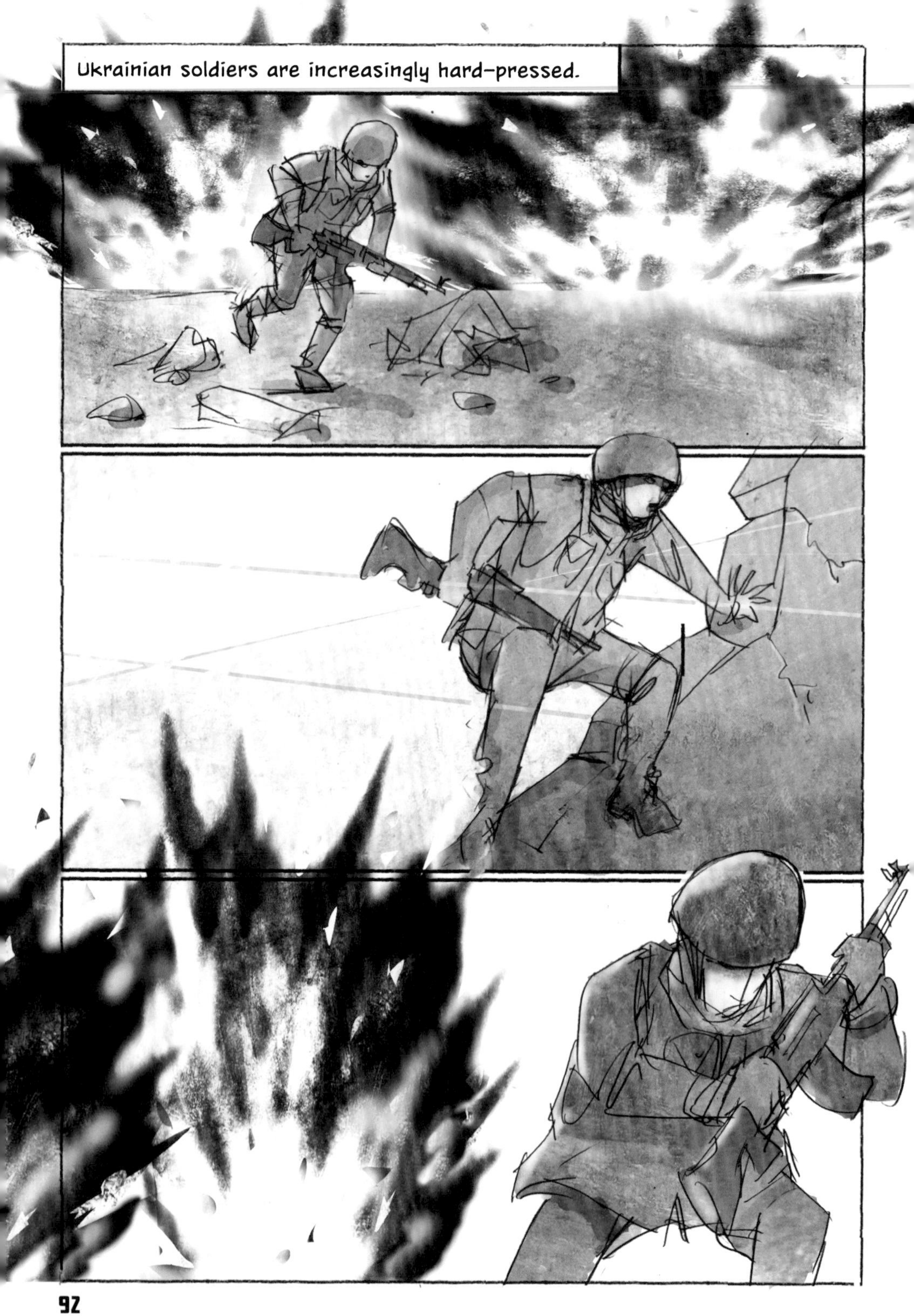
Ukrainian soldiers are increasingly hard-pressed.

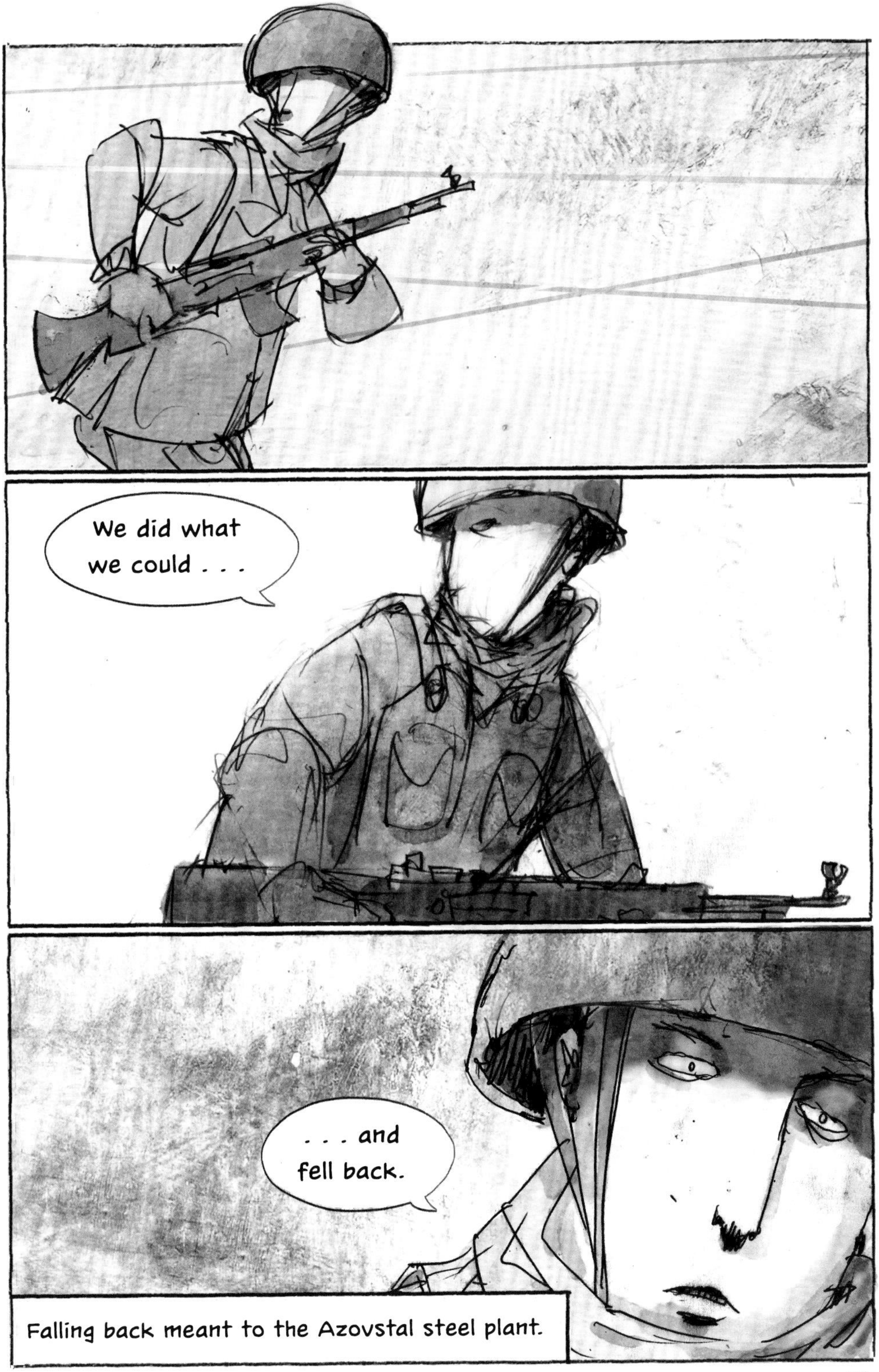
We did what we could . . .
. . . and fell back.
Falling back meant to the Azovstal steel plant.

Battered and shattered, the plant has become something of a shelter of last resort for both civilians and soldiers.

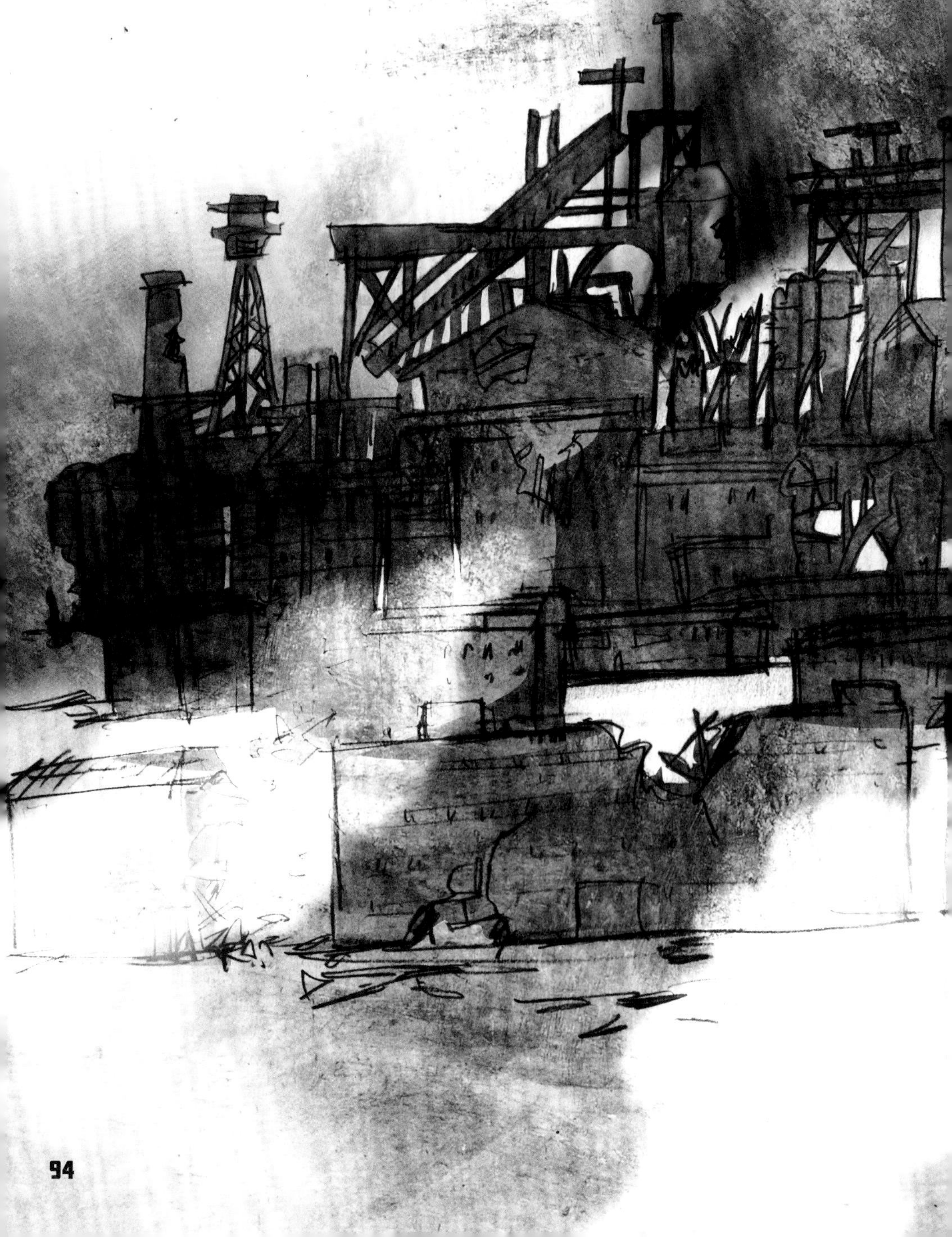

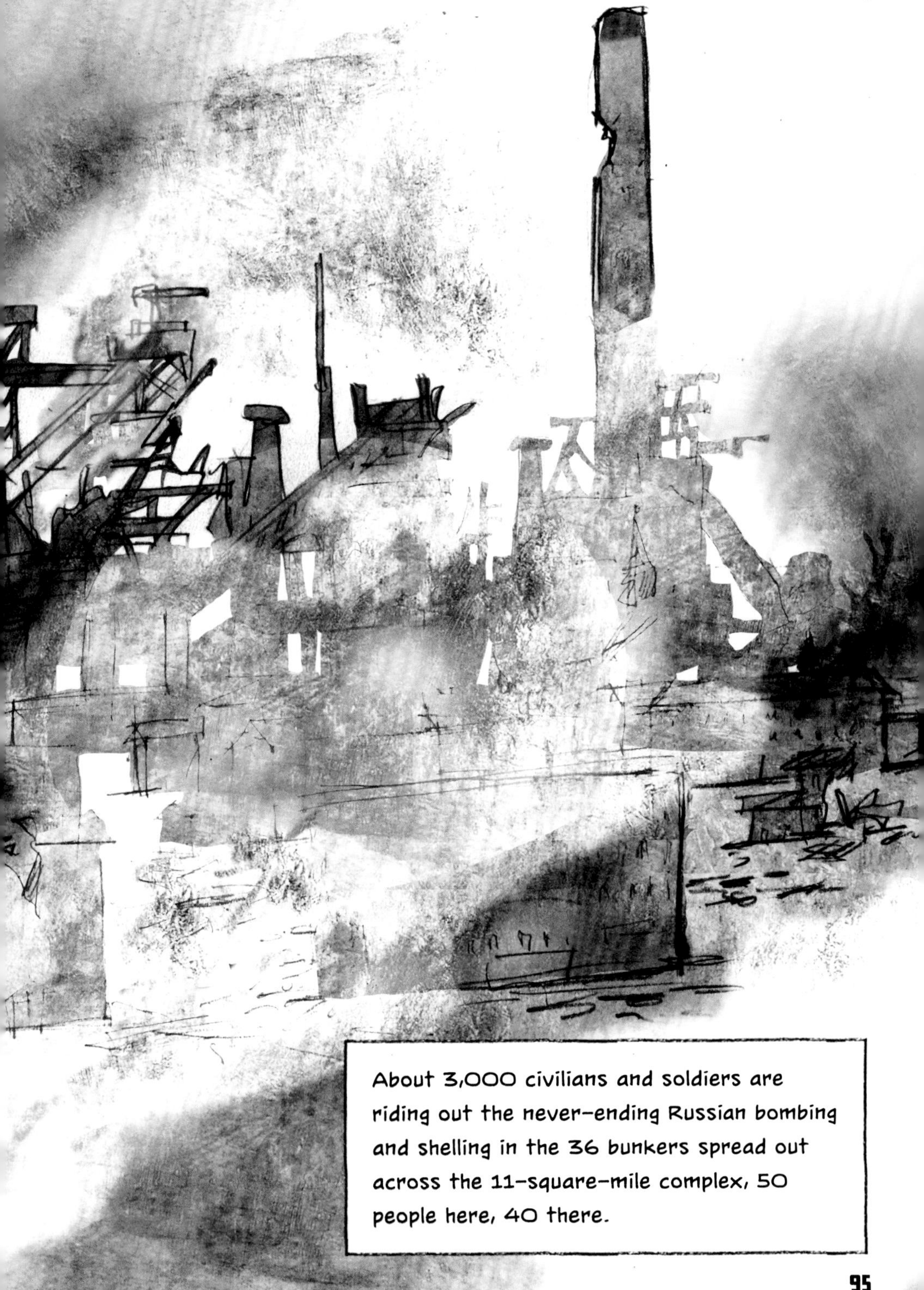
About 3,000 civilians and soldiers are riding out the never-ending Russian bombing and shelling in the 36 bunkers spread out across the 11-square-mile complex, 50 people here, 40 there.

Staying fed and watered means foraging aboveground with the risk of being shot, shelled, or bombed.

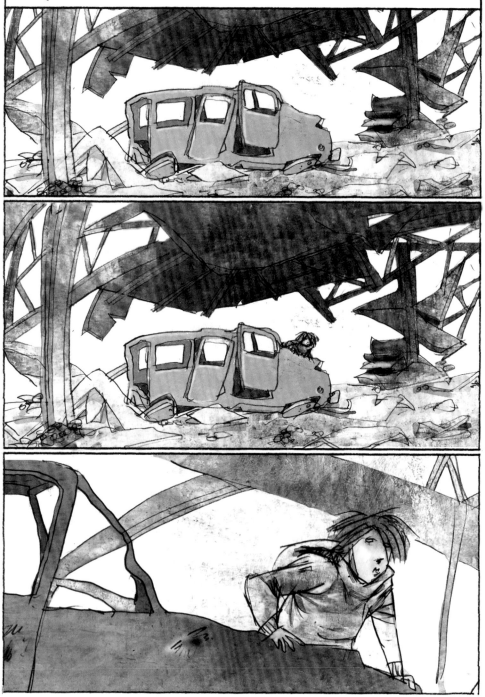

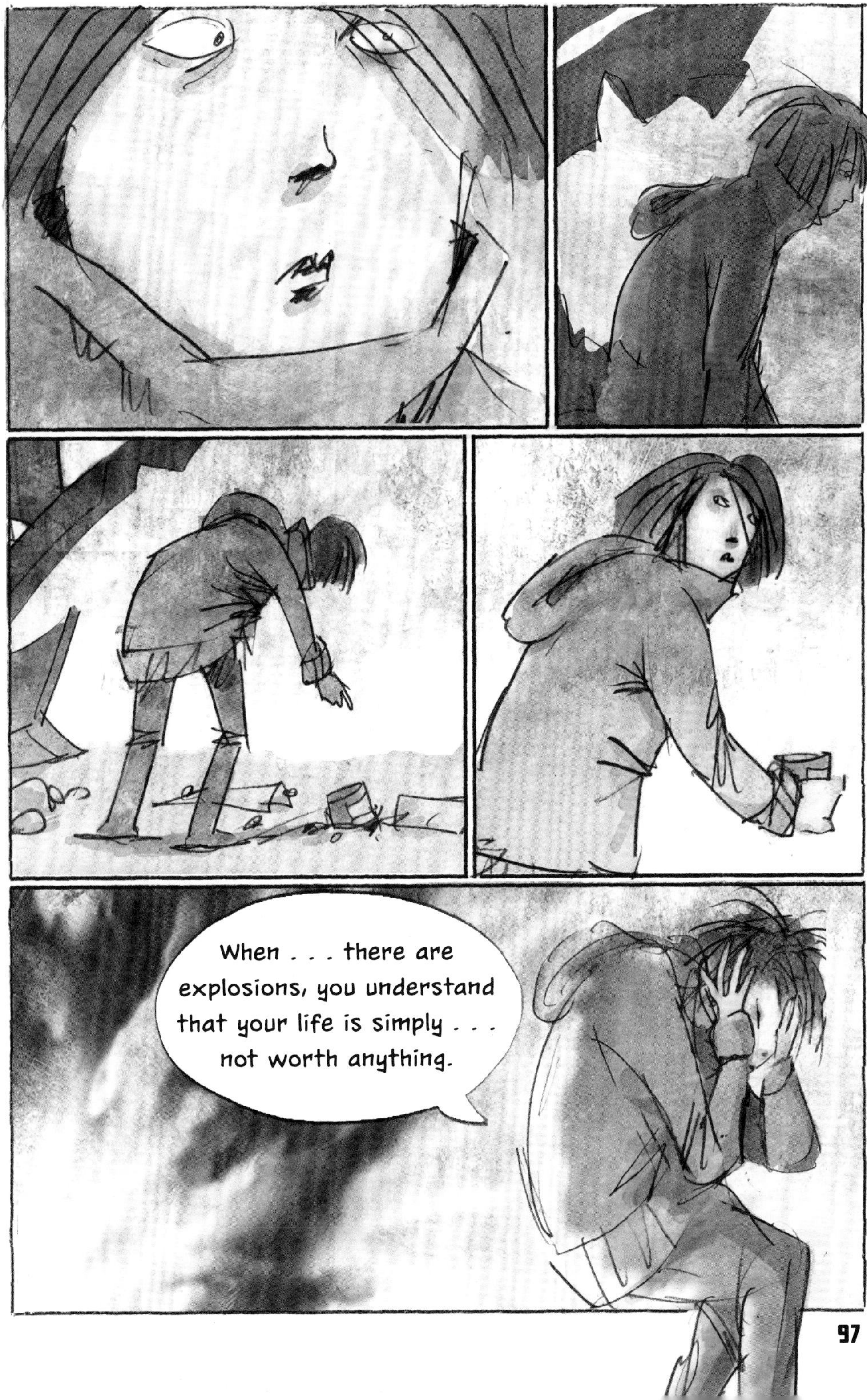
When . . . there are explosions, you understand that your life is simply . . . not worth anything.

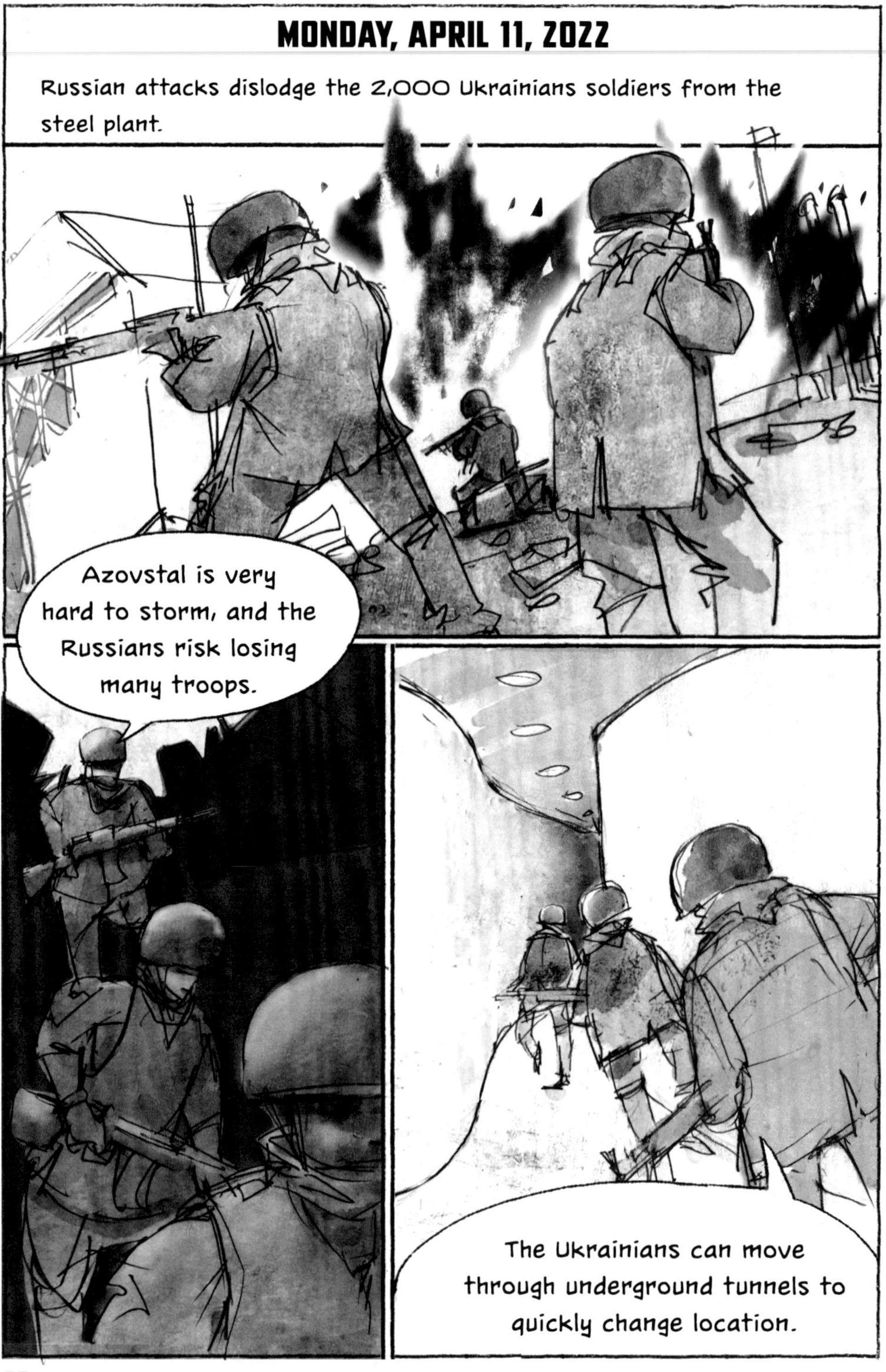
MONDAY, APRIL 11, 2022
Russian attacks dislodge the 2,000 Ukrainians soldiers from the steel plant.
Azovstal is very hard to storm, and the Russians risk losing many troops.
The Ukrainians can move through underground tunnels to quickly change location.

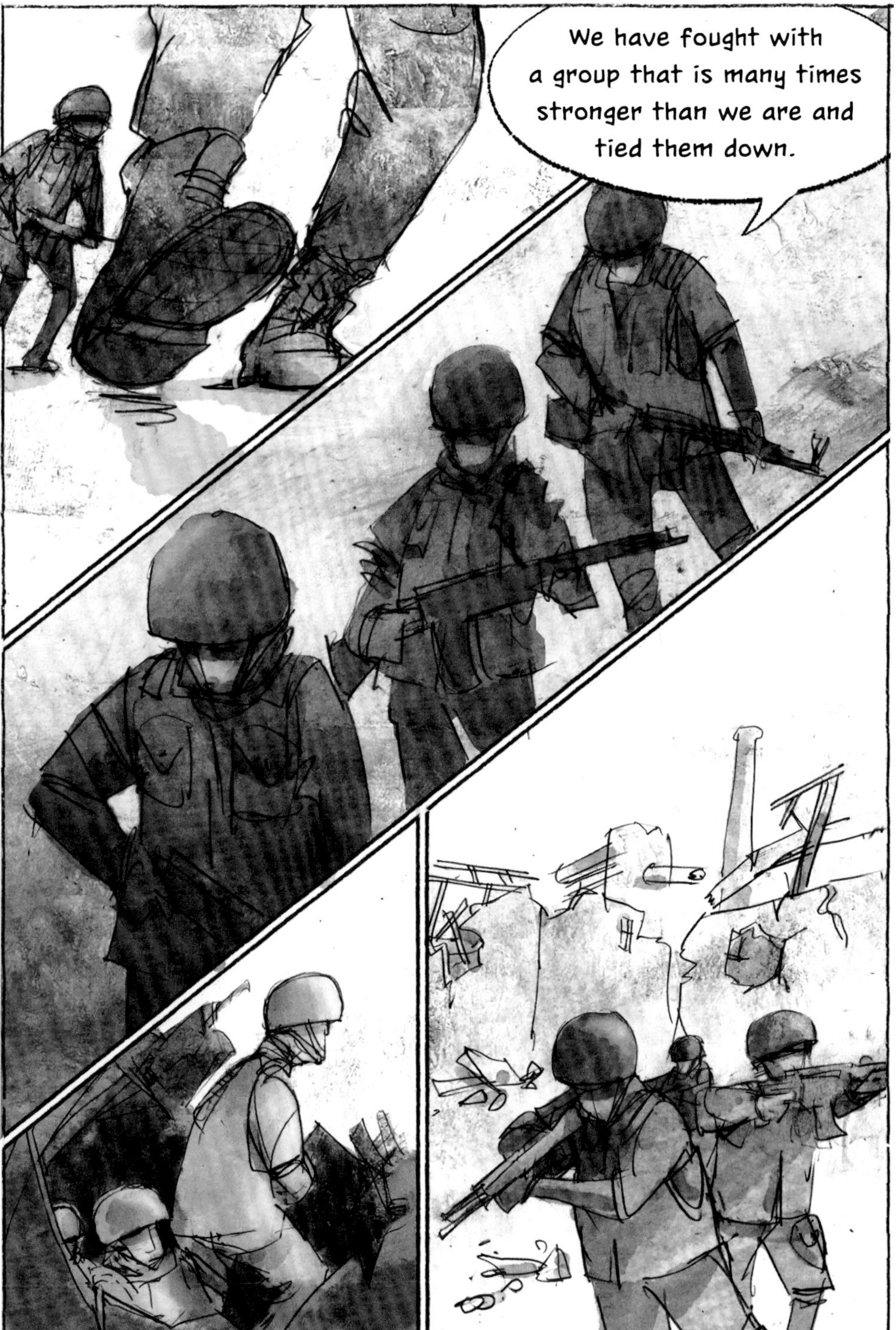
We have fought with a group that is many times stronger than we are and tied them down.

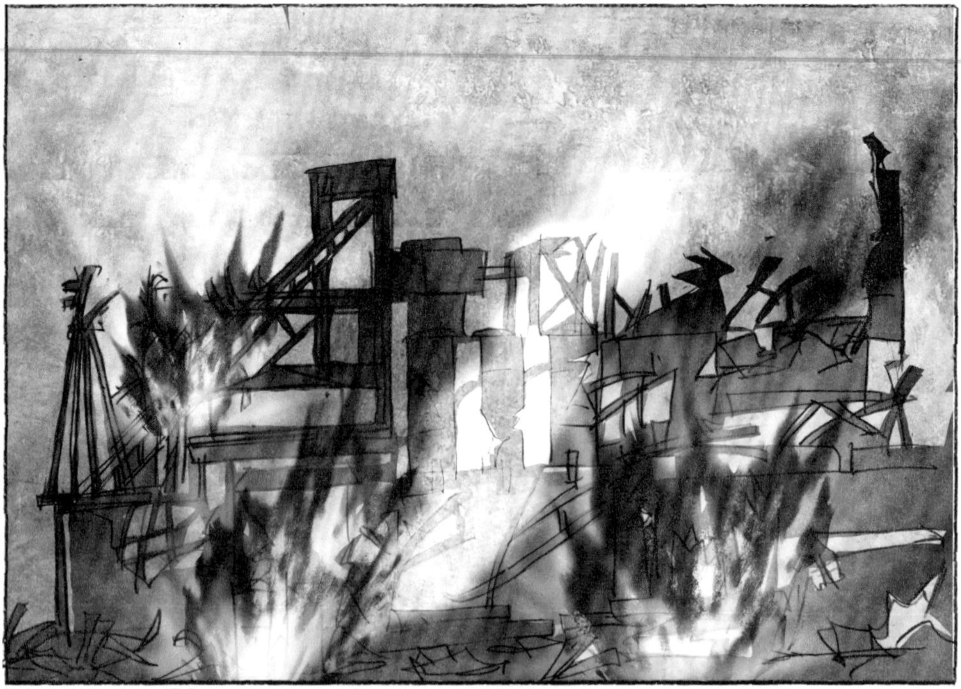

SATURDAY, APRIL 23, 2022

The Azovstal steel plant is a refuge . . . and a trap. Russians surround it, and there is little hope of escape for the Ukrainians. Ammunition, food, and water are dwindling. The soldiers fight on. The civilians endure. The constant shelling keeps them inside a dark and dank world, quaking with explosions.

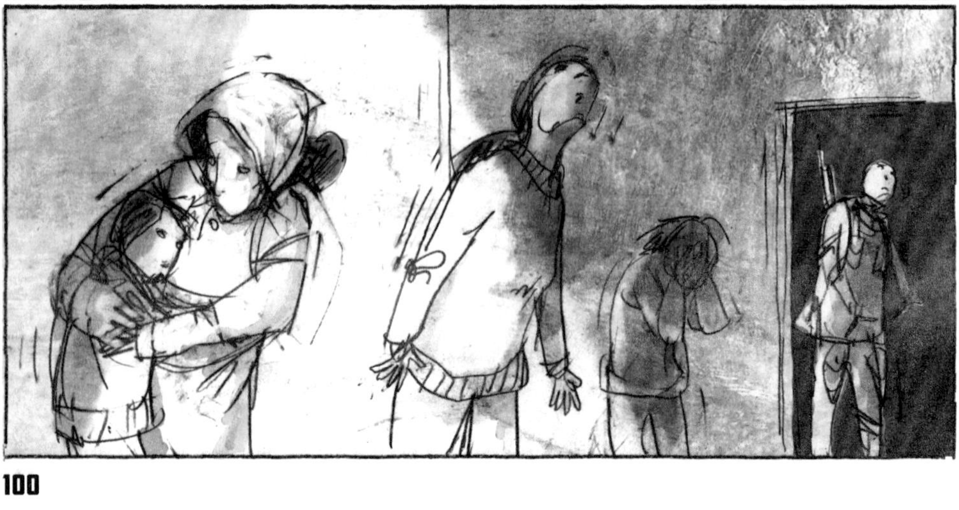

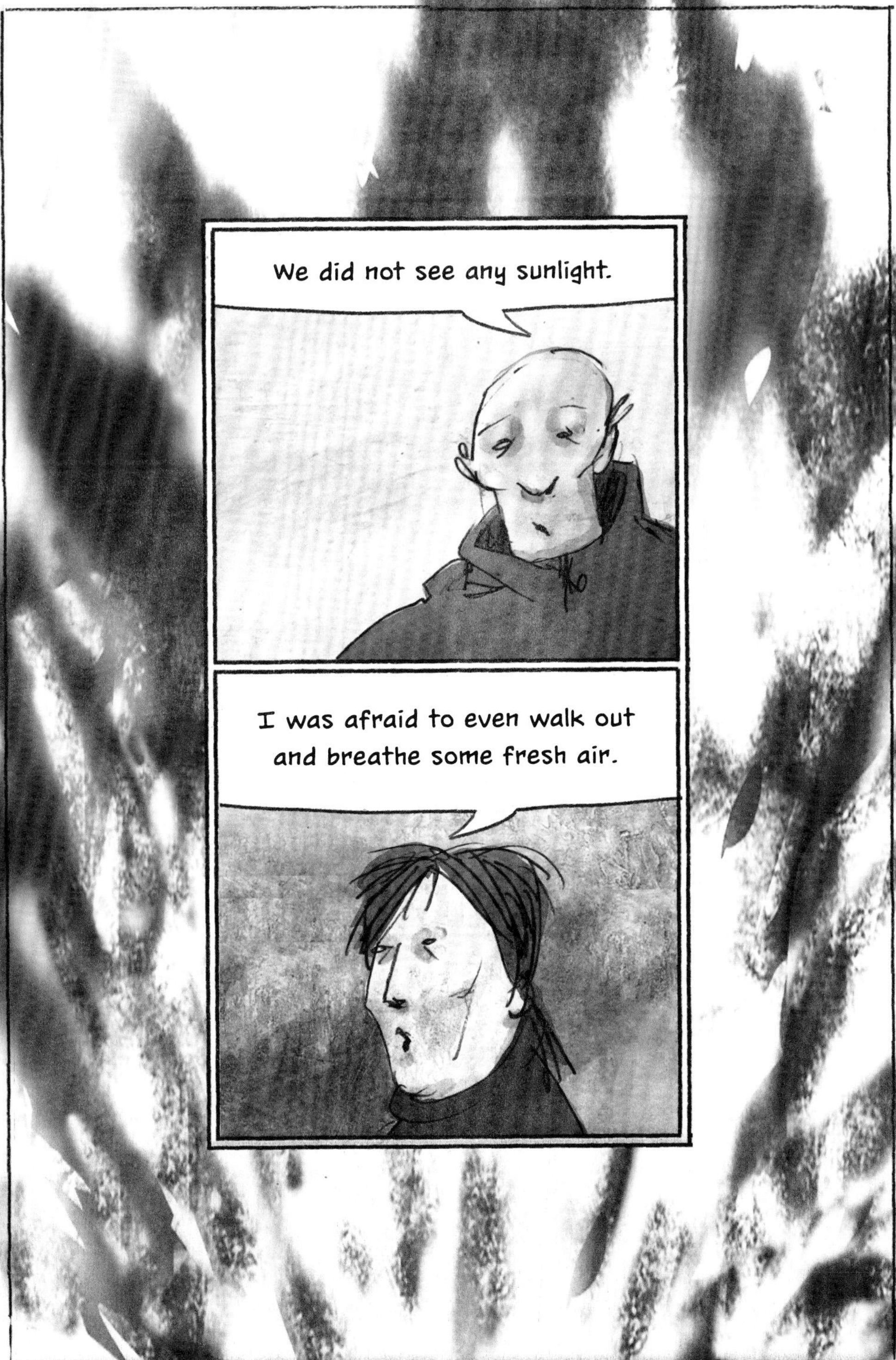
We did not see any sunlight.
I was afraid to even walk out and breathe some fresh air.

SUNDAY, MAY 1, 2022

Sixty-seven days into the siege, perhaps 100,000 live among the Mariupol rubble, risking epidemic disease from poor sanitation. At the steel mill, about a hundred civilians flee during an agreed-upon cease-fire.

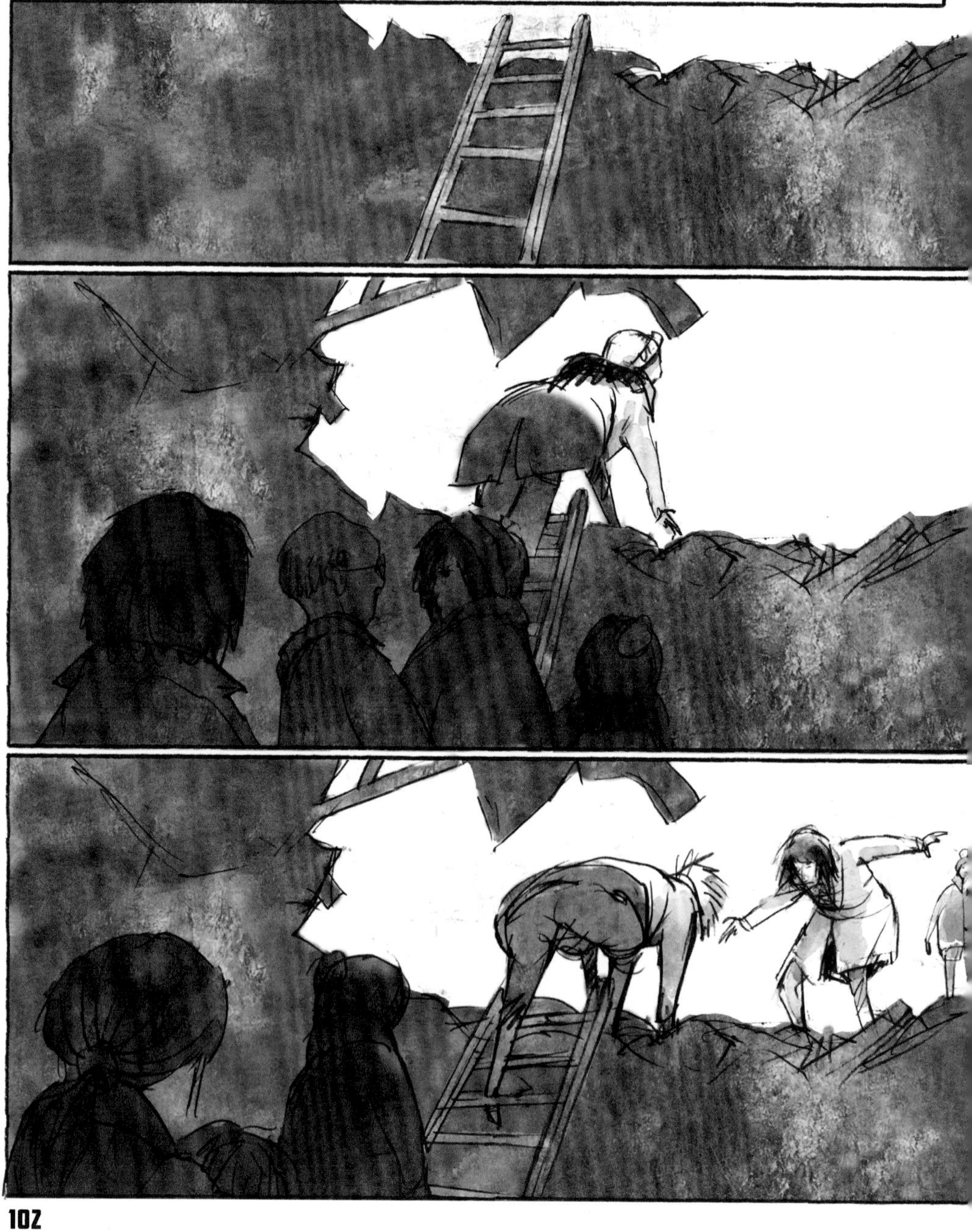

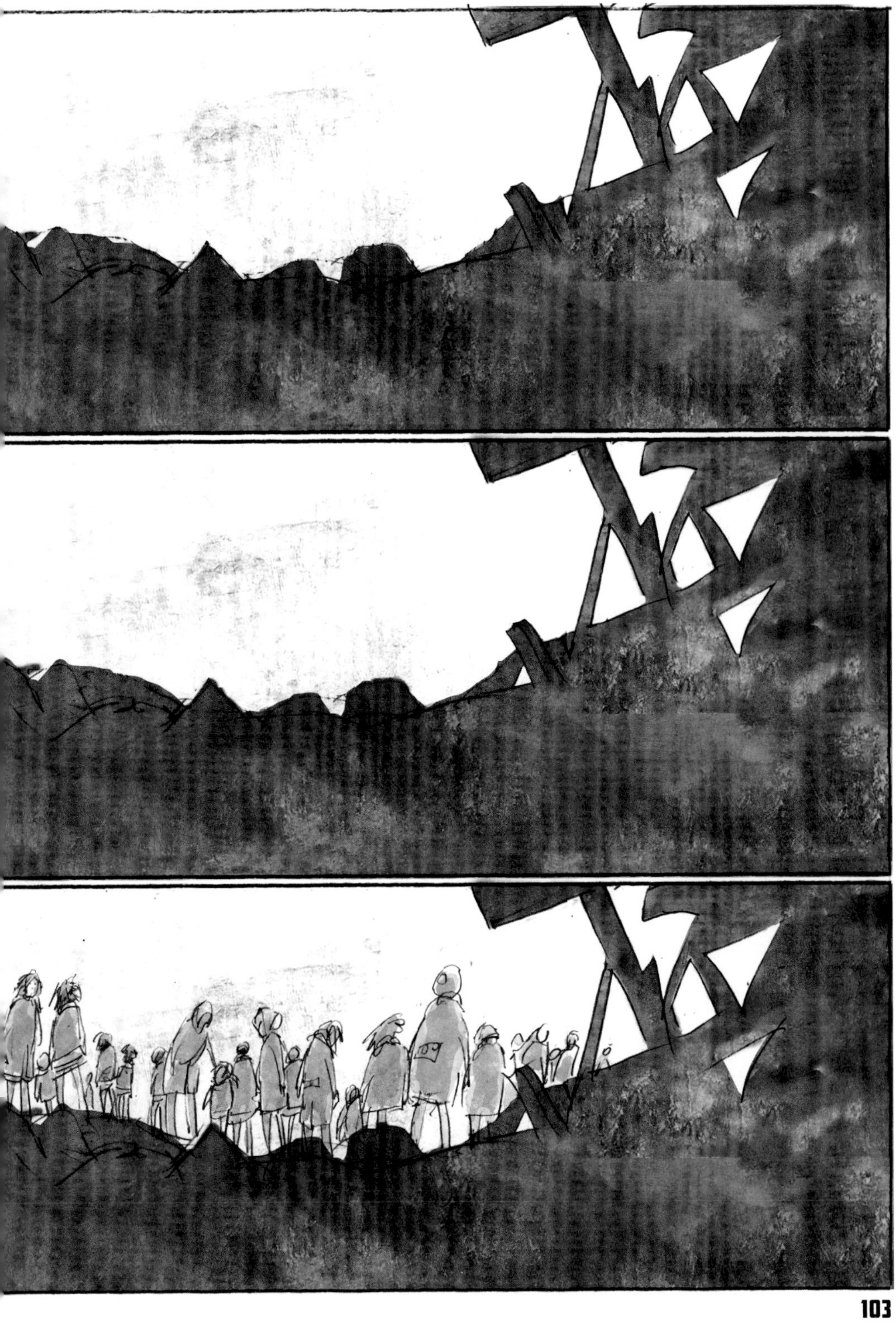

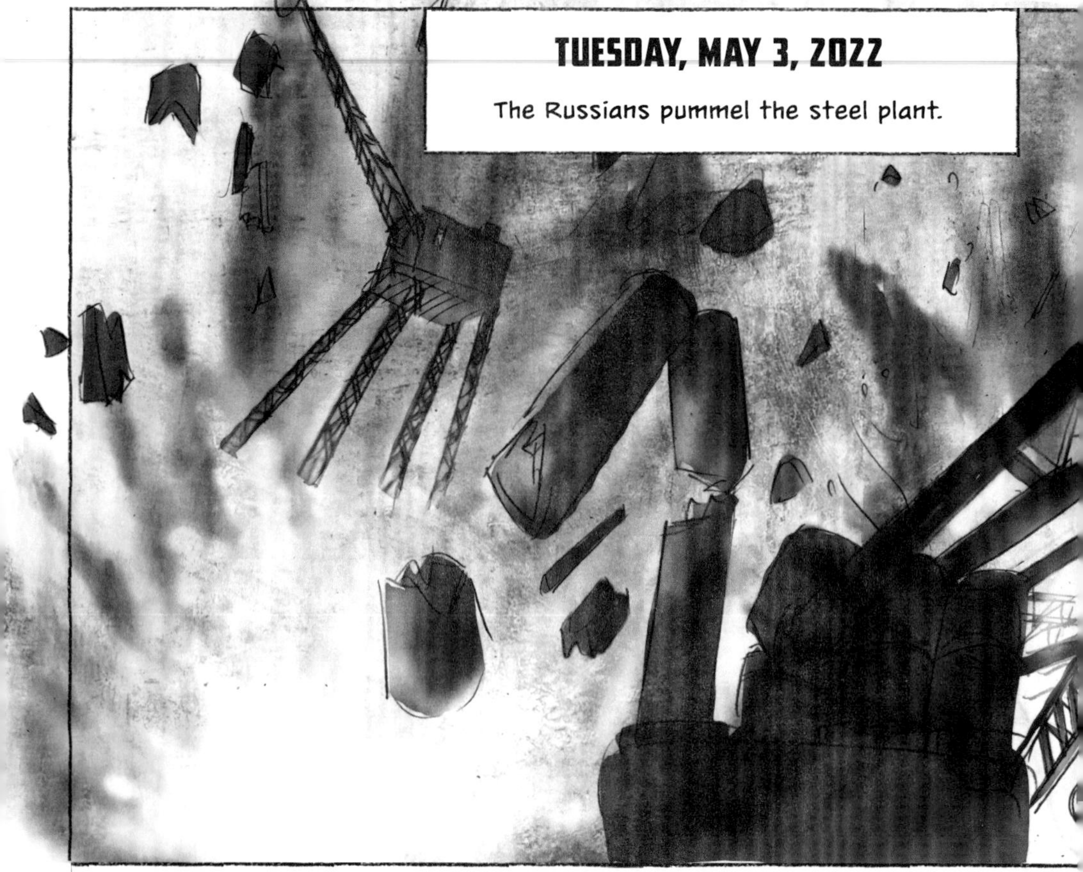
TUESDAY, MAY 3, 2022
The Russians pummel the steel plant.

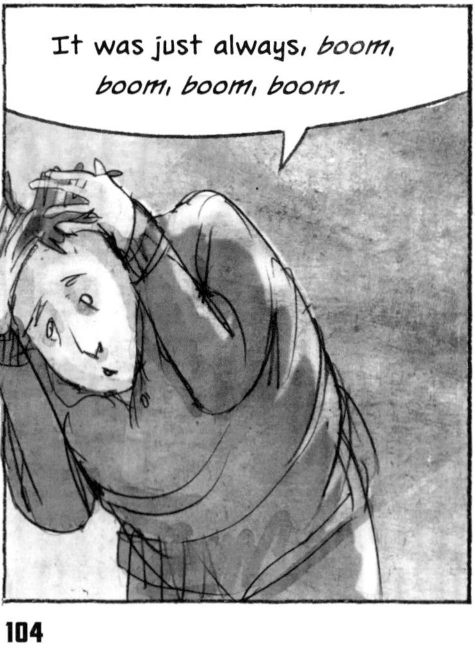
It was just always, *boom, boom, boom, boom.*

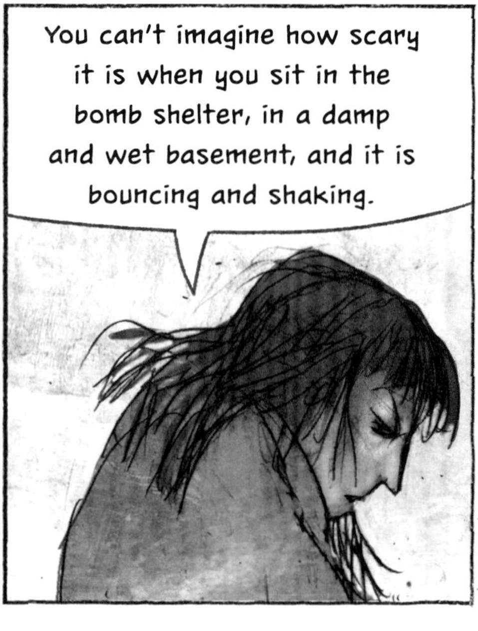
You can't imagine how scary it is when you sit in the bomb shelter, in a damp and wet basement, and it is bouncing and shaking.

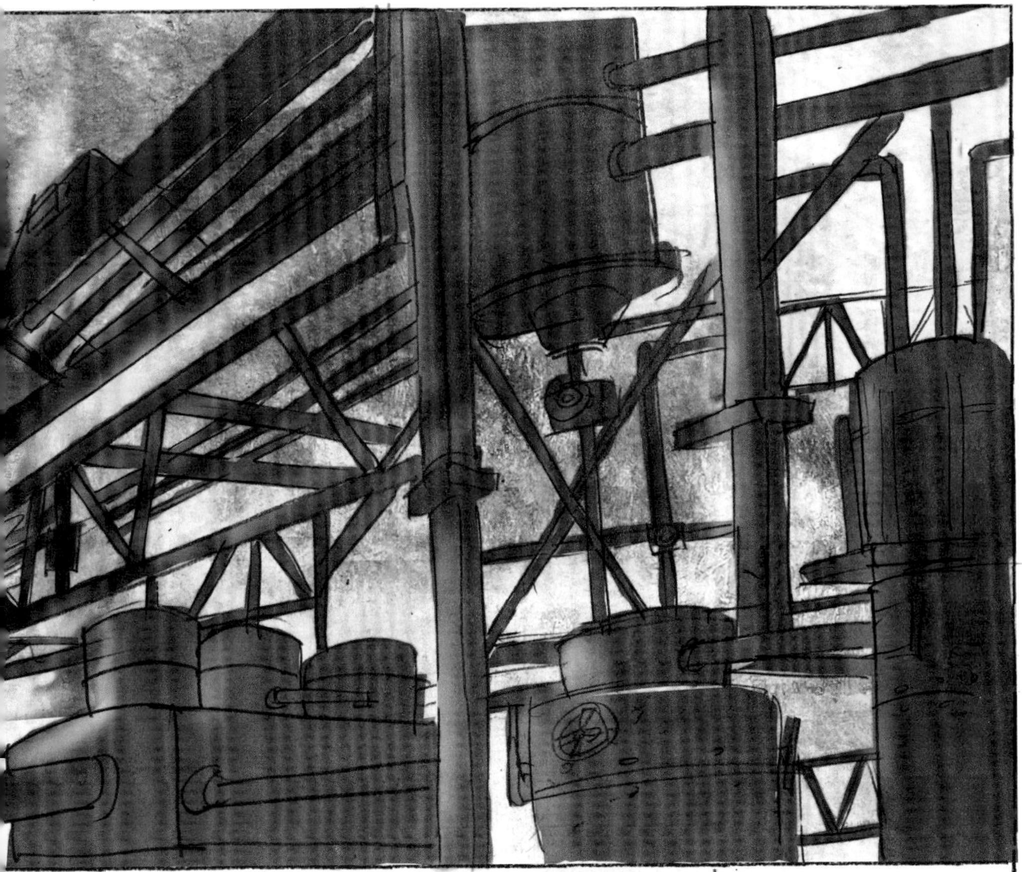

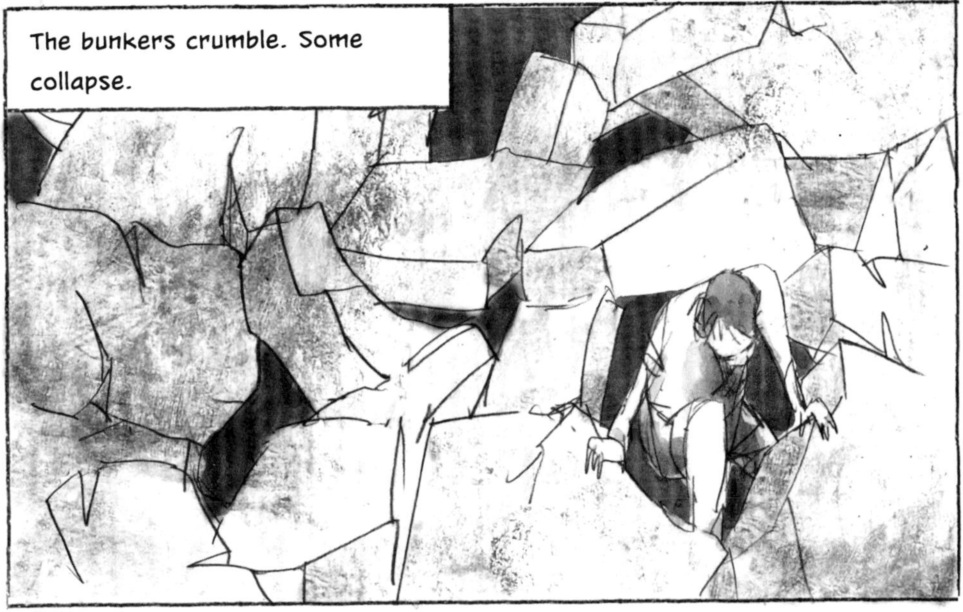
The bunkers crumble. Some collapse.

The Russians break into the heart of the plant. The Ukrainians fight back. Heavy, bloody battles rage.

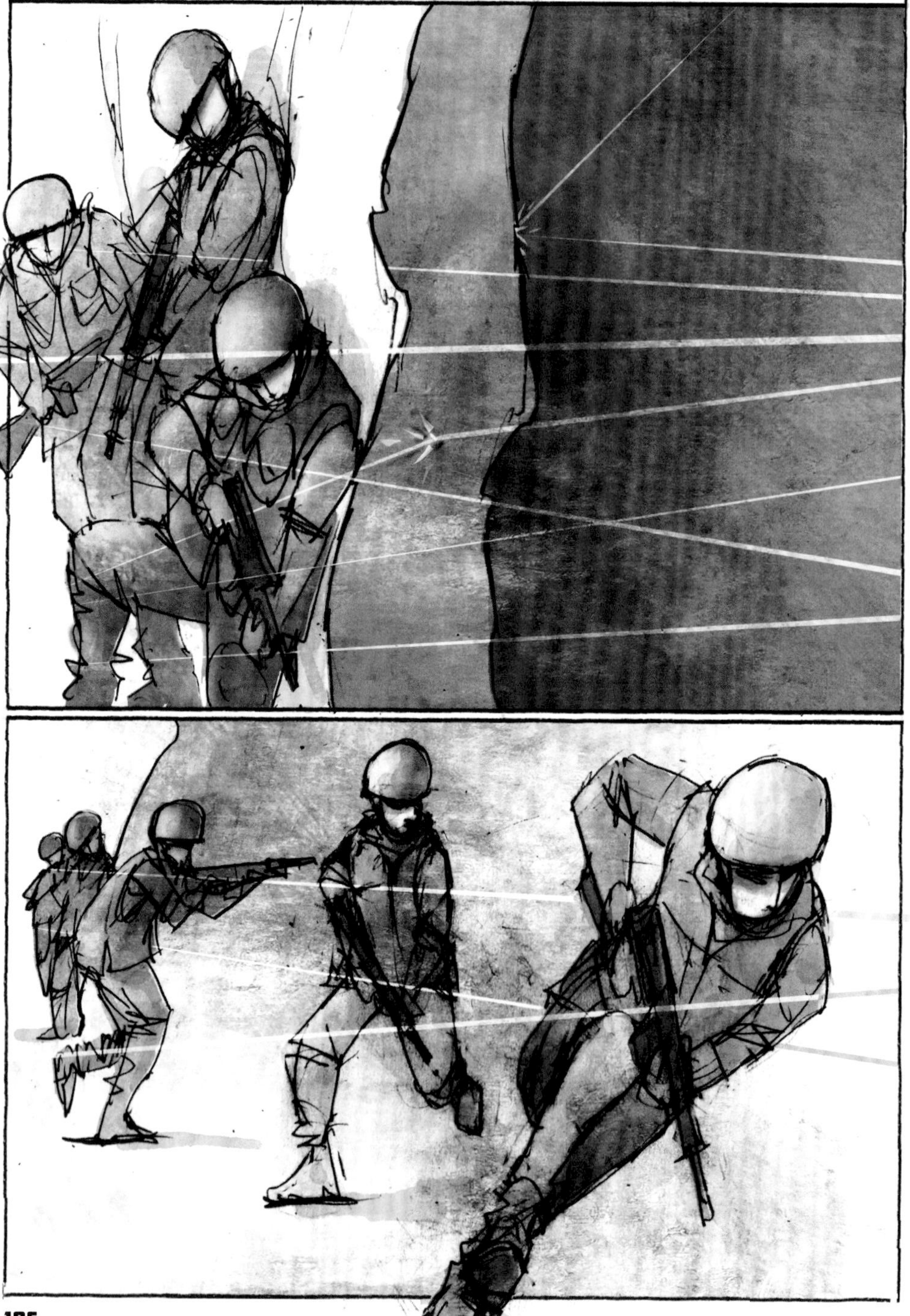

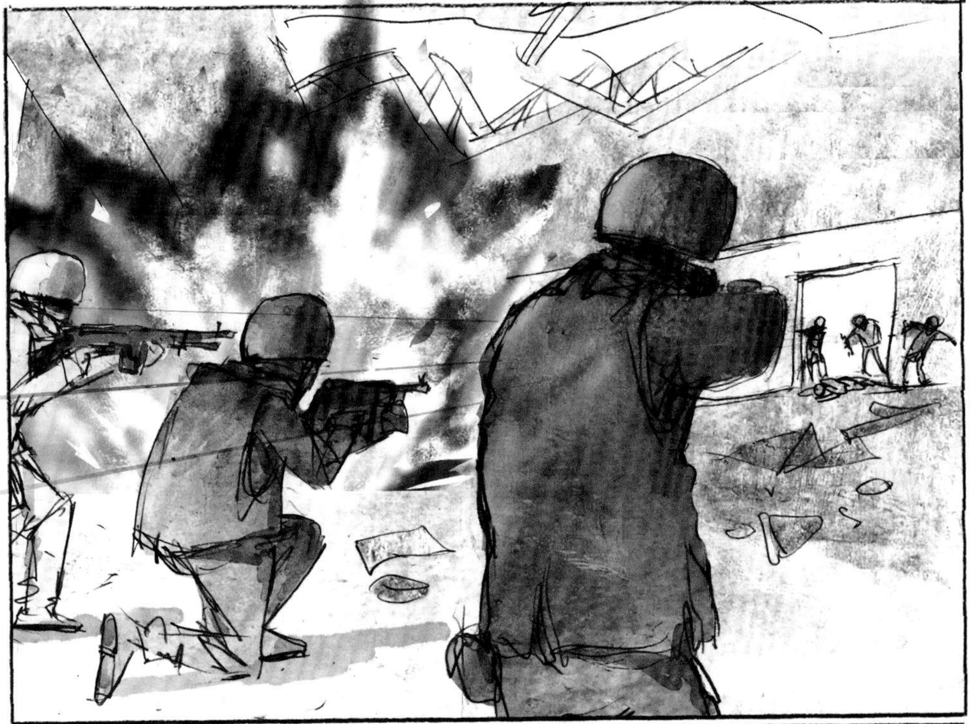

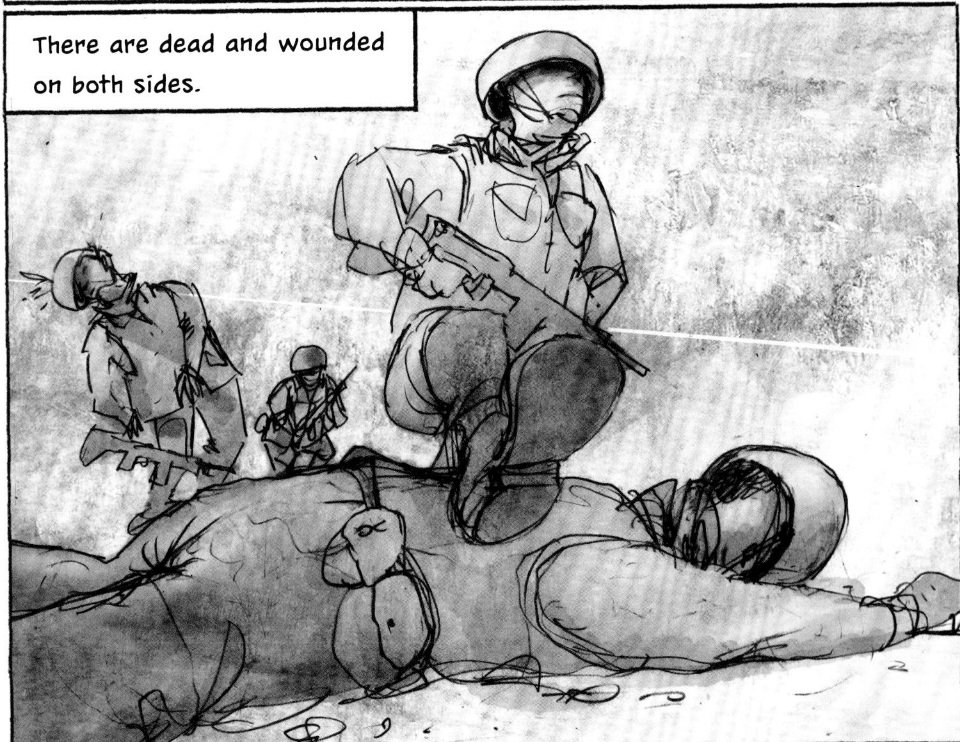
There are dead and wounded on both sides.

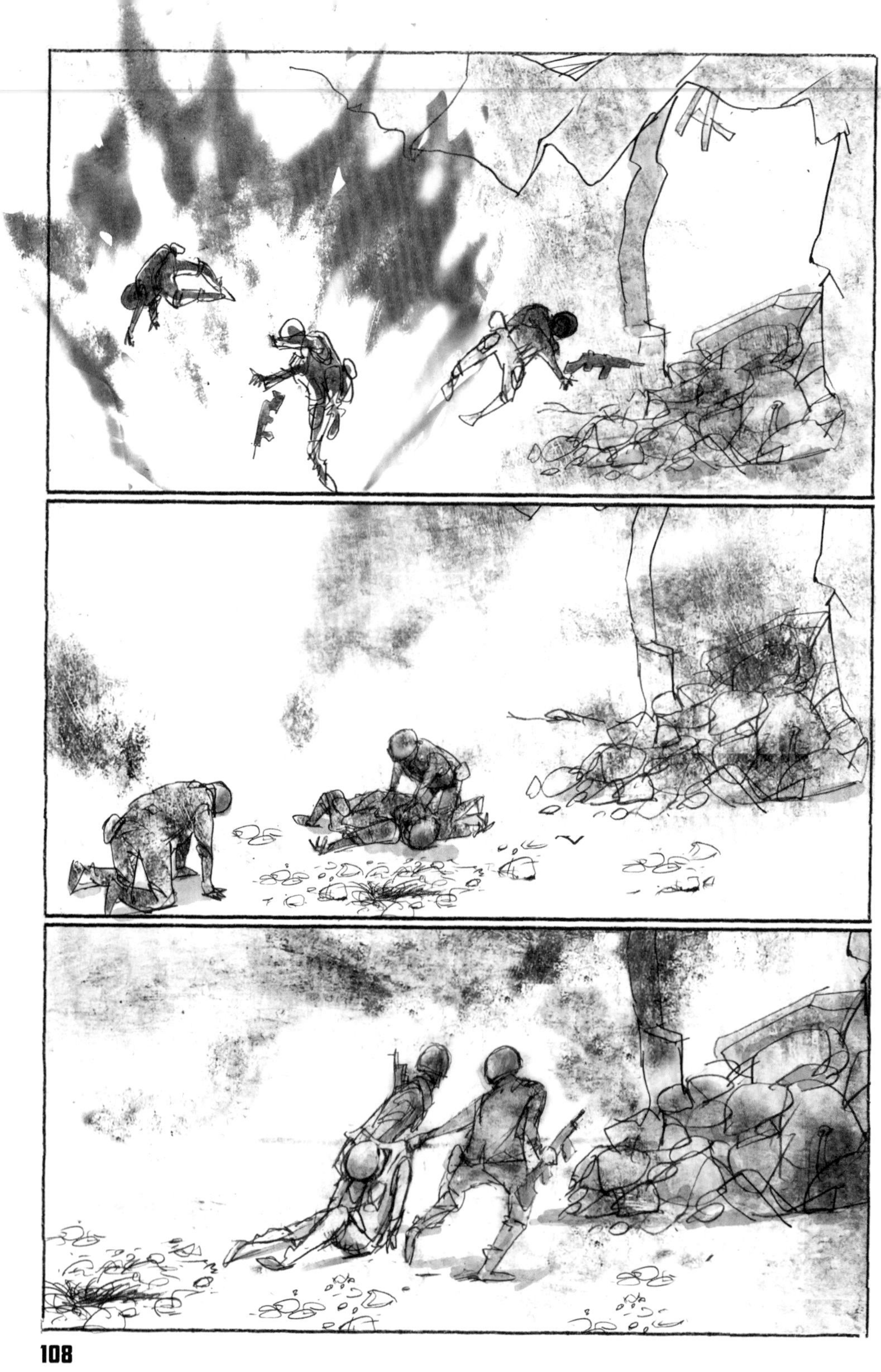

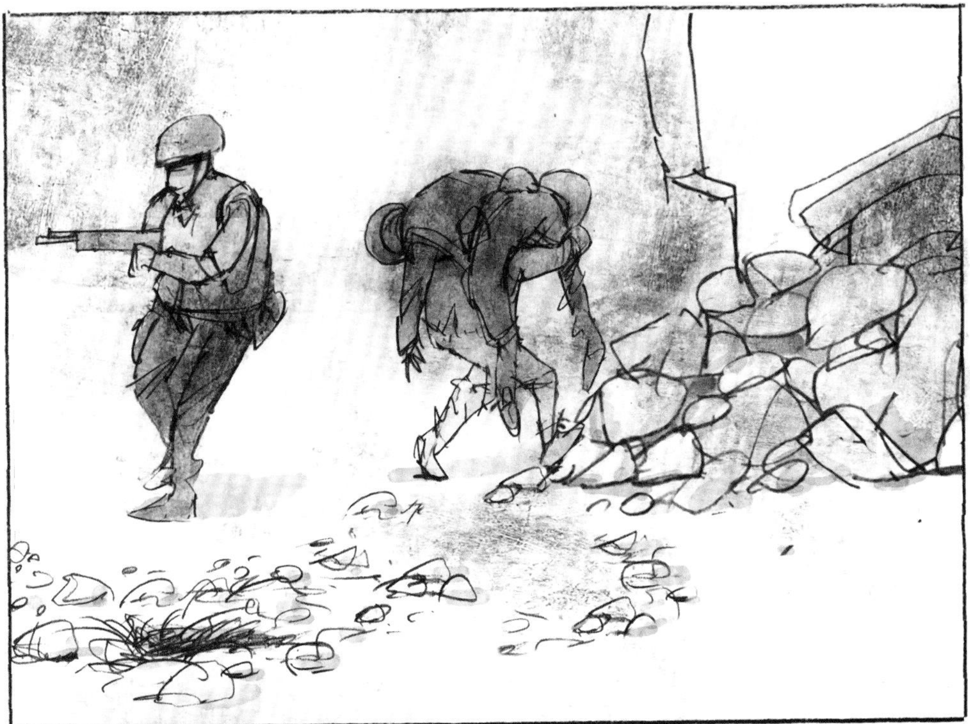

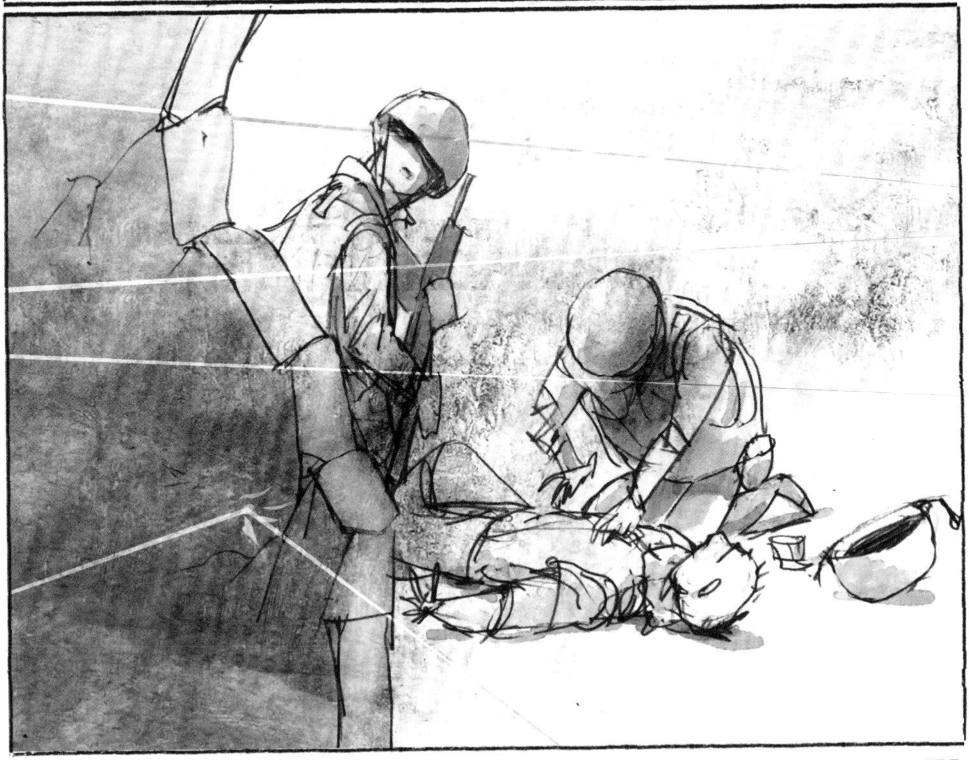

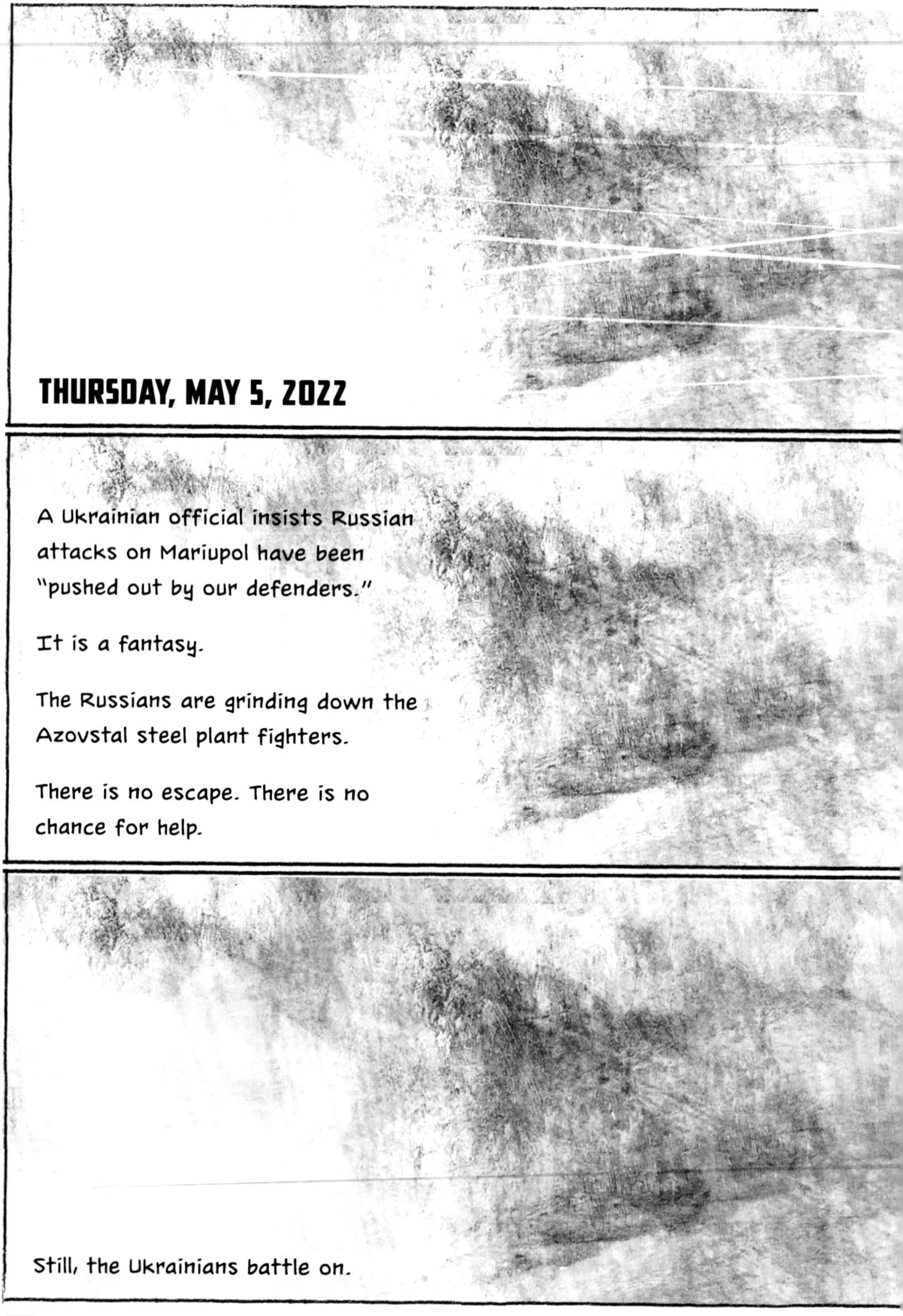
THURSDAY, MAY 5, 2022
A Ukrainian official insists Russian attacks on Mariupol have been "pushed out by our defenders."
It is a fantasy.
The Russians are grinding down the Azovstal steel plant fighters.
There is no escape. There is no chance for help.
Still, the Ukrainians battle on.

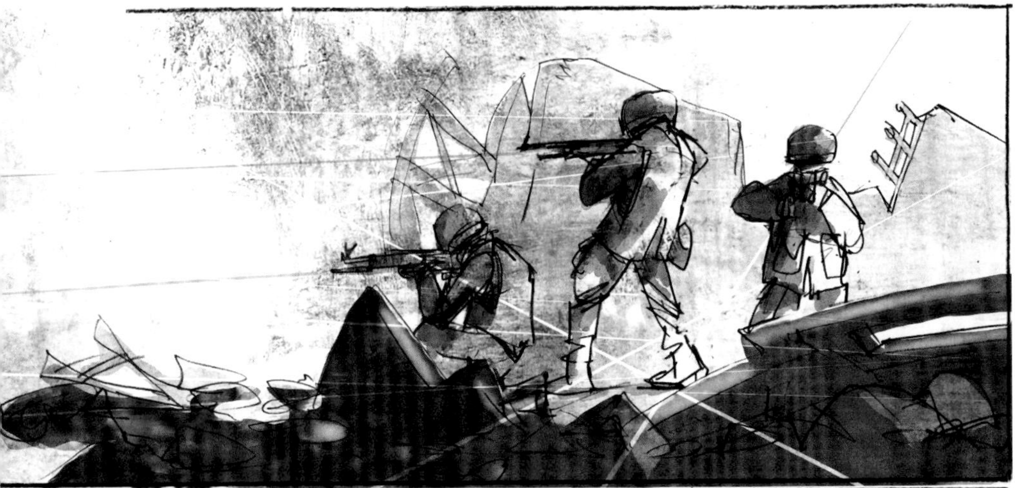

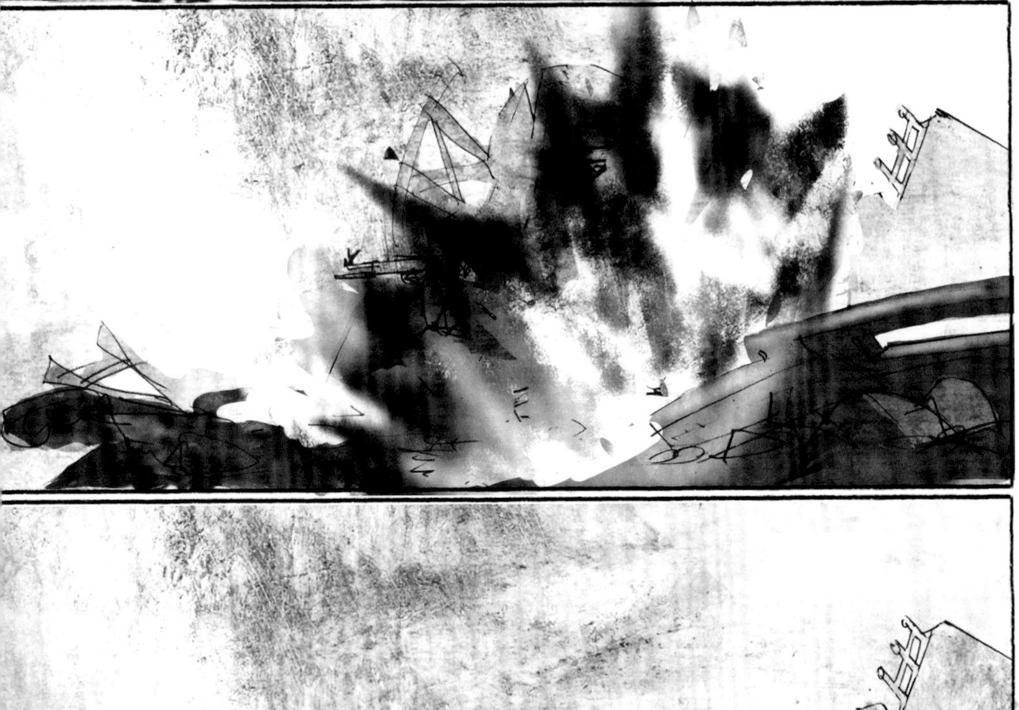

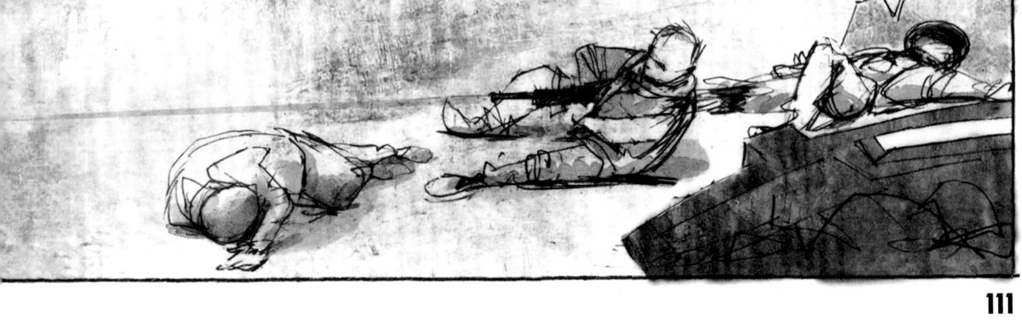

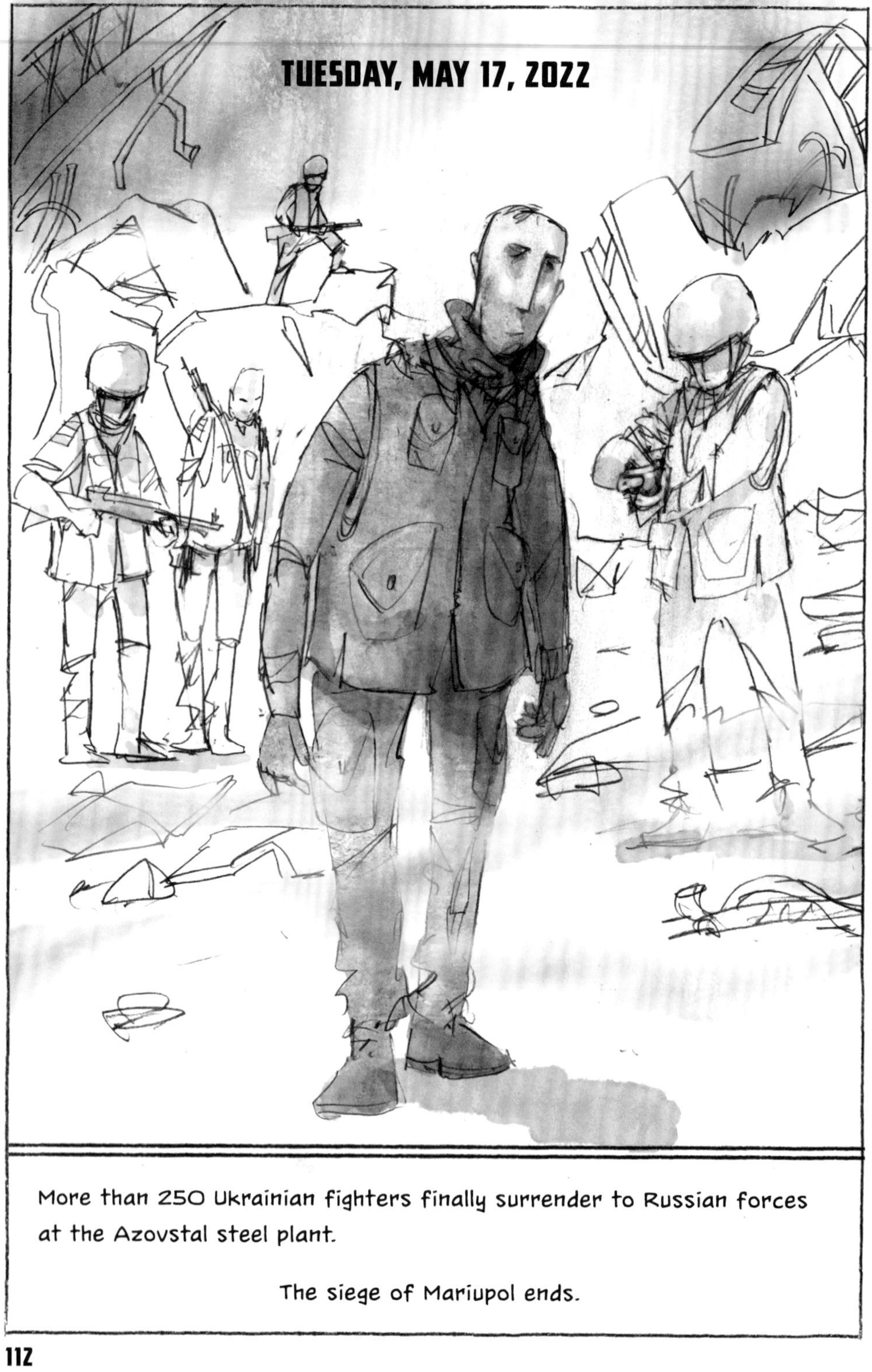
TUESDAY, MAY 17, 2022

More than 250 Ukrainian fighters finally surrender to Russian forces at the Azovstal steel plant.

The siege of Mariupol ends.

Over the next two days, another 1,730 Ukrainian fighters surrender.

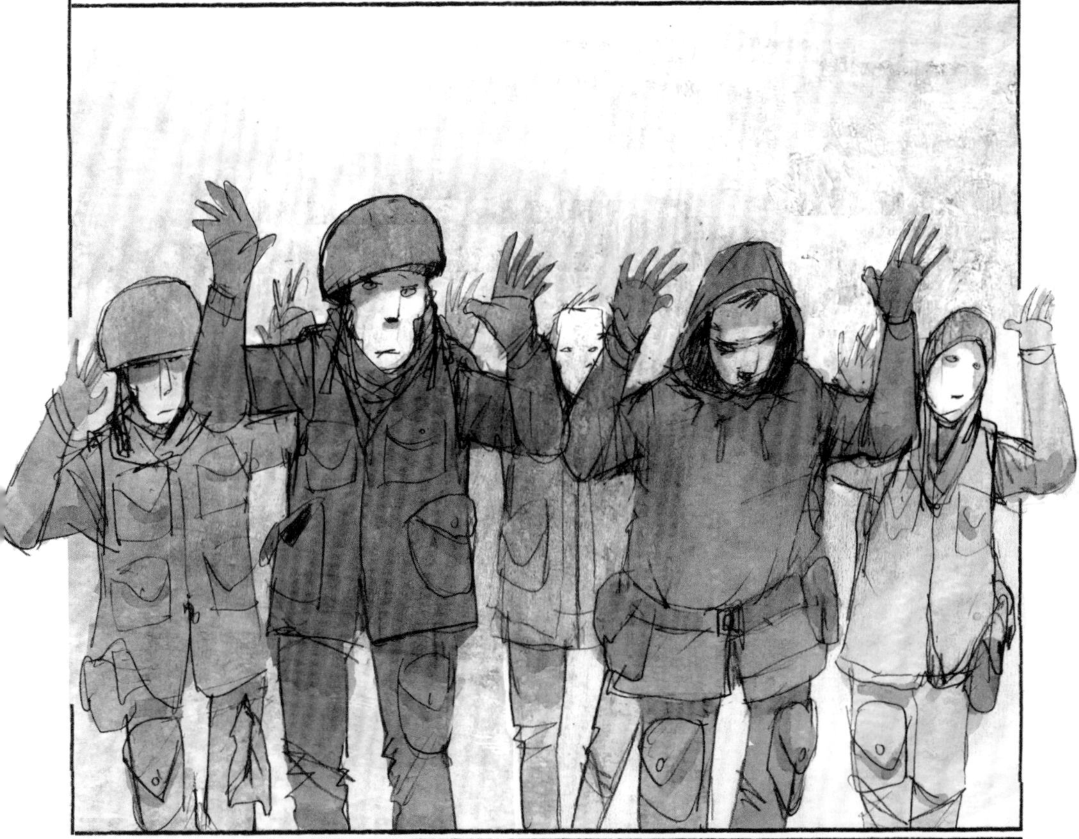

Civilians across the city fall under Russian control.

Russian president Vladimir Putin claims a victory, a bright spot in his otherwise stumbling war campaign.

With the fall of Mariupol, the Russians are rewarded with complete control of the Sea of Azov and a continuous stretch of land across eastern Ukraine.

The city of Mariupol is ruined. Ukrainian officials estimate that the brutal 83-day siege killed 20,000 civilians and destroyed 90 percent of the city. The World Health Organization warns it could now face outbreaks of cholera. Remaining residents are forced to work for the Russians in exchange for food while cats and dogs feast on corpses.

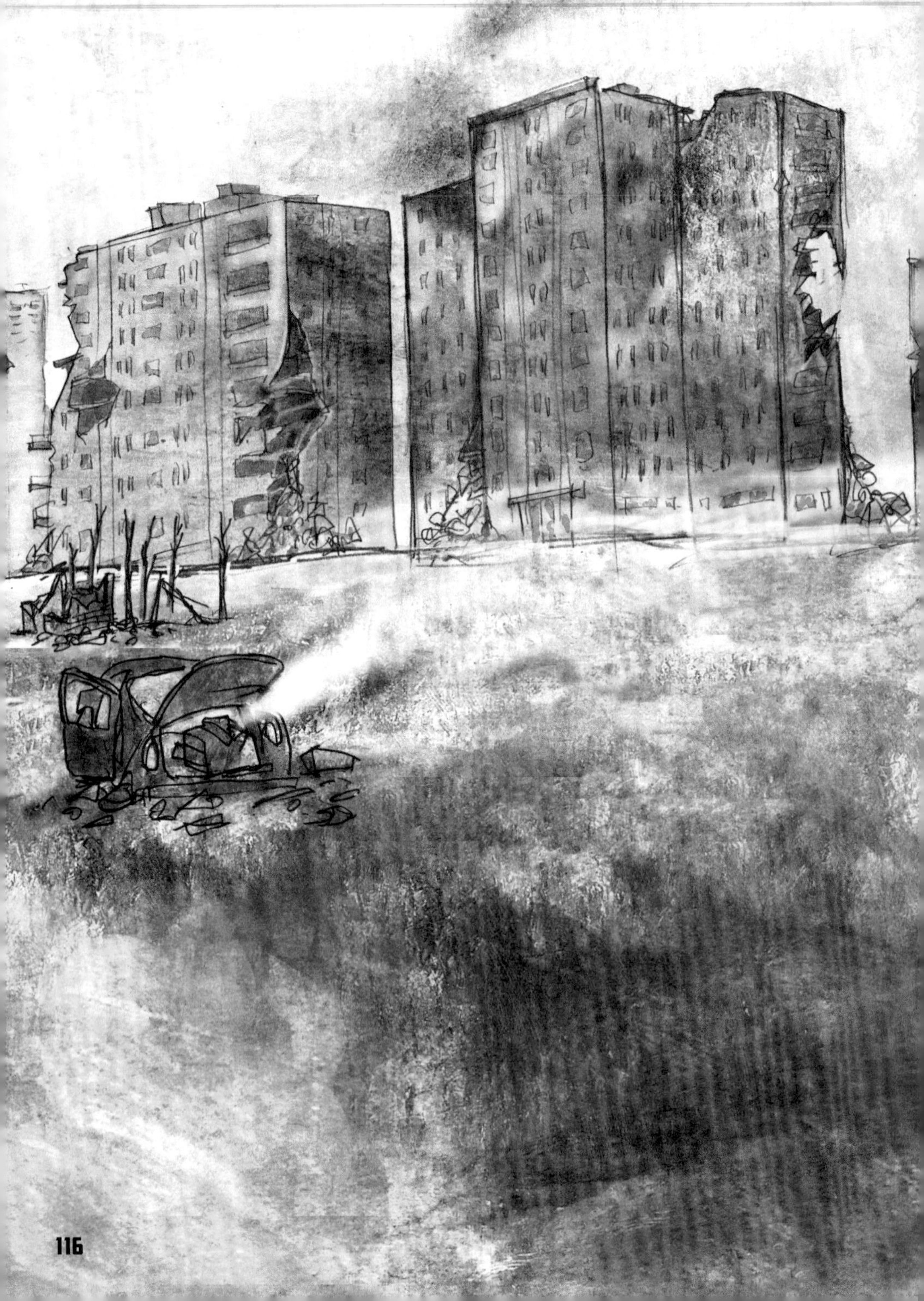

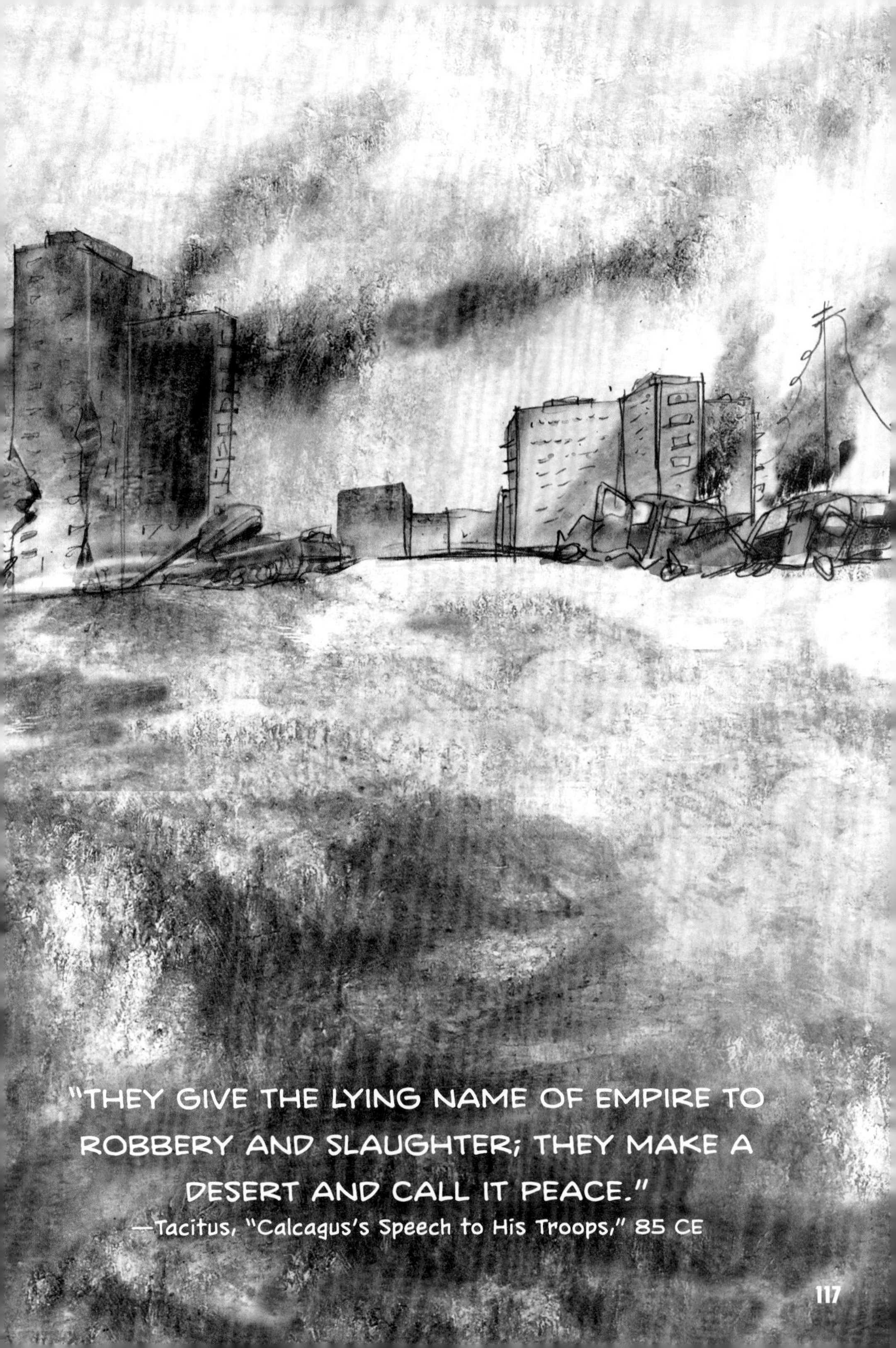

"THEY GIVE THE LYING NAME OF EMPIRE TO ROBBERY AND SLAUGHTER; THEY MAKE A DESERT AND CALL IT PEACE."

—Tacitus, "Calcagus's Speech to His Troops," 85 CE

AFTERWORD

As of January 2023, Mariupol remains under Russian control and its chance of liberation appears remote. But the city's two-and-a-half month resistance pointed to something unexpected and radical: Russian military incompetence and weakness.

At the war's outset, observers and pundits all around described Russia as a modern superpower boasting a massive military and employing a daunting collection of advanced weapons. Surely, Russian soldiers would sweep across Ukraine and seize its capital in mere days. And Russia did enjoy some early successes, especially near the Russian-Ukrainian border. But advances west and toward Kyiv—Ukraine's capital—stumbled in the face of Ukrainian nationalism and anti-Russian fervor.

Soon after, the United States and her allies of the North American Treaty Organization (NATO) flooded Ukraine with lethal, modern weapons. With advanced arms, Ukrainians struck back, killing poorly led Russian troops in astonishing numbers and forcing survivors to flee and abandon equipment. Some Ukrainian towns were freed from Russian occupation, revealing evidence of Russian brutality, torture, rape, and murder.

Continuing Russian battlefield casualties depleted its military manpower, forcing Russia to employ unpopular military conscription to fill the ranks. Ill-trained and ill-equipped troops were sent to fight, while tens of thousands of others fled the country rather than serve in Ukraine. Beyond the battlefield, trade penalties—or sanctions—imposed against Russia by America, parts of Asia, and much of Europe forced the closure of some Russian businesses and cost Russian jobs. To Russian leader Vladimir Putin's annoyance, NATO support of Ukraine has persisted while the alliance is looking to grow with the addition of Sweden and Finland.

Yet despite military incompetence and economic and political setbacks, Russia still controls roughly 20% of Ukraine and has claimed to have annexed that land into Russia. And its capacity to inflict pain on Ukraine, her allies, and international order is still formidable. The removal of Russian oil from much of the world market has driven up the cost of the much-needed commodity and worsened widespread price inflation, making millions of people pay more to heat their homes and drive their cars. Fighting has disrupted grain exports from Ukraine, a major grower, upending supply and raising the cost of food for many.

But with the likelihood of military victory over Ukraine dimming, Putin has turned to intimidation and naked cruelty to turn the tide of the war; he threatens the use of nuclear weapons and orders attacks on power plants, public utilities, hospitals, and apartment complexes in a brutish bid to crush Ukrainians' will to resist by robbing ordinary civilians of heat, electricity, water, healthcare, and housing.

Cold weather looms.

Bombs, rockets, and explosive drones fall across Ukraine.

Mariupol awaits liberation.

Death is common currency.

Peace seems far off.

SOURCE NOTES

"We will seek to demilitarize": Bloomberg News, "Transcript: Vladimir Putin's Televised Address on Ukraine," Feb. 24, 2022.

"No, that is impossible": Anastasiia Mokhina et al., "Sixteen Days in Ukraine," *New York Magazine*, Mar. 13, 2022.

"The first thing my father did": Mokhina et al., "Sixteen Days in Ukraine."

"But we'd been living on the front line": Darya Kurennaya, "Escape from Mariupol: 'The Dead Were Buried in the Yards,'" Radio Free Europe/Radio Liberty, Mar. 26, 2022.

"There is no panic": Mstyslav Chernov, Evgeniy Maloletka, and Lori Hinnant, "'Why? Why? Why?' Ukraine's Mariupol Descends into Despair," AP News, Mar. 16, 2022.

"I moved to the basement": Khaleda Rahman, "Zelensky Receives Standing Ovation from EU Parliament in Emotional Scenes," *Newsweek*, Mar. 1, 2022.

". . . fighting for our rights": Zachary Basu, "Zelensky Addresses European Parliament: 'No One Is Going to Break Us,'" Axios, Mar. 1, 2022, https://www.axios.com/2022/03/01/zelensky-video-european-parliament-address-ukraine.

"I filled the bath": Joel Gunter, "Mariupol under Siege: 'We Are Being Completely Cut Off,'" BBC News, Mar. 3, 2022, https://www.bbc.com/news/world-europe-60601235.

"There is still some bread": Gunter, "Mariupol under Siege: 'We Are Being Completely Cut Off.'"

"My city went crazy": "Escape from Hell: Women of Mariupol Tell Their Stories of Living under Occupation and Escaping the Siege," Yahoo! News, Apr. 27, 2022.

"When you need to go outside to cook": "Escape from Mariupol: 'I Didn't Want to Die on the Road,'" Reuters, Mar. 24, 2022.

"They were just killing us": AnneClaire Stapleton et al., "A Mariupol Family Fled the Horror of Russian Attacks. But They Had to Leave Their Parents Behind," CNN World, Mar. 22, 2022.

"I saw people getting water": Kurennaya, "Escape from Mariupol: 'The Dead Were Buried in the Yards.'"

"Hundreds of thousands of people": Tim Lister et al., "Mariupol Children's Hospital Bombing One of Many Attacks on Medical Facilities since Russian Invasion, WHO Says," CNN World, Mar. 10, 2022.

"I can hear shots and bombs": Joel Gunter, "Mariupol: Fires, No Water, and Bodies in the Street," BBC News, Mar. 6, 2022, https://www.bbc.com/news/world-europe-60637338.

"I didn't know this was going to happen": Yousur Al-Hlou, Masha Froliak, and Evan Hill, "'Putin Is a Fool': Intercepted Calls Reveal Russian Army in Disarray," *New York Times*, Sept. 28, 2022.

"We were fucking fooled": Al-Hlou, Froliak, and Hill, "'Putin Is a Fool': Intercepted Calls Reveal Russian Army in Disarray."

"[They are] killing civilians": Al-Hlou, Froliak, and Hill, "'Putin Is a Fool': Intercepted Calls Reveal Russian Army in Disarray."

"Schools, apartments, private houses": Anastasiia Lapatina, "Voices of Besieged Mariupol: 'It's Not Even Comparable to Hell.'" *Kyiv Independent*, Apr. 9, 2022.

"Every day and night we have spent in the cellar": Lapatina, "Voices of Besieged Mariupol: 'It's Not Even Comparable to Hell.'"

"There was a lot of burned equipment": Sabrina Tavernise, "'I Don't Have the Right to Cry': Ukrainian Women Share Their Stories of Escape," *New York Times*, Mar. 20, 2022.

"Houses are burning": Gunter, "Mariupol: Fires, No Water, and Bodies in the Street."

". . . are destroying us": Alessandra Prentice, "From Bombarded Basement, Mariupol Mayor Tries to Help Besieged Residents Flee," Reuters, Mar. 6, 2022, https://www.reuters.com/world/europe/bombarded-basement-mariupol-mayor-tries-help-besieged-residents-flee-2022-03-06/.

"I heard screams constantly": Loveday Morris and Anastacia Galouchka, "Inside the Terror at Mariupol's Bombed Theater: 'I Heard Screams Constantly,'" *Washington Post*, Mar. 25, 2022, https://www.washingtonpost.com/world/2022/03/25/ukraine-mariupol-theater-deaths/.

"I saw bodies": Luke Harding, "Escape from Mariupol: The Man Who Swam to Safety from the Russian Terror," *The Guardian*, Apr. 7, 2022.

"A little baby": "Fighting Reaches Center of Mariupol as Putin Puts Up Defiant Appearance," Radio Free Europe/Radio Liberty, Mar. 18, 2022.

"We asked if it was possible to stay": Mary Ilyushina, "'Treated Like Captives or Some Criminals': Ukraine Says Russia Forcibly Relocates Thousands from Mariupol," *National Post*, Mar. 30, 2022.

"They photograph you from all angles": Eliza Mackintosh et al., "Russia or Die: After Weeks under Putin's Bombs, These Ukrainians Were Given Only One Way Out," CNN World, Apr. 7, 2022.

"They tell you that you have to be grateful": Mary Ilyushina, "Ukraine Says Russia Forcibly Relocated Thousands from Mariupol," *Washington Post*, updated Mar. 30, 2022.

"It is as if your whole body is pricked": Carlotta Gall, "Six Weeks of 'Hell': Inside Russia's Brutal Ukraine Detention," *New York Times*, Aug. 15, 2022.

"Every second was hellish": Alessandra Prentice, "'Moles in the Dark': Survival and Escape from the Mariupol Steelworks," Reuters, May 13, 2022.

"Planes went past": Lucy Williamson, "Ukraine War: Mariupol's Refugees Carry Wounds of Battered City," BBC News, Mar. 31, 2022.

"We cook what we find": "Eking Out an Existence and Mourning the Dead in Besieged Mariupol," Reuters, Mar. 31, 2022.

"I just sobbed": Valerie Hopkins, "As Mariupol Is Bombed and Besieged, Those Trapped Fight to Survive," *New York Times*, Mar. 21, 2022, https://www.nytimes.com/2022/03/21/world/europe/ukraine-mariupol-russia-war.html?searchResultPosition=2.

"The food was running out": Prentice, "'Moles in the Dark': Survival and Escape from the Mariupol Steelworks."

"Nobody is in a position to count": Kurennaya, "Escape from Mariupol: 'The Dead Were Buried in the Yards.'"

"Either you die in the city": Yousur Al-Hlou, Masha Froliak, and Evan Hill, "A Desperate Escape from Mariupol," *New York Times* video, 05:20, Mar. 26, 2022.

"I realized that nobody will save you": Josh Kovensky, "'Nobody Will Save You': One Refugee's Account of Escaping Mariupol," Talking Points Memo, Mar. 28, 2022.

"My wife pushed our youngest girl": "Ukraine Family Tells of Epic Escape from Mariupol on Foot," *Gulf News*, Apr. 23, 2022.

"We did what we could": Michael Schwirtz, "Last Stand at Azovstal: Inside the Siege That Shaped the Ukraine War," *New York Times*, July 24, 2022, https://www.nytimes.com/2022/07/24/world/europe/ukraine-war-mariupol-azovstal.html.

"When . . . there are explosions": Schwirtz, "Last Stand at Azovstal: Inside the Siege That Shaped the Ukraine War."

"Azovstal is very hard to storm": Associated Press, "Why the Battle for Mariupol's Azovstal Steel Plant Matters in Russia's War against Ukraine," *The Globe and Mail*, Apr. 21, 2022.

"The Ukrainians can move through underground tunnels": Associated Press, "Explainer: Why the Battle for Mariupol's Steel Mill Matters," AP News, Apr. 21, 2022, https://apnews.com/article/russia-ukraine-putin-business-europe-moscow-67da12473ccd75fe02992f0eb751c5f4.

"We have fought with a group": Schwirtz, "Last Stand at Azovstal: Inside the Siege That Shaped the Ukraine War."

"We did not see any sunlight": Eliza Mackintosh, "'Two Months of Darkness': Mariupol Residents Arrive in Russian-Held Bezimenne," CNN, May 2, 2022, https://www.cnn.com/europe/live-news/russia-ukraine-war-news-05-02-22/h_0828aa7762c41eaa4f7655d7e4c25442.

"I was afraid to even walk out": Mackintosh, "'Two Months of Darkness': Mariupol Residents Arrive in Russian-Held Bezimenne."

"It was just always, boom, boom, boom, boom": Michael Schwirtz, "Evacuees from Mariupol's Steel Plant Tell of Horrors and Survival," *New York Times*, May 3, 2022.

"You can't imagine": Cara Anna and Yesica Fisch, "Russia Storms Mariupol Plant as Some Evacuees Reach Safety," AP News, May 3, 2022.

"They give the lying name": D. H. Montgomery, "'They Make a Desert and Call It Peace,'" Wise Words.

SELECTED BIBLIOGRAPHY

Al-Hlou, Yousur, Masha Froliak, and Evan Hill. "A Desperate Escape from Mariupol." *New York Times* video, 05:20, Mar. 26, 2022. https://www.nytimes.com/video/world/europe/100000008269834/escaping-mariupol.html.

———. "New Evidence Shows How Russian Soldiers Executed Men in Bucha." *New York Times*, May 19, 2022. https://www.nytimes.com/2022/05/19/world/europe/russia-bucha-ukraine-executions.html.

———. "Putin is a Fool." *New York Times*, September 28, 2022. https://www.nytimes.com/interactive/2022/09/28/world/europe/russian-soldiers-phone-calls-ukrainehtml.

Anna, Cara, and Yesica Fisch. "Russia Storms Mariupol Plant as Some Evacuees Reach Safety." AP News, May 3, 2022. https://apnews.com/article/russia-ukraine-business-europe-donetsk-organization-for-security-and-cooperation-in-5de7bbc536a8da94c0d9586b95817612.

Arraf, Jane. "A Family of Six Walks for Days to Escape the Besieged City of Mariupol. Here Is Their Story." *New York Times*, Apr. 24, 2022. https://www.nytimes.com/2022/04/24/world/europe/mariupol-ukraine-family-escape.html.

Associated Press. "Why the Battle for Mariupol's Azovstal Steel Plant Matters in Russia's War against Ukraine." *The Globe and Mail*, Apr. 21, 2022. https://www.theglobeandmail.com/world/article-russia-ukraine-war-mariupol-steel-factory/.

"'At Night I Dream of Mariupol': Nine Accounts of Surviving a Russian Siege." *New York Times*, Apr. 6, 2022. https://www.nytimes.com/2022/04/06/opinion/international-world/mariupol-ukraine-russia.html.

Bilefsky, Dan, Richard Pérez-Peña, and Eric Nagourney. "The Roots of the Ukraine War: How the Crisis Developed." *New York Times*, Oct. 12, 2022. https://www.nytimes.com/article/russia-ukraine-nato-europe.html?action=click&pgtype=Article&state=default&module=styln-russia-ukraine&variant=show.

Bondarenko, Khrystyna, et al. "Mariupol Residents Are Being Forced to Go to Russia, City Council Says." BBC World, Mar. 19, 2022. https://edition.cnn.com/2022/03/19/europe/mariupol-shelter-commander-ukraine-intl/index.html.

Chernov, Mstyslav. "Journalists Who Documented Mariupol's Agony Flee Russian Kidnappers." *Boston Globe*, Mar. 21, 2022. https://www.bostonglobe.com/2022/03/21/world/ap-journalists-who-witnessed-mariupols-agony-flee-russian-hit-list/.

Chernov, Mstyslav, Evgeniy Maloletka, and Lori Hinnant. "'Why? Why? Why?': Ukraine's Mariupol Descends into Despair." AP News, Mar. 16, 2022. https://apnews.com/article/russia-ukraine-war-mariupol-descends-into-despair-708cb8f4a171ce3f1c1b0b8d090e38e3.

"Eking Out an Existence and Mourning the Dead in Besieged Mariupol." Reuters, Mar. 31, 2022. https://www.reuters.com/world/europe/eking-out-an-existence-mourning-dead-besieged-mariupol-2022-03-31/.

Ellyat, Holly. "Russian Forces Invade Ukraine." CNBC, Feb. 24, 2022. https://www.cnbc.com/2022/02/24/russian-forces-invade-ukraine.html.

Engelbrecht, Cora. "Civilians Who Escaped the Besieged Plant in Mariupol Describe a Harrowing Life Underground." *New York Times*, Apr. 20, 2022. https://www.nytimes.com/live/2022/04/20/world/ukraine-russia-war-donbas#civilians-who-escaped-the-besieged-plant-in-mariupol-describe-a-harrowing-life-underground.

———. "Thousands of Civilians Are Holed Up with Ukrainian Troops in Mariupol, Officials Say." *New York Times*, Apr. 18, 2022. https://www.nytimes.com/live/2022/04/18/world/ukraine-russia-war-news?name=styln-russia-ukraine&region=MAIN_CONTENT_2&block=storyline_latest_updates_recirc&action=click&pgtype=Article&variant=show&index=2#ukrainians-mariupol-steel-plant.

"Escape from Hell: Women of Mariupol Tell Their Stories of Living under Occupation and Escaping the Siege." Yahoo! News, Apr. 27, 2022. https://www.yahoo.com/video/escape-hell-women-mariupol-tell-110400333.html?guccounter=1&guce_referrer=aHR0cHM6Ly93d3cuZ29vZ2xlLmNvbS88&guce_referrer_sig=AQAAAJBsjGlwhWZEyDasGIDQmizJBqKYq0v6R6a03efqrMBjQ0q4d92Em-aRdqESAehTMNEcYs-w3EXn9Rtyoau9XvsMbIJUWzDYViprwRZQG_iiaiXExAy2WmPo5f6z3E-IqiJdJWgJHgHG_oEc8u51Ge83011jcZdiTlzgnjBzMqfJ.

"Escape from Mariupol: 'I Didn't Want to Die on the Road.'" Reuters, Mar. 24, 2022. https://www.reuters.com/world/europe/escape-mariupol-i-didnt-want-die-road-2022-03-24.

"Fighting Reaches Center of Mariupol as Putin Puts Up Defiant Appearance." Radio Free Europe/Radio Liberty, Mar. 18, 2022. https://www.rferl.org/a/ukraine-missile-lviv-russian-invasion/31759094.html.

Fisher, Max. "Putin's Case for War, Annotated." *New York Times*, Feb. 24, 2022. https://www.nytimes.com/2022/02/24/world/europe/putin-ukraine-speech.html.

Foer, Franklin. "The Horror of Bucha." *The Atlantic*, Apr. 4, 2022. https://www.theatlantic.com/ideas/archive/2022/04/russia-bucha-killings-war-crimes-genocide/629470/.

Gall, Carlotta. "Six Weeks of 'Hell': Inside Russia's Brutal Ukraine Detention." *New York Times*, Aug. 15, 2022. https://www.nytimes.com/2022/08/15/world/europe/ukraine-russia-detention-prisoners.html.

Gardner, Simon. "In Ukrainian Street, a Corpse with Hands Bound and a Bullet Wound to the Head." Reuters, Apr. 5, 2022. https://www.reuters.com/world/europe/ukrainian-street-corpse-with-hands-bound-bullet-wound-head-2022-04-03/.

Gunter, Joel. "Bucha Killings: 'I Wish They Had Killed Me Too.'" BBC News, Apr. 6, 2022. https://www.bbc.com/news/world-europe-61003878.

Harding, Luke. "Escape from Mariupol: The Man Who Swam to Safety from the Russian Terror." *The Guardian*, Apr. 7, 2022. https://www.theguardian.com/world/2022/apr/07/ukraine-escape-from-mariupol-man-swam-russian-terror.

Hinnant, Lori, Mstyslav Chernov, and Vasilisa Stepanenko. "AP Evidence Points to 600 Dead in Mariupol Theater Airstrike." AP News, May 4, 2022. https://apnews.com/article/Russia-ukraine-war-mariupol-theater-c321a196fbd568899841b506afcac7a1.

Hopkins, Valerie, Ben Hubbard, and Gina Kolata. "How Russia Is Using Ukrainians' Hunger as a Weapon of War." *New York Times*, updated Mar. 30, 2022. https://www.nytimes.com/2022/03/29/world/europe/mariupol-ukraine-russia-war-food-water.html.

Ilyushina, Mary. "'Treated Like Captives or Some Criminals': Ukraine Says Russia Forcibly Relocates Thousands from Mariupol." *National Post*, Mar. 30, 2022. https://nationalpost.com/news/world/treated-like-captives-or-some-criminals-ukraine-says-russia-forcibly-relocates-thousands-from-mariupol/wcm/21948df3-a59f-4086-ac3b-c6f68cb21a7e/amp.

———. "Ukraine Says Russia Forcibly Relocated Thousands from Mariupol." *Washington Post*, updated Mar. 30, 2022. https://www.washingtonpost.com/world/2022/03/30/ukraine-mariupol-russia-evacuation-filtration/.

Kovensky, Josh. "'Nobody Will Save You': One Refugee's Account of Escaping Mariupol." Talking Points Memo, Mar. 28, 2022. https://talkingpointsmemo.com/prime/nobody-will-save-you-one-refugees-account-of-escaping-mariupol.

Kramer, Andrew E. "They Died by a Bridge in Ukraine. This Is Their Story." *New York Times*, Mar. 9, 2022. https://www.nytimes.com/2022/03/09/world/europe/ukraine-family-perebyinis-kyiv.html.

Kurennaya, Darya. "Escape from Mariupol: 'The Dead Were Buried in the Yards.'" Radio Free Europe/Radio Liberty, Mar. 26, 2022. https://www.rferl.org/a/mariupol—escape-russian-siege-ukraine/31771645.html.

Lapatina, Anastasiia. "Voices of Besieged Mariupol: 'It's Not Even Comparable to Hell.'" *Kyiv Independent,* Apr. 9, 2022. https://kyivindependent.com/national/voices-of-sieged-mariupol-its-not-even-comparable-to-hell.

Lewis, Lauren. "Now Ukraine Accuses Putin of Kidnapping 2,500 Children: Kyiv Makes New 'Nazi' Allegations after Claiming Ukrainian Refugees Were Being Deported from Mariupol to 'Filtration Camps' in Russia." *Daily Mail* video, 0:58, Mar. 21, 2022. https://www.dailymail.co.uk/video/news/video-2643339/Video-Russians-spotted-checking-people-border-Nazi-tattoos.html.

Lister, Tim, et al. "Mariupol Children's Hospital Bombing One of Many Attacks on Medical Facilities since Russian Invasion, WHO Says." CNN World, Mar. 10, 2022. https://www.cnn.com/2022/03/10/europe/russia-invasion-ukraine-03-10-intl/index.html.

Mackintosh, Eliza, et al. "Russia or Die: After Weeks under Putin's Bombs, These Ukrainians Were Given Only One Way Out." CNN World, Apr. 7, 2022. https://www.cnn.com/2022/04/07/europe/ukraine-mariupol-russia-deportation-cmd-intl/index.html.

Maloletka, Evgeniy. "Amid Heavy Shelling, Ukraine's Mariupol City Uses Mass Grave." AP News, Mar. 10, 2022. https://apnews.com/article/russia-ukraine-war-mariupol-mass-graves-286b84d5d795ef91fb8c9ee48ed26612.

"Mariupol Refugee Recounts Hardship, Devastation." AP News video, 01:29, Mar. 28, 2022. https://apnews.com/article/videos-4be371b9f422476c9141ec7c2be82901.

Mokhina, Anastasiia, et al., "Sixteen Days in Ukraine." *New York Magazine*, Mar. 13, 2022. https://nymag.com/intelligencer/article/ukraine-war-diary.html.

Montgomery, D. H. "'They Make a Desert and Call it Peace.'" Wise Words. https://englishlanguageandhistory.com/?id=dh-montgomery-roman-britain-desert-peace-1.

Morgan, Jayne. "Ukraine War: Children in Mariupol 'Drank Rainwater from Puddles.'" CNN, May 2, 2022. https://nwlsclrddc.tudasnich.de/news/uk-wales-61250092.

Morris, Loveday, and Paul Sonne. "Voices from the Siege of Mariupol." *Washington Post*, Mar. 31, 2022. https://www.washingtonpost.com/world/2022/03/30/mariupol-siege-voices-ukraine-war/.

Murphy, Zoeann, and Dan Rosenzweig-Ziff. "How Ukrainian Children Understand the War." *Washington Post*, Mar. 15, 2022. https://www.washingtonpost.com/world/interactive/2022/ukraine-war-children-refugees/?itid=hp-top-table-main.

Prentice, Alessandra. "'Moles in the Dark': Survival and Escape from the Mariupol Steelworks." Reuters, May 13, 2022. https://www.reuters.com/world/europe/moles-dark-survival-escape-mariupol-steelworks-2022-05-13.

Rahman, Khaleda. "Zelensky Receives Standing Ovation from EU Parliament in Emotional Scenes." *Newsweek*, Mar. 1, 2022. https://www.newsweek.com/zelensky-receives-standing-ovation-eu-parliament-1683607.

Rainsford, Sarah, et al. "Safe Passage for Civilians to Leave Mariupol Under Way—UN." BBC News, May 1, 2022. https://www.bbc.com/news/live/world-europe-61252785.

Rosenzweig-Ziff, Dan, and Julia Alekseeva. "As Refugees Flee into Poland, Some Ukrainians Have Decided to Do the Unexpected: Go Home." *Washington Post*, Mar. 13, 2022. https://www.washingtonpost.com/world/2022/03/13/ukrainians-return-russia-war/.

"Russia Bombs a Maternity Hospital in the Ukrainian City of Mariupol." BBC Newshour, Mar. 9, 2022. https://www.bbc.co.uk/programmes/w172xv5mwl543g1.

Sauer, Pjotr. "Hundreds of Ukrainians Forcibly Deported to Russia, Say Mariupol Women." *The Guardian*, Apr. 4, 2022. https://www.theguardian.com/world/2022/apr/04/hundreds-of-ukrainians-forcibly-deported-to-russia-say-mariupol-women.

Schreck, Adam, and Mstyslav Chernov. "Ukrainian Defenders in Mariupol Defy Surrender-or-Die Demand." HuffPost, Apr. 18, 2022. https://www.huffpost.com/entry/mariupol-surrender-defy-ukraine_n_625ce197e4b0be72bff7ac7a.

Schwirtz, Michael. "Evacuees from Mariupol's Steel Plant Tell of Horrors and Survival." *New York Times*, May 3, 2022. https://www.nytimes.com/2022/05/03/world/europe/mariupol-azovstal-survivors-evacuated.html.

Sommerville, Quentin, and Darren Conway. "Watch: Our Correspondent Goes into No-Man's Land with the Ukrainian Army." BBC News video, 05:16. Mar. 10, 2022. https://www.bbc.com/news/av/world-europe-60699588.

Stapleton, AnneClaire, et al. "A Mariupol Family Fled the Horror of Russian Attacks. But They Had to Leave Their Parents Behind." CNN World, Mar. 22, 2022. https://www.cnn.com/2022/03/22/europe/mariupol-ukraine-family-escape-intl-cmd/index.html.

Tavernise, Sabrina. "'I Don't Have the Right to Cry': Ukrainian Women Share Their Stories of Escape." *New York Times*, Mar. 20, 2022. https://www.nytimes.com/2022/03/20/world/europe/ukraine-women-escape-stories.html.

Terajima, Asami. "One Onslaught, One Family, One Lucky Chance: Surviving Mariupol Theater Bombing." *Kyiv Independent*, Apr. 17, 2022. https://kyivindependent.com/national/one-onslaught-one-family-one-lucky-chance-surviving-mariupol-theater-bombing.

"Ukraine Conflict: Russian Forces Attack from Three Sides." BBC News, Feb. 24, 2022. https://www.bbc.com/news/world-europe-60503037.

"Ukraine Family Tells of Epic Escape from Mariupol on Foot." *Gulf News*, Apr. 23, 2022. https://gulfnews.com/world/europe/ukraine-family-tells-of-epic-escape-from-mariupol-on-foot-1.87391303.

van Brugen, Isabel. "Russian Occupiers March through Destroyed Mariupol to Mark Victory Day." MSN, May 9, 2022. https://www.msn.com/en-us/news/world/russian-occupiers-march-through-destroyed-mariupol-to-mark-victory-day/ar-AAX4uSA.

Voitocich, Olga, et al. "'Mariupol Is Now Just Hell': Survivors and Drone Footage Reveal the Scale of Destruction." CNN, Mar. 15, 2022. https://www.cnn.com/2022/03/15/europe/ukraine-mariupol-destruction-footage-intl.

Williamson, Lucy. "Ukraine War: Mariupol's Refugees Carry Wounds of Battered City." BBC News, Mar. 31, 2022. https://www.bbc.com/news/world-europe-60935734.

Zinets, Natalia. "Ukrainians Hang on at Mariupol Steel Plant." Reuters, Apr. 15, 2022. https://www.reuters.com/world/europe/fortress-city-ukrainians-cling-steel-plant-mariupol-2022-04-15/.

THIS BOOK IS DEDICATED TO THE UKRAINIAN PEOPLE.

Clarion Books is an imprint of HarperCollins Publishers.

83 Days in Mariupol
Copyright © 2023 by Don Brown
All rights reserved. Manufactured in Canada. No part of this book may be used or reproduced in any
manner whatsoever without written permission except in the case of brief quotations embodied in
critical articles and reviews. For information address HarperCollins Children's Books, a division of
HarperCollins Publishers, 195 Broadway, New York, NY 10007.
www.harpercollinschildrens.com

Library of Congress Control Number: 2023930001
ISBN 978-0-06-331156-5

The artist used pen and ink with digital paint to create the art for this book.
Design by Whitney Leader-Picone
23 24 25 26 27 FSN 10 9 8 7 6 5 4 3 2 1

First Edition